What others are saying about *The Performance Culture:*

This is the book I've been looking for. This book will become required reading for my graduate management students. It is filled with practical approaches to team implementation and team maturity challenges. Dr. Ray's writing and insights support academic research on team performance.

Prof. Herbert Tuttle
Associate Director, Assistant Professor
Graduate Engineering Management Program
The University of Kansas, Edwards Campus

Darrel Ray's highly practical book offers real-world insights into human behavior in the workplace, the dynamics prevalent in modern organizations, and the keys to building a productive culture where both the business and its members can grow and succeed.

Jeffrey Boyd, Ph.D.
Director – Workplace Solutions
Georgia-Pacific Corporation

This is an approach that works! Built on solid practice and basic human principles. Following Dr. Ray's prescription has allowed our associates and company to grow in ways not even imagined. All the pieces are there to solve the 'Human Dynamics' puzzle. Although he presents a detailed plan for change, it is not so rigid that you can't take a few side trips without getting lost. It is logical and detailed, yet common sense on steroids.

Paul Heacock, President
Human Dynamics, Inc.

D1512163

Dr. Ray's new book is an invaluable resource for leaders at every level in both labor and management. Management and union leaders will find not only candid portrayals of what really happens in the workplace, but nuts and bolts ideas for making their organizations successful.

Bob Jacobi, Executive Director
Labor–Management Council of Greater Kansas City

In a time where breakthrough performance is a requirement, Darrel Ray gives us an easily executable roadmap. He shows what managers need to do to develop a Performance Culture. This book covers the waterfront from team dynamics to managing change, influencing culture and the role of leadership, including that of Team Developers. It is an important fieldbook in the area of human performance.

Cheryl Highwarden
Cheryl Highwarden Consulting
The Woodlands, TX

The Performance Culture

Maximizing the Power of Teams

The Performance Culture

Maximizing the Power of Teams

Darrel W. Ray, Ed.D.

with

Howard Bronstein

IPC PRESS

www.teaming-up.com

IPC PRESS
www.teaming-up.com

Publisher's Cataloging-in-Publication

Ray, Darrel.
  The performance culture : maximizing the power of
teams / Darrel W. Ray with Howard Bronstein ;
illustrations by Zeb Hodge. – 1st ed.
  p. cm.
  Includes bibliographical references and index.
  LCCN: 2001012345
  ISBN: 0-9709505-0-0

  1. Organizational behavior. 2. Corporate culture.
3. Teams in the workplace. I. Bronstein, Howard.
II. Title.

HD58.7.R39 2001   658.4'02
                  QBI01-200576

Cover and interior design by Tappan Design

Illustrations by Zeb Hodge

Dedicated to

Mark Phelps – in work
Bus May – in life
Gene Ray – in love

Bus:
    You were one of the three most important men in my life. Thank you for showing faith in me and seeing more in me than I saw in myself. The pitching lessons have lasted a lifetime.

David

Table of Contents

Acknowledgments

Many people played an important part in this project but the one who paid the highest price and spent the most time is my dearest wife, Fran Ray who has helped me at every step of the way. My co-author, Howard Bronstein, did a great job of tracking down many very busy people to interview and gather data. His input and tenacity allowed us to share the experience of many people through his excellent interviewing and writing skills.

I want to thank the many people who read and contributed their insights and thoughts. Most of them have been involved in teams and Teaming Up® in some way for years and gave me valuable feedback based on their firsthand experience. Barb Bridger, vice president of human resources at Butler Mfg., Michael Selway training manager at Sverdrup, Corp. at Cape Canaveral (NASA), and Lou Haddad, labor relations manager for the city of West Palm Beach, did a most complete read with volumes of feedback. Paul Heacock, president of Human Dynamics, Inc., read the manuscript numerous times even as he was implementing teams in his organization and gave valuable firsthand feedback. Dr. Jeff Boyd of Georgia Pacific, Herb Tuttle of the University of Kansas, Janine Connolly of General Electric, and Lee Bowman of iPhotonics all spent many hours on the manuscript commenting and offering their experience.

Four of the people closest to me: Dave Wolfe, Jack Seymour, Brian Wolfe, and my wonderful daughter, Adrienne Carey – offered not only great feedback but also the moral support only true lifelong friends can provide.

Many others read or provided comments or experiences that proved valuable: Ray Montjoy of Luxfor, Inc., Mary Winterle and

Eric Sills of Standard Motor Products, Eileen Dakan of Region III, Dan Genin at Circle Seal, and Gary Henrie of South Central Behavioral Services.

The quality of this process was greatly enhanced by a top-notch team who helped take this project from rough manuscript to polished book. Terrill Petri, project lead, Kirsten McBride, editor, Kim Tappan, book and cover design, and Pola Firestone, marketing guru, not only worked very closely with me but illustrated what teamwork looks like through their incredible cooperation and synergy. They took ownership of this book like it was their own, providing great feedback and many quality suggestions.

Zeb Hodge, of Human Dynamics, Inc., thank you to a wonderful illustrator whose excellent listening skills greatly complement his artistic talent.

Thanks also go to the many people who were interviewed by Howard Bronstein. Their contributions, whether included in the book or not, proved a strong foundation for the concepts and examples.

Finally, I want to acknowledge the great influence Mark Phelps, Bus May and my father, Gene Ray, have had on my life and my career. Without these three mentors I cannot imagine what life would have been like. While none played a direct role in the writing of this book, the lessons and learnings they gave me have lasted a lifetime and are clearly the foundation of much you read in these pages. And last but not least my mother, whose child rearing practices have provided many great stories for my books and seminars.

Darrel Ray

Introduction

Corporate culture is serious business in business, but don't look at it too closely. You will find that most organizations have great difficulty understanding how to sustain a corporate culture that supports high performance.

Early in my career I had the opportunity to work for a leader, Mark Phelps, who understood how to develop an entire organization to high performance. When he came into the mental health organization where I worked as a clinical psychologist, it was under legislative investigation, had several lawsuits pending and had attracted the attention of nearly every newspaper reporter in the region. It was a miserable place to work and had great difficulty attracting strong employees even in times of high unemployment. No one wanted to work there.

Over the course of four years Mark was able to systematically create a goal-focused organization that placed great value on recognizing people and measuring what many thought was unmeasurable. The result was an organization that performed far above others and received accolades and recognition from many corners. Soon recruitment became much easier and people actually liked to come to work. Mark had created a culture of performance where people knew what the goals were and how to measure them. I learned what a Performance Culture could look and feel like as people began to take pride in their work and show care for the clients and one another.

My next lesson occurred when Mark left. Since the corporate organization was not committed to high performance, they paid no attention to the culture that had been developed under Mark's leadership. The new leader, in his first speech to the organization, indicated that he intended to stay until he retired. He then proceeded to retire while holding his position! It only took six months for him to tear down the trust, goal focus and sense of purpose that people had come to feel. I am sure his intentions were good, but the results were a disaster that hurt many people and left many cynical and unwilling to give any extra effort for the organization. The sense of betrayal was immense. People had come to feel a great deal of pride in what they had accomplished in four years only to have new leadership undermine it. Soon morale declined and conflicts became the order of the day once again. That was the second lesson. It is hard to sustain a Performance Culture through changes in leadership if the organization is not committed.

Since then I have seen the same problem over and over again. One leader creates a positive, producing culture only to see the next less skilled leader tear it down. How does an organization develop and sustain a Performance Culture through leadership transitions?

How does one build a sustained culture where people feel the power of teamwork and give their best to the organization? How does an organization sustain high quality leadership that fosters and continues the growth and development of the culture? How does an organization avoid putting leaders in place who might destroy the trust on which high performance is based?

There are really two cultures in most organizations – the official and the informal culture. I call these the intentional and endemic cultures. Both of these cultures have their own set of beliefs and assumptions that are not talked about or shared between them.

When the intentional and endemic cultures come into conflict, tremendous energy is wasted. Conflicts take the place of performance and people spend a good deal of time and energy protecting themselves. In addition, major communication problems develop between the leaders, middle management and the workforce.

Go to the lunchroom some time and listen to how people talk about management. It is mostly complaining, isn't it? Unfortunately, when those same people return from lunch they are not focused and ready to do their best after having spent the lunch hour complaining about management.

This book is about integrating these two cultures to avoid such problems. It is about the power of a system that supports teamwork at every level, a Performance Culture. A culture that values open communication and works to eliminate hidden beliefs that cause cultural conflict, undermine trust and prevent people from giving their best. High-performing organizations have traditions and structures that open the dialogue between the endemic and intentional cultures and keep it open. With an open dialogue, hidden beliefs have to compete in the light of day against more legitimate concerns.

DILBERT reprinted by permission of United Feature Syndicate, Inc., Scott Adams, 2000, p. 96.

What hidden beliefs are driving the behavior of these characters?

High-performing organizations reduce or eliminate culture conflict by means of several organizational disciplines we will discuss in this book. In less than one year, using these ideas, most organizations can eliminate a great deal of the conflict and begin focusing the organization's energy in more productive ways.

A few years ago I was asked to evaluate a state mental hospital. My investigation found tremendous problems including incredibly high staff and patient suicide rates! The state legislature was investigating, lawsuits were filed, the union leadership was frustrated, and most people felt it was a very depressing place to work.

With a leadership change, Dr. Barbara Ramsey took over and began to systematically use some of the disciplines discussed in this book. When I conducted a followup evaluation a year later, I found an organization that had made phenomenal progress. The union leadership was very satisfied with labor relations. The legislature was pleased with the performance indicators. Middle management felt a sense of direction. Programs were developing rapidly – and employees said it was a much better place to work. The culture conflict that had created complaining, grievances and lawsuits was gone. In its place was an organization that was helping patients and reaching out to the community. But what will happen when Dr. Ramsey leaves? Will the organization place a high value on the new culture? Will the new leader be chosen for his or her ability to further develop the organization?

This book will help you understand your organization and learn how to minimize the culture conflict and create sustained performance even when leadership changes. It will show you how to harness the power of teams even as you create an entire system to support teamwork through changes in leadership. This book is the product of over 20 years of helping organizations make the transition to high performance systems.

You are probably wondering, "What is a Performance Culture?"

A Performance Culture is one in which everyone knows the goals and consistently values and achieves high performance. The culture and its leaders have an strong belief that they control their own destiny.

Performance Cultures waste little energy on culture conflicts but instead focus that energy on common goals and performance. They are cultures where people enjoy coming to work, feel good about their accomplishments and find teamwork rewarding.

Organizations that develop cultures of performance report:

- Dramatically improved communication throughout the organization
- Increased productivity and faster turnaround times

- Less focus on conflict, territory or turf protection
- Greater ability to innovate and respond quickly to market conditions
- Far less strife between managers and nonmanagers
- Far less gossip and rumor mongering

I have helped many companies make the transition to team-based, performance-focused systems. Hundreds of times I have had individual team members and managers tell me they would never go back to doing it "the old way." High performance is far too rewarding and fun. It makes most traditional workplaces seem boring and wasteful by comparison.

I have been involved with and assisted some organizations on an ongoing basis for as long as 10 years. During that time I have seen these organizations not only sustain their culture of performance but continuously grow and develop through multiple leadership changes. While I continue to believe that leadership is critical, I also feel that it is not everything. There are far too few charismatic leaders to depend on them to develop our organizations and when they leave the organization often suffers. Leaders can learn to lead and cultures can be developed that do not require charismatic leadership to be able to perform at a high level. Tools and methods are available through which leaders can learn to develop their organizations to use the power of teamwork. This book will give you some of those tools.

As a leader trying to find the key to motivate and direct your organization, you may have asked yourself:

- Why did the team miss its goals again after all the planning and work we did?
- We have gone over and over the goals for this year, why is it that no one seems to know what our goals are?
- Why do people seem to see managers so negatively?
- Why is it so hard for people to be honest with me and tell me what they are thinking?
- Why does the union continue to protect and defend an employee who even they feel is incompetent?

- How can I be sure I know what is going on in my organization?
- Why doesn't the group see things the way I see them?
- Why did that manager do exactly what I told him NOT to do?

When you have finished reading this book, you will have the knowledge to answer many of these questions. The mystery behind many group and individual behaviors can be found in the structure of your organization and in your own behavior as a leader.

How to Read this Book

This book has been divided into three sections that build on each other. Section I looks at how culture affects behavior. These concepts are essential to understanding how groups work and how you as the leader can facilitate team development. Section II outlines and explains the basic ingredients required of any productive and profitable Performance Culture. Section III shows what teams actually look and sound like and what leader behavior should be within a Performance Culture. If you want a sense of how a Performance Culture looks, feel or sounds you might want to read Chapter 10 right now. Regardless, after reading just the first few chapters you may see your organization in a very different way.

Throughout this book, at the end of each chapter there will be several questions to help you assess your own organization. Read the questions and try to answer each one as honestly as possible. By applying these questions, you will be able to better understand your own organization and identify skills or changes necessary to move to a Performance Culture.

What you will learn:

1. How leaders can create a culture that values performance and goal achievement.
2. How to avoid unintentionally hurting motivation and performance.
3. Methods for enhancing teamwork and creating the conditions for high performance.

4. How to avoid common errors that leaders make in trying to develop teamwork in their organizations.
5. Techniques and methods that will help you develop more and better teamwork.
6. How to ensure your efforts are sustained after you leave.

Learn a few of the techniques and concepts in this book and practice them consistently, adding a few ideas as you gain experience and confidence. In over 20 years of work and study with teams and leaders, I know of no one who has mastered these concepts completely. Yet I know many who have become good leaders instilling a Performance Culture in their organizations.

SECTION I

THE CULTURE
AND PSYCHOLOGY
OF ORGANIZATIONS

CHAPTER 1

Is Your Work Group a Team?

In order to understand how to create a Performance Culture we must understand how people work in all types of groups, but especially in teams.

"Team" is a much overused term. Most so-called teams are nothing more than single-leader work groups with few team skills and a strong dependence upon the leader. More importantly, most organizations do not have the infrastructure to support successful teams, so if true teams are somehow created, they are doomed to frustration and lack of support.

A true team has an internal structure that allows it to function semi-autonomously. The team participates in measuring its own processes and goals and engages in some level of self-discipline, including training and performance feedback. When managers confuse a single-leader group with a team, they lose the confidence of the members in the group. Most people can easily recognize when they are being treated as a team and when they are being treated as a single-leader work group although called a team. They may not know the technical terms but they know the feeling of being manipulated by a leader who maintains the controls but spouts the language of teamwork. Many organizations use the language of teams without practicing the discipline of teams. Your organization may be one of them.

When an organization attempts to create true teams inside the structure of a non-team environment, it is like mixing oil and water.

Many organizations fundamentally misunderstand the basis of the team concept and team systems. They define teams as simply a group of people working together on a project or in a department with little consideration of how they should be structured and what supporting human and physical infrastructures need to be in place for the process to succeed.

For example, performance feedback comes from the leader in most organizations but in a team-based environment it comes from many sources. Team employees are expected to do things like goal setting and measurement that non-team employees do not. Because they have greater responsibilities and freedom, team members may also have more privileges and discretion about work and schedules than non-team employees. Certain tasks are expected of team members that are not expected of non-team employees, such as work scheduling, input of team data, attending business planning meetings or meeting with customers. Further, team employees may be allowed to make certain decisions for themselves, that are off limits to non-team employees such as scheduling vacations, making hiring recommendations, and so forth.

> *We believe that teams – real teams, not just groups that management calls "teams" – should be the basic unit of performance for most organizations, regardless of size. Teams are more productive than groups that have no clear performance objectives because their members are committed to deliver tangible performance results. Teams and performance are an unbeatable combination.*
>
> **Jon R. Katzenbach and Douglas K. Smith,**
> **1993, p. 15.**

All these differences add up to conflict and misunderstanding. It is impossible to develop a Performance Culture when the leadership is undecided about what type of work system it has – team or single-leader work group?

People will follow neither enthusiastically until the leadership makes up its mind.

The Performance Culture is markedly different from a single-leader work group system. Decision making, accountability, goal focus, and discipline are all different. When managers and employees in a team structure try to work inside a traditional single-leader structure, the result is enormous friction, hidden costs and non-value-added activity. Both types of systems work better alone than together. While the team process generally gets better results than a traditionally organized system, this only happens when the culture supports the process. Without this, teams may work no better than single-leader work groups.

One reason an organization moves to a team-based system is that it is about the only way to create a Performance Culture. Traditionally organized, single-leader systems have never been able to step up to a Performance Culture.

Types of Teams

Generally, there are four types of teams:

1. Task or project teams
2. Dynamic teams
3. Virtual teams
4. Self-directed teams

The following discussion will look at each type of team, including its strengths and weaknesses.

Task or Project Teams

Task or project teams are time-limited with a specific goal. They are the most commonly used teams in all types of organizations. A task team is given a project or assignment to research or complete with a time assigned in which to complete it. The team may be comprised of volunteers or the best people with the most expertise for a given task. Participants may be given release time and special resources to get the job done. Often a chairperson or leader coordinates activities but does not exercise strong authority over the group. The group works fairly independently and outside of the normal bureaucratic structure of the organization.

These types of teams often do quite well. Unfortunately, when they are finished they usually must turn their product or plan over to the organization. This handoff is dangerous and often fails. Since the team made decisions and plans that did not include those in

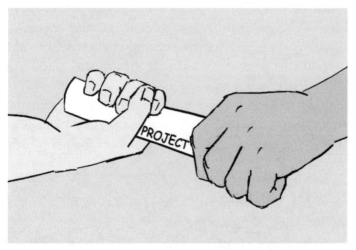

Handing off a project is a difficult problem between a task
or project team and those who must implement the project.

power within the structure, the plans may not be adopted whole-heartedly and may be modified or improperly implemented without regard to the plan. As a result, there may be resentment toward the task team for the time, money, resources and special training it receives.

I once witnessed a task team work for months on a product roll-out, only to turn it over to a vice president who felt it was a direct challenge to his authority. His response was to underfund the project and disband the implementation team. The result was a still-born project with the commensurate waste of time and resources. Not surprisingly, there was a good deal of anger at the vice president, and morale declined among those who had worked so hard to bring an exciting product to market.

When using such teams, therefore, special attention must be paid to make sure there is ownership and commitment from the key figures who are charged with the implementation. Key people almost always have to put their stamp on a plan before they will agree to cooperate. This means the plan or product may experience arbitrary changes without consultation. Non-team environments have a difficult time controlling this type of behavior in managers, because the culture itself does not value consultation and cooperation after the handoff, even on important projects.

In a Performance Culture handoffs are still a concern but are not nearly as dangerous as in a traditional system. Task teams come and go as needed, but results and measurements are focused on effective implementation. The success or failure of the project is evaluated by teams, and adjustments are made by teams, with open discussion and a focus on the goal. Because people in a Performance Culture work in teams in their everyday duties, the process of forming a team, setting its mission and establishing its goals is familiar to everyone. The basic skills are already there. Everyone also knows that whatever they come up with will have to be implemented, often by the teams that developed the idea. Consequently, there is a high degree of ownership and strong consideration of how the process will be implemented.

In brief, in a Performance Culture, task teams are a way of getting the right resources together, making a plan and then taking that plan back to the teams for implementation. In a traditional hierarchical system, task teams are often a way to get around an intransigent bureaucracy or a slow-moving decision-making process. In fact, the very existence of task teams may be an indictment of the system. Handoffs are far more difficult and it is often impossible to keep managers from inappropriately modifying the product. Also, task teams in traditional systems may get too far ahead of the system and create unrealistic plans or products. Since they are not the ones that have to implement, it is easy to overlook important problems that managers and workers back in the workplace would have to deal with.

Task teams are useful in all types of organizations but must be managed differently according to the surrounding organizational structure.

Dynamic Teams

When speed, innovation and high-quality thinking are needed, along with a clear implementation or migration strategy, dynamic teams are often the answer. Seen as a more sophisticated form of task team, dynamic teams are often involved with long-term projects and their implementation. While task team projects are generally six months or less, dynamic team projects can last for years.

Dynamic teams generally consist of a core of people, two to four, who stay with the project through its completion or for a year or two. These teams get larger and smaller according to the phase of the project and what is needed. For example, software projects or major new products are often brought to market with dynamic teams. The original Ford Taurus and the Boeing 777 were products of enormous dynamic team efforts. The Lockheed Skunkworks of the 1950-1980s may be seen as a hotbed of dynamic teams.[1]

Use of dynamic teams requires innovative thinking on the part of corporate leadership. It also requires new accountability structures. For a dynamic team to work, it must have a clear purpose and be accountable directly to a high-level management group that controls adequate resources. The team's structure should be monitored and changed as needed. Dynamic teams often get in trouble because they are not accountable to a single management group. When multiple organizational entities influence and fight over the product or resources of the team, it can create chaos, and project scope often becomes a major problem. With competing political entities all trying to influence the decisions and products of the team, the team becomes a bouncing ball that never goes anywhere. Since dynamic teams often command large resources, it is a great temptation for management to interfere in hopes of getting some of those resources focused in their direction. Individual managers may compete for maximum resources, while ignoring the needs of the organization.

Many companies have found that dynamic teams need to be isolated, if not secretive, in their workings. Software companies, as well as research and development companies, use this process routinely. A few high-level, key managers are charged with keeping tabs on the project and may act as a quasi-board of directors, meeting regularly to review the team's work. As the team needs resources or personnel they ask the "board." Insulation of the team from the larger organization prevents undue influence from individual managers and insures a clearer accountability to the organization as a whole.

Dynamic teams seem to work well in all types of organizations provided the structure supports them.

Virtual Teams

Virtual teams are increasingly popular as our systems of electronic communication become more efficient. Members of virtual teams are not co-located and may never see one another, but are charged with working on a common goal or process. To be successful, virtual teams must have a clear focus and a reason for being. Software development teams often work across a wide geographic range. One client company uses a virtual team across several offices to maintain computer systems, coordinate software acquisition and ensure standards are maintained. They meet weekly in a conference call.

These teams have to work harder in coordinating and communicating than a co-located team. For example, meetings must be well planned and well led. Since members do not know each other very well, they may not develop as much trust in one another as a co-located team. For this reason the synergies of a virtual team may not be as strong as those of a co-located team. Where possible, it is helpful for a virtual team to meet physically on occasion to build effective working relationships.

The larger the virtual team, the more face-to-face contact is needed. A small team of four or five may do fine without ever meeting as long as the goals are clear and the evaluation process is tied to how well they function as a team in meeting their goals. But a larger virtual team of 8-12 becomes too disjointed. Electronic communication, while easy, is no substitute for face-to-face contact. Large virtual teams inevitably generate electronic communications that grow exponentially with the size of the group. When the team meets obstacles or has interpersonal conflict, this tendency becomes quite pronounced. In general, large teams have difficulty maturing. Indeed, large virtual teams may find it impossible to mature without some personal contact.

Some virtual teams are poorly designed as they do not have a clear common goal or have too wide a range of projects or tasks. In such cases it may be useful to examine the team and determine if it could be split into two or more smaller teams to achieve a more narrow scope and a more clearly defined goal. This way each team could function as a smaller team meeting once a week, while the larger group meets by teleconference once a quarter.

Virtual teams are more difficult to manage when the team member's local manager often views the virtual team member as his captive employee. This makes it difficult for team members to participate fully in the team without constantly looking over their shoulder at the local manager, who may or may not see any importance in what the virtual team is doing.

Virtual teams must have a clear focus and reason for being and, if possible, team members should meet to establish trust and build relationships.

Self-Directed Work Teams

Although all of the above teams are often self-directed or at least have some level of shared leadership, they are different in many ways from self-directed work teams (SDWT).

SDWTs are co-located and generally work on a common product or process. They closely coordinate their work and have the ability to plan, coordinate and perform many of the basic tasks formerly carried out by a supervisor. I see the difference between task teams and SDWTs as similar to that between marriage and dating. The task team is together for a limited period of time and maybe only a few hours a day or week, hence the similarity to dating.

SDWTs, on the other hand, spend eight hours a day together over an indefinite period of time, making it similar to marriage.

The skills required to function in a SDWT are much more sophisticated and difficult than those needed to work on a task team. While each of the other types of teams can and does exist within a more traditional structure, SDWTs require a different, dedicated infrastructure and a management system.[2] Self-directed teams are generally better trained than any of the other types with great emphasis on cooperative skills, goal setting and measurement. The management of the SDWT is also highly trained and behaves more as a coach than as a manager. If the manager has done a good job, the team eventually can do well with only minimal contact with the manager.

For long-term success, SDWTs require some major changes in the organizaton. SDWTs may function inside a single-leader environment for a while but sooner or later the friction with the rest of the organization will tear them apart. Most efforts at SDWTs are stillborn or marginally successful if the organization is not structured to support them.

Self-directed work teams are an important means of developing a Performance Culture.

Natural Teams

The term "natural teams" has been used throughout industry as an excuse for avoiding the difficult task of redesigning the organization to support true teams. In many cases the use of "natural teams" indicates a desire to create teams, but leave the current systems in tact, albeit downsized at times.

Natural teams have been defined as groups where interdependencies exist. The theory is that employees can be put into a team and develop teamwork, hence the concept of "natural." But no organizational structure is natural. All organizational structure is, by design, a human invention that can be configured in an infinite number of ways. Only human conventions constrain the possibilities. For example, the design of an accounting department can be quite different from company to company, and from country to country. In most cases the rules of accounting often dictate that certain functions be performed in certain ways but they do not dictate the organizational structure and those rules do not come from any natural imperative.

Instead of talking about such an unnatural thing as a "natural team," it is more productive to look at what needs to be accomplished and structure the work system to achieve that objective. If the work can best be done with a cross-functional team, then structure it that way. Design the coaching role for the team carefully and be very aware of the tendency of most organizations to move back to the old way of doing things. Do NOT use the word "team" unless that is, in fact, what you intend to create and you are willing to do what it takes to make it happen. If all you really want is a single-leader work group, you fool no one by using the language of teams, but only undermine credibility. Think of it as a sports team. The coach is on the sidelines, runs practices, and coaches for skill improvement, but when the game starts only the players are on the field. How are you going to structure the team to ensure the players are able to play without constant interference from the manager?

> *Accounting is a field in which the technical imperatives are weak: historically based conventions are more important to it than the laws of nature. So, it is logical for accounting systems and the ways they are used to vary along national cultural lines.*
> **G. Hofstede, 1997, p. 157.**

I once did an informal survey of five companies that claimed to use natural teams. I found that none had reduced the amount of management oversight. None had done significant work to change or redesign management roles. Although there had been a good deal of training of managers, their behavior and expectations were largely the same. Moreover, none had seen anything more than modest gains in productivity since their efforts began. In one case, product measurements had improved but there were no clear rewards or even recognition for the efforts of the group. In every case the performance appraisal system was the same as was the compensation system. Managers had full control over all appraisals and compensation recommendations. In other words, there were no structural changes or incentives for true teamwork and no significant change in management. They all had single-leader work groups but called them "natural teams."

No organizational structure is "natural," hence the term *"natural team"* is often a misnomer.

Some Quick Theory on Groups

Teams have been around a very long time, but modern industrial society with its segmentation and Taylorist[3] organizational structure has all but eradicated the natural tendencies of humans to work in teams. We are fundamentally group creatures and function best in a setting where we feel secure and confident.

In practice, managers often ignore some pretty basic aspects of human behavior. As a result, they end up behaving in ways that are diametrically opposed to the natural tendencies of the people they are leading.

For example, when you ignore the natural communication tendencies of people, you miss the major source of influence and communication with the culture. Many leaders' efforts to communicate the values and direction of the company are a waste of time because no one is listening. It is not enough to tell people something, your words must become a part of what they believe and do. That takes a different kind of communication.

Communications problems occur when:
- A work group is created that is far too large.
- There are barriers to effective communication across divisions.
- The level of unhealthy competition within the organization gets out of control.
- Individualistic performance and appraisal systems encourage people to withhold information from others.
- Abusive or poorly trained managers are allowed to stay in place for years.

> *In the work of Frederick Taylor we have, I believe, the first clear statement of the idea that society is best served when human beings are placed at the disposal of their techniques and technology, that human beings are, in a sense, worth less than their machinery.*
>
> **Neir Postman,**
> **1992, p. 52.**

To manage these problems we have historically created supervisors, middle managers, mediators, labor relations, and human resource departments. While these roles may be necessary in any design, the work they do is often not forward-looking, but focused on putting out fires and correcting misunderstandings and problems resulting from the design or discipline of the organization.

An engineer with a major technology company noted example after example of mistakes, redundancy and inefficiency in his organization. Most of this waste could be prevented with only small changes in the communication patterns of his organization. His comment was interesting, "This level of waste is very demotivating to my group and keeps us in the middle of the pack in our industry instead of the leaders we could be." He went on to say, "What would happen if we were able to develop a system that could control this waste and allow people to take the time and energy they currently spend being frustrated and angry at management and direct it toward producing more and better products?"

Group Size Does Matter!

In our highly urbanized society we easily forget that most people in North America lived not in cities but in rural villages until the early 1900s. We have grown to see large groups as being natural when, in fact, they are quite unlike most of our past history as a species or civilization. While our view of the history of the world has been written from the city perspective, until about 1950 most people lived their entire lives in small towns and villages.

The "big is better" mentality creates major problems for productivity and trust in the workplace. There are optimal sizes for groups of people as they go about their work. Larger organizations often ignore the natural size and simply group people in large departments or corporate structures with little thought to how this affects productivity.

The "Industrial Village"

What is the optimal size for human groups? Over eons of time the village or clan group has stayed remarkably close to 150 people, usually ranging from 100-200. In agricultural times, this size group could provide for mutual protection from low-level conflicts and allowed the residents to get to and from their fields safely. In hunter-gatherer societies, the clan was often 150, with subclans of 30-40 coming together on regular occasions for various rituals, social occasions and large game hunting. This size allowed the clan to fully exploit the environment without concentrating too many humans in one place and thereby overtaxing natural resources.

In modern organizations a unit size of 150 or less (village size) allows people to get to know one another and develop some degree of trust. Larger unit sizes inhibit trust and cooperation by creating a more anonymous environment. The more anonymous the environment is, the more easily people can hide from accountability and avoid responsibility for the goals of the organization. Authors such as Hackman and Oldham[4] and Richardo Semler have noted, organizational structures of about 150 people seem optimal for the most efficient level of leadership and management.

> *The essence of the new role, I believe, will be what we might call manager as researcher and designer. What does she or he research? Understanding the organization as a system and understanding the internal and external forces driving change. What does she or he design? The learning processes whereby managers throughout the organization come to understand these trends and forces.*
> **Peter Senge, 1990, p. 229.**

This closely matches my own observations. In a number of cases when client companies redesigned themselves into smaller business units, the ability to focus the group's goals and to communicate effectively improved almost immediately. The reason for this change is that smaller business units can help an organization focus its resources and people at a level that is comprehensible to the average person. Most people cannot comprehend or relate to an organization of thousands or even several hundred, but they can identify with their "village" or business unit.

The Family Group

The second size consideration is the family group. In the past the family group was far larger than today's nuclear family. In most cases the family group consisted of 8-12 people living in the same physical structure. In some cultures this could be as many as 20. People identify most closely with their family group. In the workplace they identify with an equally small number of people. You often hear people say that those they work with are like family. Some workers claim that they feel closer to their coworkers than their own family. True or not, this says something about the depth of identification people feel with their immediate group and their natural tendency to focus their emotions, loyalties and energy on a small group.

Team Size and Communication Overhead

An effective, high-performance work group needs to communicate very efficiently to avoid mistakes, rework and conflict. Looking at this mathematically, the number of possible communication channels equals six when three people are involved.

When the group expands to six people, the number of channels increase to 30! With 10, it expands to 90! This means that for any individual in the group, there are 90 possible ways to communicate or miscommunicate. If the group expands to as many as 20, the communication overhead balloons to an impossible 380 combinations.

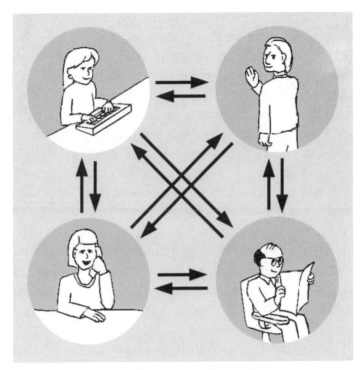

In a group of 4 there are 12 possible ways
to communicate or miscommunicate.

Considering that it takes time to communicate, learn, understand and trust one another, it is obvious that the larger the group,
the longer it will take for such communication, familiariza-
tion and trust to develop. At some point, the size of a group
will overwhelm the process and the group will never mature
into a strong team. Organizations that try to put teams
together in sizes of 20 or 30 violate this important principle.
The result is a team that never matures, where a significant
number of people hide and avoid taking responsibility for
the work or the decisions of the group. In my experience,
optimum team size is from 6 to 12 people. If they are larger
than that, the benefits of teams are diminished.

For example, a team of 12 or more has trouble getting all members to take ownership. Team decisions take a lot of time, and con-

practical tip

sensus becomes difficult. When last-minute changes or high levels of responsiveness are needed, the team has trouble adjusting. Conflicts are more difficult to resolve. Also, it is easier for two to six of the team members to hide or avoid responsibility while actively criticizing or resisting the team's decisions.

On the other end, the smaller the team size, the less efficient it can be. One of the major advantages of a Performance Culture is its ability to load balance. Especially in cross-functional teams, load balancing can greatly increase efficiency. For example, a four-member team with one person on vacation loses 25% of its capacity and must make up for it with the other 75%, a 8.33% increase in everyone's workload. A team of 10 with one person absent only loses 10% of its capacity and can theoretically spread that among the other 90%, resulting in only a 1.1% increase in workload.[5] If you wish to get the most advantage out of the load balancing effect, it is best to stay in the 6-12 range for a team.

Sometimes, simply adjusting the size of the team back to the "family group" dimensions will help a team mature and become more functional. People who have trouble being team members in an outsized group may be effective in a more appropriately sized group.

The Cost of Violating the Rules

Middle managers are often charged with managing the problems created by inappropriately sized work units. That is, the role of many middle managers or supervisors is to do for the group what the group itself cannot do because it is too large, or too poorly trained, or because the design of the work prohibits or inhibits natural cooperative communication and trust building.

Ethical Aspects of Organizational Culture

Simply to look at an organization as something to be managed and manipulated is to miss the essence of human groups and humans in general. In many organizations efforts to "empower" employees have fallen flat because these efforts are seen for what they are – a way to manipulate people. Creating a Performance

Culture is not the same as developing a high-performance car or new software. Unlike a car or software, people sense when they are being manipulated or used. People respond most productively when they feel respected and accepted and they believe that the system values their efforts.

As management theorists have been saying for 30 years, leaders must strive for a balance between focus on task and focus on people. Proper balance facilitates trust between management and the worker. Too much emphasis on task can lead to unethical or harmful decisions that undermine trust between the leadership and employees. Too much emphasis on people leads to

> *Eliminate slogans, exhortations, and targets for the work force asking for zero defects and new levels of productivity belong to the system and thus lie beyond the power of the work force.*
> **Dr. Edwards Deming (in Neave, 1990), p. 45.**

poor goal focus and wasted effort catering to the whims of individuals or subgroups, rather than the good of the organization.

A Performance Culture has a strong, open communication structure that helps maintain this balance for both leaders and followers. With open communication, people are much less likely to feel manipulated or used, and the trust necessary for high performance can take hold. Questions of proper treatment and ethical behavior should be openly discussed with opportunities for growth and development for everyone in the system. Hiding mistakes, talking behind one another's back or constant complaining about management can be greatly reduced, while openness and honesty in communication is increased.

Questions

1. Do you have work units that are far larger than 150 people or work groups that are larger than 12?
2. What effect does that size have on performance and communication in your organization?
3. How would you know if group size is causing performance or communication problems in your organization?

4. Can you identify places in your organization where there is too much communication overhead?

5. Where do you see frequent communication problems in your organization? Could size be creating some of the problems?

6. Does management do most of the load balancing for your work groups? How could this overhead be eliminated with a more appropriate design?

7. If you work in a non-team environment, how many times have you seen the word "team" misused? How do people respond in your organization when their work group is called a team, but it remains a single-leader group?

8. Which of the four types of teams are used in your organization? How have they worked? Based on what we have discussed in this chapter, why do you think they have worked or failed to work?

Two Cultures
in Conflict

Th culture that arises without planning and little influence
from the leadership is called "endemic." The endemic culture has little interest in business but is interested in relationships and social status. The task of leadership is to effectively
communicate and involve the endemic culture so that a
Performance Culture can develop that is more in line with the business' focus. The key to understanding the endemic culture lies in
recognizing the importance of security to humans.

The Endemic Culture

Cultures develop when people are in extended, intense social
contact. Place 50 people on an island for 100 years with minimal
contact with the outside world and you will soon have a unique
culture, different from all others on earth. This island culture
would generate many new words and ideas. It would develop a
unique hierarchy, marriage and courtship rituals, child-rearing
practices, and a political system. Humans are culture-making creatures, it is a deeply embedded part of our being.

Culture that arises out of an organization with no planning or
significant influence from the leadership is called the natural or
the "endemic culture." This culture is neither good nor bad, it is

simply the culture that arises when leadership is not paying attention. In some cases it is positive and productive, in many others it is quite unbusinesslike. Endemic culture is not formed out of response to a business plan or a well-thought-out approach to corporate values and behavior. It arises because a group of people are in intense and intimate contact for long periods of time just like the people on the island.

Endemic Culture Defined

Endemic culture refers to that part of the organization that is outside the control of the formal management or leadership system. The endemic culture is most often observed when authority figures are not present, in places like the lunch room, break rooms and around the water cooler.

Endemic culture exists independent of business needs or even common business sense. There is no necessary relationship between endemic culture and good business practices. Unless the company intentionally creates the conditions in which good business practices are incorporated into the culture, a strong business-focused culture is not likely to form. By ignoring the important role of culture formation, companies succumb to the whims of the endemic culture.

Let's look at two examples

1. For years, a unionized beer distributor had experienced unexplained periodic shrinkage in inventory. Management had its suspicions but could never prove anything until one day a new employee complained of harassment. Upon further investigation management uncovered an initiation scheme (rite of passage) by union members that had been in operation for many years. New employees were told, "you cannot become an accepted member of the group until you prove yourself." The ritual went like this: The new employee was required to steal a significant amount of beer from the company and then invite the other union members over for a beer

party. After carrying off the party successfully, the new employee was accepted as a full-fledged member of the group.

In this case, the union members were harassing the new employee because he would not abide by the ritual. The failure of management to develop a positive, business-focused culture allowed the employees to create their own culture complete with its own rites of passage.

"You cannot become part of the group until you prove yourself."

2. A long-term worker in a government organization discovered a sexual affair between a popular supervisor and an employee. When the two employees were transferred out of the department for disciplinary reasons, the group quickly turned on the person who reported the affair and made life so miserable for her that she soon took a demotion to get a transfer out of

the department. They expressed anger at her exposure of the affair that had upset a very cozy arrangement whereby they had been able to play bridge for several hours each day with the supervisor's approval and involvement. With the new supervisor, the bridge games came to an abrupt halt.

Learning Point: The endemic culture cares little about goals or performance. It is primarily concerned with status and the ordering of relationships. Without guidance it can go in directions counter to the good of the company.

Endemic culture comes from two primary sources (a) leadership within the employees themselves and (b) middle management or supervisory-level people. The military has recognized this for centuries. Any well-trained officer knows that the troops respect and follow the sergeant much more readily than an officer. Similarly, an experienced upper-level manager knows that middle management and the supervisory staff set the tone for the organization. At the same time, leaders among the work force can exert strong influence as is illustrated in the following story.

One engineering group I worked with had a series of very poor managers over a period of several years, yet this group of 40 engineers and technicians continued to be among the highest performing in the company. When I studied the group, it quickly became apparent that everyone had a great deal of respect for one of the senior engineers, a quiet but very intelligent and wise man. Throughout all the leadership turmoil, the group looked to him for the real leadership and responded to his direction regardless of who was in charge. He never wanted to be a manager and refused several promotions throughout his career. He was a strong and positive leader of the endemic culture.

The Intentional Culture

Intentional culture is designed and implemented by the leadership of the organization. It is often seen in the policies and procedures, in the disciplinary and appraisal systems, as well as in the hiring and promotion systems. Thus, it represents an attempt of the leadership to guide and direct the organization.

Intentional Culture Defined

Intentional culture is that part of the culture that is designed by upper-level management to meet the business and social needs of the organization.

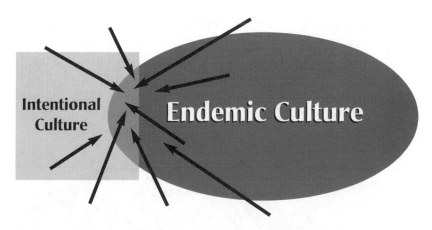

Poor integration of the two cultures leads to mistrust and poor communication about the goals of the company.

Most organizations try to create an intentional culture but find that the endemic culture is far stronger. Since the intentional culture comes from top management whereas the endemic culture comes from middle management, unions and employees, there is already a major disparity in numbers. There are far more people to carry the endemic culture.

The only way to integrate the two cultures is to include the endemic culture. All the power and memoranda from corporate headquarters (intentional culture) will do little to budge a well-established endemic culture. Endemic cultures are at times so strong that they persist in the face of eminent closing of the business.

One family-owned business had such strong negative labor relations that no one in management or labor could find it within themselves to change their abrasive relations despite the possible loss of the entire business. It was like two dogs, so busy fighting that they never noticed the lion about to eat both of them. The intentional culture was too fragmented and confused to have any real influence on the endemic.

Culture Carriers

Surprisingly, employees are not the primary carriers of the endemic culture. Instead, middle managers are generally the culture carriers. They reside between the intentional culture the leadership wants to develop and the endemic culture of the workforce. These middle managers are the key to cultural change.

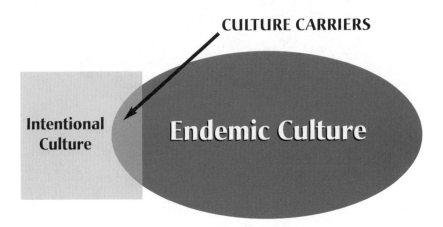

Middle managers and other informal leaders are always between the intentional and endemic cultures. They have the power to implement the agenda of the intentional culture.

As every modern U.S. president has discovered, middle management in the federal bureaucracy has a tendency to continue on its own course that even presidents find hard to influence. When Ronald Reagan fired the air traffic controllers in the union dispute of the early 1980s, he was using an enormous amount of power to try and change a relatively small part of the federal bureaucracy. Many would say that it still did not change much.

John Sculley, by his own admission, found it impossible to influence or change the engineering culture he inherited from Steven Jobs at Apple Computer in the 1980s. Two other CEOs also tried and failed miserably. Not until Jobs returned did the culture respond and make the changes necessary for Apple to regain market competitiveness. What did Jobs do to change the culture? He got the attention of the culture carriers. For starters, most of the board was asked to leave. Next, many of the middle managers responsible for the endemic culture were pressured out. A new focus was then brought to bear on indoctrinating new employees and regaining the vision of Apple Computer.

Unless you get the attention of the culture carriers, it is doubtful that the existing culture will respond or change. Middle management, the professional ranks, and union leadership, especially the stewards, foremen or leads, are the people who have the most influence over who gets hired and how employees are indoctrinated into the system and evaluated.

The training department, labor relations, and human resources are not primary culture carriers. They have little clout in the day-to-day enforcement of the endemic culture and are often seen as superfluous by middle management. It is for this reason that we focus most of our own transition efforts on middle management. Too many organizations attempt to change the culture by training line workers. This is generally a waste of time. Until line supervisors and middle managers change their behavior, nobody else is likely to do so. This is especially true in union shops. While the union has a part in carrying the endemic culture, most union activities are in direct response to manager and supervisor behavior. Change the behavior of managers and you quickly see a change in the behavior of the union!

To achieve true and permanent management change there has to be a clear path and a strong incentive for change. Such change can be accomplished in six to nine months if properly focused with consistent business results. Once the culture begins focusing more on business issues than relationships, many things become possible. Therefore, the objective is to teach the endemic culture how to be business-focused rather than relationship-focused.

Note:

From this point on, for brevity's sake, I will use the term "culture" when referring to the endemic culture except where a distinction is important.

The Performance Culture

The Performance Culture avoids the dichotomy of intentional and endemic cultures by creating a wide range of opportunities for the two cultures to blend and cooperate. The Performance Culture is created when leadership involves key leaders of the culture at all levels. The goal is to create a culture that is largely unified with little "we" and "they" and a focus on common goals.

The following are the characteristics of a Performance Culture compared to more traditional cultures.

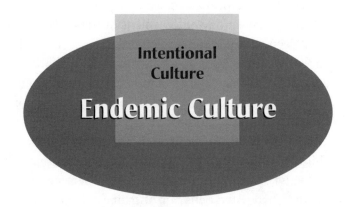

A Performance Culture merges the endemic and intentional cultures so that they work toward the same goals.

Performance Culture Defined

A Performance Culture is one in which everyone knows the goals and consistently values and achieves high performance. The culture and its leaders have an strong belief that they control their own destiny

Contrasting Cultures

Performance Culture

- High levels of involvement in planning and execution from key players in the endemic culture.

- Strong focus on goals, goal setting and achievement at every level.

- Public and frequent reporting on goals including financial information.

- Real-time direct feedback on performance from multiple sources.

- Strong emphasis on "treatment of others" issues. That is, how people should be treated and how they should treat others.

Traditional Cultures

- Employee involvement at the discretion of the local manager.

- Goals are the responsibility of the leader and local manager.

- Information on finances, performance and goals controlled by the local manager and leadership. May or may not be made public. Goal reporting not systematic or frequent.

- Feedback is generally from manager or leader down to employees with long delays, as much as a year.

- People issues treated at the discretion of the local leader.

• No focus on position status, emphasis on performance status, recognition and status based on current or recent performance.

• Status an important part of position. System uses status as a reward and control method.

• High value on cooperation and team responsibility for goals.

• Cooperation encouraged but not part of the work design. Functionalized work and individual responsibility.

• High levels of recognition and praise from all directions.

• Praise and recognition at the discretion of the local manager.

• Use of both individual and team accountability processes.

• Accountability only at the individual level.

• Significant involvement of non-management in hiring decisions.

• Hiring entirely controlled by management, involvement at management discretion.

• Leadership potential emphasized in everyone.

• Leadership in the formal leaders and managers or at their discretion.

• Focus on individual and group responsibility.

• Focus on entitlements and management direction.

• Accountability for leadership to act as stewards of the human as well as the physical resources.

• Manager accountable mostly for results, less regard for human resource development.

• Use of a developmental model for employee and organizational growth.

• Use of a more mechanical or rigid model of employee and organizational development.

Security and the Organization

To fully understand human behavior in any work group we must also look at behavior through the lens of security. It is virtually impossible to gain high performance from a group that is feeling insecure. Insecurity breeds fear and drains energy and focus. When there are rumors of layoffs or downsizing, lost productivity can almost always be seen if not measured right away - people spend more time talking and thinking about their fate than in producing or thinking about their work.

Faced with insecurity, middle managers and workers become suspicious of the leadership and of one another as reflected in dissention and turf protection. If there has been a historic lack of trust in an organization, insecurity increases the problem. The culture will tend to blame management and fall into internal conflicts between subgroups. And a suspicious and mistrusting workforce does not readily accept threats to the company. When management claims a threat to the company, employees may see management as crying wolf just to get more production out of them or to justify more layoffs.

In a Performance Culture the leadership is trusted, as are the workers. Since both the endemic and intentional cultures become integrated toward a common goal when a crisis occurs, people believe what management tells them and trust that their coworkers are working toward the same goals. People respond with appropriate actions to stem the threat.

> *Security comes from being with other people. There's a lot to be said for knowing that everybody's in the same boat with you, that you aren't an island, that you don't have to do it all on your own.*
> **Jack Stack, 1992, p. 50.**

At Patchwork Traditional Foods in Wales, United Kingdom, the company moved into a new and expensive facility and experienced a market downturn at the same time. Management and the teams quickly realized that there was trouble. They were able to pull together and overcome huge difficulties because management was totally honest with them about the situation and involved them in the solution. Margaret Carter, founder and owner of the company, says they were able to do a very rapid turnaround and recover from a potential disaster not just because of the team's dedication and hard work but because of the skills they had already developed as a Performance Culture.

Steve Hall, president of Boelte-Hall Lithography, in Roeland Park, Kansas, has a similar story. When a major fire destroyed half their facility and all the computer and preproduction equipment, the teams were able to get the plant back to full production with only five lost work days. Steve credits strong self-direction on the part of the teams for this incredible accomplishment. Management gave the teams a budget and told them, "do what it takes to get us back in business." This freed Steve and other managers to deal with the insurance company and reassure customers. Amazingly, the company was able to show a profit that year despite the huge setback.

When a loss of major customers and a change in the market forced Harmon Industries to announce that it would close its Riverside, California, plant, the workforce was initially shocked. Jeff Utterback, then vice president and general manager, got together with the leadership team and the steering committee to make sure all communications were clear through this difficult time. They had worked

> *There is no necessary trade-off ... between community and efficiency: those who pay attention to community may indeed become the most efficient of all.*
>
> **Francis Fukuyama,**
> **1995, p. 32.**

hard to integrate the endemic and intentional cultures into a Performance Culture and it paid off.

The leadership created an environment where people could feel secure even as they were transitioning to new jobs or leaving the company. All the traditional supports were offered such as outplacement and severance pay. But far more was done to support, recognize and praise good performance throughout this period.

Teams were given awards, recognition was continuous and material support was offered in many small ways. When employees from sister plants came to learn the work and took it back to their plants, they reported a remarkable level of cheerfulness and cooperation among the very people who were losing their jobs. What was going on? What could cause people who are losing their jobs to be cheerful about helping someone else learn the tasks so they could take them to another plant?

Tom Short was a team developer in the Riverside plant during this time. Here is what he said about the culture and the plant closing:

"We had grown a lot in the team process over the last two years. We understood how to maintain our morale and take care of business in the face of adversity. We had a lot of pride in our work and had a culture that took pride no matter what happened. We had meetings once a week to keep up with the events. We did tons of recognition every week with dozens of recognition awards. We gave awards for maintaining on-time delivery and safety. We gave 110% awards to those who went above and beyond to help train or produce. We did everything we could to be helpful to those who were literally taking our jobs. We gave out awards for training the people from the other plants. We even gave awards to the people we were training. In some areas we actually improved production. I have worked for a lot of managers over the years and I have never worked for someone like Jeff Utterback or the Riverside leadership team. They worked hard to maintain dignity and respect in the work force throughout the plant closing. Some managers gave out recognition awards at their own level. Joe Bass, my manager, gave several $50 gift certificates for work going beyond. Dan Genin, purchasing manager, also gave out certificates. It seemed like everybody was being recognized. It created a great feeling clear up to the last day we were open."

The remarkable thing we can learn from these examples is that security is created by the climate management creates. Most plant closings do not maintain, much less increase productivity. This was only possible because a Performance Culture was in place that took pride in its work and valued recognition and praise as a primary driver of behavior. The work force trusted management and recognized that a business decision had been made for better or worse. Even in the worst of situations, when leaders develop a solid Performance Culture in which workers feel secure, many things can be accomplished. Jeff Utterback and his team used the fund of goodwill and trust they had built up over two years to bring the plant to a smooth close. Steve Hall used his fund of trust to rebuild after a disaster and Margaret Carter used it to come back from the brink when the market suddenly fell. All three leaders say it was only possible because they had built a culture that could thrive in adversity.

While I hope it does not take a plant closing or major crisis for you to find out how positive your culture is, it is important to create a focus and structure within your organization that allows people to take the kind of pride in their work seen at Patchwork, Boelte-Hall and Harmon.

Questions

1. In what ways does the culture of your organization work against the goals or the efficiency of your organization? Can you see any evidence or cite examples?
2. How well do the culture carriers of your organization develop and carry the culture toward high performance?
3. How well integrated are your two cultures?
4. How many of the Performance Culture characteristics fit your organization?

CHAPTER 3

Influencing the Endemic Culture for the Good of the Organization

In the absence of a positive, business-oriented culture, work groups become defensive and suspicious due to excessive amounts of gossip, rumor mongering and poor information sharing on the part of middle and upper management. Poorly focused cultures quickly abandon company goals in the face of threat because the only unifying factor is social relationships.

If leadership can learn to use the energy of the culture, change will happen much more rapidly and permanently. The objective is to create a culture that corresponds to the needs of the market and keeps the organization healthy and competitive. To achieve that goal the organization needs to be intentional about consciously constructing the culture with a business purpose in mind. It is not a culture that is designed in every detail, but one that encourages the kinds of behavior needed to enhance the business position of the company and keep it on an increasingly profitable course.

Think of a culture as a series of relationships and practices, like a phone network where lines and switches govern the flow of information and communication. In the early days of phone communication, telecommunications companies laid transoceanic cables to allow direct phone communication between the continents. Each cable allowed more and better communication. As continents became "wired," communication increased. In World War I, one of the first things the British did was cut the direct transatlantic cables from Germany but left those that ran through Great Britain intact. This allowed the British to monitor communication between Germany and the Western Hemisphere. By cutting the cable, Great Britain changed and restricted the pattern of communication.

In corporate culture, middle management functions like the British by restricting the flow of communication. That is not to say that middle managers have bad intentions, but the culture says they are responsible and should know everything going on in their department. The only way to know what is going on is to make sure everything goes through them. That is why the British cut the cable and that is why middle managers often cut off direct communication between employees of their department and the department down the hall or upper management.

Getting the Culture Carriers' Attention

Most organizations with any size or history have strong cultural inertia, making it difficult to make even small changes. The only way to change such systems is to get the attention of the culture carriers.

practical tip

I have found that up to 30% of culture carriers in any organization cannot or will not adjust to major cultural change – they are far too committed to the current culture. For this reason, leadership needs to develop a plan to work with these people. Most are technically skilled and have a strong loyalty to the organization, they just can't seem to make the behavioral change to the new culture. By design or not, they hold the change process back.

Learning Point: To change the culture you must change the way the culture carriers communicate.

Several activities can help create new communication patterns for the culture carriers.

These activities include:

- Opening some management and leadership meetings to non-managers
- Using skip-level meetings where upper management meets with line workers regularly to discuss their concerns.
- Survey feedback on the key issues
- 360 degree feedback for the culture carriers

These simple activities do a great deal to help the two cultures begin to understand one another. With guidance and restructured communications, the organization often sees positive changes very quickly. Much more is required to make a permanent change in the culture, but these are generally a good start and fairly clear indicators of how positively the culture carriers respond to change.

One sure way to get the attention of the culture carriers is to literally reindoctrinate them to the new culture. There are several ways to do this. First, the organization can ask all supervisors and managers to reapply for positions in the new organization and receive comprehensive training in their new role. This is pretty strong medicine but it has worked well in some organizations.

The second method I call "transition management." All the culture carriers remain in their positions but are required to go through a course of study and behavioral feedback over six to eight months. Each person takes written tests and receives evaluation feedback from their boss, subordinates and peers on specific new behaviors they are asked to practice. During this time, the organization redesigns itself and those managers who have successfully completed the training are assigned to positions in the newly created structure. This is a broad outline of the process. The idea is to get people's attention and change their behavior before beginning the new organizational structure.

This approach provides strong support and clear guidance for change. Those who are capable of making the change will easily pass the various evaluations and tests.

The Special Case of Union Environments

Union environments have the strongest cultures, often built on mistrust of management, especially middle management. In such cases there are two important culture carriers – the line managers and the union representatives. Both groups vie for control of the culture as a means of gaining security, but neither has the power to dominate the system. In fact, if one or the other succeeds in dominating the system, it may lead to a major strike or financial collapse and a real crisis in security. Both groups waste a great deal of energy and time trying to achieve superiority with little hope of succeeding, and systemic failure is likely if they do. If they could succeed in developing a joint culture, a Performance Culture, much of the non-value-added activities and waste could be eliminated. A joint culture can provide more of the security both parties crave while allowing both to get more of what they want.

It is important for management to keep in mind that union leaders are first loyal to the endemic culture. In order for union leaders to feel secure, they must sense that they are seen as loyal to their membership. In bargaining or working on joint projects, management should make sure that they provide support for the union leadership. This may take the form of special joint training for union and management or involvement of union leadership in high-profile decisions. Above all, control the anger, negative comments and stereotypes that often characterize discussions in union or management meetings after the bargaining session is over. What is said outside the bargaining meeting often has more influence on the work force and membership's attitudes and behavior than anything said at the table. Posturing and bad-mouthing can quickly tear down trust that took months or years to develop.

Communicating with the Endemic Culture

The endemic culture is not monolithic but it has a very effective communication network. What you tell the receptionist may travel wide and fast. How you treat the janitor will be noted by him and everyone who sees you interact with him. How you treat the engineer differently from the delivery person will be carefully noted and conveyed to many others within hours if not days.

Learning Point: What you say to one person in the culture, you say to everybody. Make sure what you say is what you want everyone to hear.

The endemic culture shows itself most clearly
in the rumor and gossip system it supports.

Influence the culture through effective modeling of what you want. A trusted leader has tremendous influence. Even when people disagree with a leader or dislike him, they may still trust him because they see values consistent with his actions.

The Informal Communications Network

The culture shows itself most clearly in the rumor and gossip system it supports. Whether the culture is positive and business-oriented, or negative and relationship-oriented, is reflected in the gossip of the organization. It is extremely important to usurp the informal communications network by creating official communication systems that people can trust.

Paul Heacock, president of Human Dynamics, Inc., implemented self-directed work teams in his company, Margie McDaniels, a new employee, commented, "I have worked here for several months and I could not figure out what was different about this company. Then I received some training in the communication process we use here and it came to me: There is little or no gossip. People don't talk behind one another's backs and problems are expressed openly."

Paul Heacock remarked, "That really pleased me because it tells us that we have succeeded to some degree in learning how to communicate directly and openly in our company. People don't feel a need to back bite or gossip because they are not afraid to talk openly about issues and problems."

An open and trustworthy official communications system greatly diminishes the fuel needed for the informal rumor mill. Management gains influence in the culture by opening up the information and decision-making processes. This allows people to see what is happening and greatly reduces the urge to gossip or spread rumors.

When people lack trustworthy sources of information, they feel insecure. They don't know what is going on and feel "out of control" or "out of influence" in their work environment. Their natural response is to seek information from any source – no matter how unreliable – and maybe to act on that information. In most cases that information is unreliable and negative. Positive rumors do not seem to spread as effectively as negative ones. By their very nature negative rumors foster insecurity, which in turn creates more rumors and insecurity. It becomes a negative feedback loop that only good, positive, regular management communication practices can counteract.

The Performance Culture creates a structure that encourages direct and open communication and helps people build strong and supportive business-focused relationships.

People Want to Belong

Most people have a strong desire, even a need, to belong to a group. This desire is so powerful that it drives people to do extraordinary things to gain membership and maintain status with a group. Examples include hazing rituals of fraternities and sororities, boot camp in military organizations, and assignments given to "rookies" in many trade groups or professions. Few people want to spend eight hours a day with a group of people who do not accept them. And if they are not accepted, they go to great efforts to find out what will help them get accepted. If they cannot find any way to gain acceptance, most leave or change their work circumstances until they find a way or place to feel accepted.

The need for continued acceptance is just as powerful as the need to be accepted in the first place. Therefore, threats of being rejected or unaccepted by the group have a powerful influence, keeping individuals in line with the norms and expectations of the rest of the group.

Rites of Passage

Rites of passage are the ways in which a culture determines if you are acceptable to the group, whether you will be admitted, or on what terms you will be admitted. Whether it is a work group, a self-directed work team, the Masonic Order, or Knights of Columbus, all groups have some requirements for acceptance. When the United States Marines say, "The few, the proud, the Marines," they are essentially playing on one of the most ancient of social rules: In order to be seen as elite and valuable, an organization must be selective in its admission processes. Rites of passage are important, or the process would not have been so pervasive for thousands of years. What is their function?

Rites of Passage in Modern Society

Modern society has seriously downplayed rites of passage thinking of them as primitive and unnecessary to modern life. But this long-standing human tradition serves important psychological functions. Without rites of passage people do not feel connected to their world. They are not oriented to the values, norms and traditions of their organization. This lack of orientation, in turn, leaves people feeling like a ship without a rudder, tossed about with no sense of direction.

In general, the less rites of passage are emphasized, the less commitment the individual shows to the group. All cults recognize this and therefore make their initiates go through long and often elaborate initiation rites, sometimes spanning many years and many levels.

Rites of Passage and the Corporate Organization

While modern organizations do not, indeed should not, create dangerous or overly rigorous rites of passage, those that do nothing to indoctrinate new members of the organization get exactly nothing back in terms of loyalty and commitment to the norms and values of the organization. Rites of passage tap into the very powerful human need to belong and be respected by the group. They are an essential ingredient in a Performance Culture. A culture that carefully orients and educates new members creates high expectations and strong commitment. If there are no requirements for belonging, how can there be any pride in belonging?

Organizations that have little consciousness of their norms and values see no need to indoctrinate and educate new members. It seems like a waste of time and resources. I call these companies "warm body" organizations. That is, any warm body who meets the minimum qualifications for the job is hired without regard to his or her willingness to commit to the values and norms of the organization. This is a fatal mistake and will undermine a Performance Culture.

Management and teams must set and maintain specific requirements for new employees to ensure that all feel they have earned their way into the organization. If membership is too easy, then there is little sense of accomplishment and acceptance. What value is it to be accepted into an organization that takes in anyone, regardless of competence or skill? It is like the Groucho Marxs quote: "I sent the club a wire stating, 'please accept my resignation. I don't want to belong to any club that will accept me as a member'."[6]

How does your culture instill pride of belonging in every employee from the day they start work?

I have seen few organizations that do this well, but those that make even a reasonable attempt to orient and indoctrinate employees see clear results. The most important time in an employee's career with your company is the first week of employment.

Without proper orientation and indoctrination, new employees may bring attitudes that are a direct threat to your organization's culture and values. They bring with them the values and attitudes of the outside world. These values are probably not completely compatible with your system. Without proper indoctrination or orientation, these well-meaning new employees will show much lower commitment to your organization than senior team members.

Learning Point: New employees bring attitudes that may be a direct threat to a Performance Culture's values. Orient them very carefully.

Failure to indoctrinate and educate new employees is most common in times of rapid expansion. In an effort to get people on line and producing right away, proper indoctrination is often reduced or eliminated with the best of intentions. When the crisis is past, management often says, "We survived without all that training and indoctrination during the crisis, so maybe we don't need that expense." Senior employees soon notice that new employees are not getting properly indoctrinated. The result is that the more committed employees end up trying to enforce the norms and values of the organization with new employees, cleaning up their mistakes and training them, even as management hires more new, improperly indoctrinated people. Soon these loyal employees may say, "If management does not care enough to uphold the values and indoctrinate new employees, why should we?"

Worse yet, sometimes the most disaffected senior people latch on to new employees and begin teaching them values and attitudes that are counter and even harmful to the organization. With no clear orientation process, and values that are not well understood, any system soon begins experiencing high levels of friction and inefficiency. Conflict, poor morale, high turnover, labor problems or an undercurrent of dissatisfaction are clear signs that the values of the organization are not well understood or followed.

In my first full-time job out of graduate school I was hired as a counselor in an institution for delinquent boys. On my first day my boss brought me to his office and gave me a quick half-hour talk, then told me he was going on vacation for two weeks! He instructed his secretary to show me to my office. As the new kid on the block, I had an office clear in the back, far from the only exit door on the floor. The tradition was that the newest employees got the worst offices. As people retired, transferred or left, junior employees could move up into more desirable offices.

On the first day I met the fellow across the hall from my office. His name was Bart Simpson (name fictitious but not the initials). Bart had been on the staff for five years and refused to buy into the system of seniority so he kept his office in the back where, incidentally, he could be least observed by the boss.

Bart invited me in for a cup of coffee and began the process of unofficially orienting me to the institution. He told me who could be trusted and who could not. He told me who fudged their time sheets, he even told me how to fudge my own if I wanted. He told me who was sleeping with the CEO, who the chief psychologist was sleeping with and who I could sleep with if I played my cards right! Yes, Bart provided an invaluable orientation to the institution.

Two weeks passed. The boss returned from vacation and immediately called me into his office where he proceeded to tell me that my job was in danger and that I could be fired at any time since I was on probation. I asked him, "Why are you telling me this?" He replied, "You have been associating with Bart Simpson these last two weeks. He is trouble and he will get you in trouble as well. Stay away from him."

I was shocked and resolved to get out of that department as soon as possible. Four months later I received a transfer to another department with one of the best managers I have ever worked for.

Every organization has its Bart Simpsons. If you, the leader, do not ensure that every new employee is properly educated and indoctrinated, the Bart Simpsons of the world will. You have no choice. New employees will get indoctrinated one way or another – it's your choice how they learn the values of your organization.

First rite of passage in an organization – hiring

practical tip

Most of our client companies do some kind of testing and prescreening before hiring.[7] From the day potential employees pick up their application, they are told, "We are a team-based organization. You will be expected to take on responsibilities and show initiative in ways that you may not have done in your previous work. If this sounds exciting and interesting to you, please apply. If it does not, the team process may not fit your work style."

An important part of this early period is the hiring and evaluation of the new employee by the team. At Human Dynamics, team members take great care in orienting, training and evaluating new employees. If the employee is not capable of performing the job, now is the time to find out. Team members help in the hiring process and take their role very seriously, since they know they may have to work with this new employee for many years.

Once the prescreening has been completed, employees and middle management take over. Procedures vary for the different organizations, but all Performance Cultures give team members a meaningful role in the interviewing of candidates, even management candidates. Modeling teamwork to the candidate is critical at this stage. If the person is hired, she recognizes that she was not hired by a manager who may not know much about the work. She was hired by people who know the work intimately and will be responsible for her training in the coming months.

At the same time the team members see that they were instrumental in hiring the new person. They feel a special ownership, realizing that the candidate's success or failure depends largely on how well the team orients and trains her.

Once the new employee is on board, training in values and attitudes is essential. Gary Henrie, CEO, and Susan O'Brien, assistant director, at South Central Behavioral Services, conduct two days of orientation training for all new employees in their organization. During those two days they clearly spell out their expectations for ethics, values, behavior toward clients and how the team process works at South Central. After two days there is little doubt about the leadership's commitment to the team process and to the values of the organization.

practical tip In other organizations pairs of line workers do the orientation of new employees. The trainers are from the shop floor and they know that they represent the values of the company to the new employees. These trainers rotate regularly so that all teams from the floor become responsible for orienting new people.

Leaders also play an important role in the orientation process. At some point in the orientation process a leader must make a significant presentation to the group and interact with them in such a way that they see and understand the values of the organization. There is no substitute for leadership presence. Cameo appearances do not send the right message. When a leader shows up for 10 minutes and gives a little "glad to have you on board" speech, new employees have no opportunity to see and feel the commitment of the leadership to the values of the organization. The future of the company lies in the hands of new employees. It is worth some significant time from the leadership to make sure the new employee understands and feels their commitment to the mission and values of the company.

No matter how you do orientation training for new employees, it must take place as soon as possible after they are hired. The longer you wait, the easier it is for bad habits and attitudes to take hold. The "Bart Simpsons" will soon do the orientation for you.

Learning Point: Someone will orient your employees. The choice is whether it will be you, the leadership, or others who may not be committed to your values.

Second rite of passage – skill development

The next step in the rites of passage should involve some action, learning or skill development on the part of the trainee over a period of three to six months. Some companies use a checklist of action items that must be completed before the person can finish the probation period. These items are important steps the trainee must take to demonstrate competence, understanding or skill. In completing the requirements, the person is demonstrating initiative and the ability to self-manage. If the employee does not or cannot complete the tasks in the expected time frame, it may indicate a poor match with the company or team. Further investigation may be needed to understand what is causing the poor performance.

Third rite of passage – celebration

The last step in the "passage" by the employee is acknowledgment and celebration of acceptance into the company. This may take the form of a meeting with an upper-level manager, a certificate of achievement, a small pay raise, a promotion from probationary to permanent and a public recognition of the employee's new status in the company. This is an important event in the life of the employee, just as getting out of boot camp alive is an important event in a Marine's life! It should be celebrated by all. New employees should be made to feel proud that they are now an accepted part of the organization – that the organization has tested them and found them to be worthy of membership. No Groucho Marx here!

Questions

1. What have you done to get the attention of the culture carriers and achieve the kind of change you desire?
2. How do your hiring practices show selectivity and commitment to quality and teamwork?
3. How do you indoctrinate new employees?
4. Does your organization create conditions where people want to join or be a part of the organization? What is the evidence?
5. What does your organization do to develop a positive and healthy culture?

CHAPTER 4

Language:
A Reflection of Culture

anguage is the heart of culture. While leadership cannot control language it can guide, develop and influence it. By developing and using a specific language in your organization you begin the process of influencing the culture. Words give people ways to describe their experience. Left to their own devices they will use the words and concepts they already know, many of which may not be congruent with the values of the organization. When language is not developed in the context of the organization's culture, it leaves a language vacuum that is soon filled by the culture. The challenge of the leadership is to develop a system of training and development that harnesses the powerful and natural creativity of every person in the organization around a common language.

The Language Vacuum

Think of your organization as a giant language vacuum that constantly seeks to be filled from somewhere. You can fill it through training and constant cultural development, or it will be haphazardly filled by the culture.

Learning Point: Leadership's challenge is to feed the vacuum so there is no room or time for language and values that undermine the goals of the organization.

A strong corporate culture is able to create a language that at the same time helps employees understand the company and its goals and creates an identity with the company. There will always be some degree of separation between the intentional and endemic cultures and their language, but a Performance Culture seeks to blend the two inextricably.

Poorly integrated cultures have two distinct languages – the intentional and the endemic. Often the endemic language includes words that are the opposite or run counter to those of the intentional culture. These are words, phrases or sayings that describe the company or management ideas but can never be said in front of a manager. In the former Soviet Union there was a common saying, "They pretend to pay us and we pretend to work" – probably not words used in front of Stalin.

They saw little value in the meetings
but loved the snacks the company provided.

One company struggled for years to develop quality circles. After five years the effort was dropped because there was no sign of results. When we interviewed employees several years later, we found that the employees called the program "cookies and donut time." By that they meant that they saw little value in the meetings but loved the snacks the company provided. They also had names for the facilitators and managers who led the effort – none of which was flattering.

The further the intentional and endemic cultures are from one another, the more the languages diverge. It is the culture carriers who determine the language of the group and use it to support or undermine the goals of the company. When trust breaks down, the endemic culture often begins making fun of management and the intentional culture. Ridicule is one way the culture lets people know who is really in charge. Union leaders, unofficial leaders and even middle management and line supervision use ridicule, sarcasm or cynicism to convey to the work force their view of corporate initiatives.

Language is an indicator of the culture; it is not the culture itself. *When the work force voluntarily and spontaneously uses positive, business-focused language, it is a sign that the leadership has done a good job of melding the two cultures.*

Group Identity and Language

People gain a sense of identity through language and make significant assumptions about others who share their language.

Kurt Vonnegut made great fun of the idea of group identity based upon geographic origin or language in his book, *Cat's Cradle*. Inventing a whole set of descriptions based upon how people create affiliation and identity-words like Granfalloon, Karass, Wampeters, and so on[8] demonstrated how people make major assumptions about others based on nothing more than the college they attended or the place they were born.

People are eager and anxious to belong and go to great lengths to learn the language customs and traditions of their group. Just as you will be more accepted in the French or German community if you can speak its language, you will be much more accepted in a company if you can speak its unique language.

If your organization's language is well developed and consistent, reflecting the values and goals of the organization, it is a powerful tool for creating group identity and focus.

Levels of Language

There are five levels of language in an organization:

1. Language of the surrounding culture
2. Industry-specific language
3. Company language – the language that is unique to the company
4. Unit language – unique to the unit, regional office, local plant, and so on
5. Work group or team language – unique to the particular group of people in a work group

In this discussion we are only concerned with the last three levels, although the first two can also have an impact upon the workplace. For example, words and terms that are part of EEOC, OSHA, and HAZMAT come into the workplace from the surrounding culture. Words from pop culture also work their way into the organization's language.

As for industry-specific language, each industry has arcane words that can convey a complex idea in a single word or phrase. For example, when an engineer talks about the number of purlins required to support a roof, other engineers quickly understand what she is saying, whereas a nonengineer might find himself lost in the conversation.

Language provides a quick and precise way to communicate complex ideas. Just as industries have their own language, so do all corporations.

Language in the Company

When an organization develops its own terms and language different from another company in the same industry, it is a sign of internal cultural development. Language development is one of the clearest signs that a group is developing its own culture. Leaders can guide this process by giving the organization specific words and phrases that are subsequently used in conducting day-to-day business to describe the values and beliefs of the organization.

I have been impressed with a number of organizations' efforts along this line. Harmon Industries, Saturn Automobile, Boeing Airlift and Tanker Programs have well-developed internal language to describe and reinforce their integration of the endemic and intentional cultures. They do an admirable job of teaching the values of the organization and help to develop a Performance Culture.

On the opposite end of the spectrum, many organizations have an entire language of blame. Scape goating and witch hunts are a regular part of management behavior. When deadlines are missed or groups or individuals do not meet goals, the focus is on who is to blame rather than on what caused the performance deficiency and how the roadblocks to performance can be removed in the future. The effect of blaming language is to drive behavior underground. People start to hide mistakes rather than learn from them with the goal of not getting caught rather than doing the right thing.

Blame language in senior management is all too common. Many senior management meetings focus on "Who is the person or department responsible for our poor showing in the market this quarter?" rather than "What is the problem and how can we learn from it?"

> *A mistake is an event, the full benefit of which has not yet been turned to your advantage.*
>
> Peter Senge, 1990, p. 154.

When senior managers model problem-focused language, they support the very team values they most want to see used in their organization. Jeff Utterback and his leadership team used a token $25 award for the "Mistake of the Month." People did not line up

The Language of Blame
Blame Frame vs. Solution Frame

When you frame language around a person, it is "blame frame" behavior, but when you frame language around a problem, it is referred to as "solution frame" behavior. Solution frame focuses on the person's behavior and avoids any judgment of the person. It is often stated using an "I" or "we" message.

Blame frame, on the other hand, is focused on the person and often begins with "You ..." It is no surprise therefore that this causes instant defensiveness. Defensive people do not learn because they cannot listen. Therefore, when you create defensiveness, you minimize the person's opportunity for learning.

Most important, blaming behavior is itself a defensive activity. As a result, the blamer or fault finder is unlikely to learn from the encounter and is doomed to repeat the mistake. When in doubt about an interaction, look first at the person initiating the blaming or fault finding. That person is likely the most defensive. High levels of defensiveness or frequent defensive behaviors indicate a lack of emotional control.

People who consistently engage in blaming behavior are their own worst enemy and are the least likely to see how their own behavior is preventing them from reaching their goals. The more they engage in defensive behavior, the harder it is to get others to help them reach the goal. This in turn creates frustration, leading to a negative spiral and ineffective interpersonal relations. This cycle of defensiveness is deadly in a Performance Culture and quickly kills teamwork.

to make mistakes, but according to Jeff, the subtle message was, "We want to openly admit mistakes and learn from them. We want to be problem-focused not blame-focused. People telling their mistakes in public has dropped the fear level. While making a mistake is not a crime, failing to learn from one could be." He goes on to say, "It is a powerful step toward creating a culture where people say, 'I made a mistake and here is what I did to fix it.' The motto here is: 'What have I done today to make tomorrow a better place?'"

Belief Systems and Their Impact on Language

Essentially, there are two ways to view oneself in relation to the rest of the world:

1. Being in control, also referred to as having an internal locus of control, or
2. Being a victim, with an external locus of control.

Language says volumes about how people or groups view themselves and their world. A person with an internal locus of control has a strong belief that "I control my destiny and am in charge of my life," whereas a person with an external locus of control believes "I am a victim of circumstances. Events and other people control my life."

Internal Control

Persons with an internal locus of control believe they are in control of their life and strive to understand their world so they can better achieve their goals. They recognize that the best way to achieve their goals is to help others achieve. Internal people listen to their inner voice and emotions but use them as points of information NOT as the final answer. While they experience as much pain and insecurity as anyone, they use these experiences as a guide to understanding themselves and their world. People intuitively trust them because they are honest with themselves and others. They do not engage in self-deception but are often brutally honest with and about themselves. They are not afraid to admit mistakes because they believe mistakes are necessary for learning to take place.

An internal locus of control allows leaders to learn and adjust to their environment because they do not have to deal with the emotional baggage of denial and defensiveness. Internals see the world accurately, including the role they play in that world. This is an invaluable skill for the Performance Culture.

External Control

This belief system can be classified as passive-defensive or aggressive-defensive. Two different ways people use to defend themselves when they feel insecure or under pressure.

Passive-defensive people have a belief system that focuses on helplessness and powerlessness. They are acutely aware of their internal pain, fears and insecurities, which prevents them from seeing the world accurately. Their greatest fear is that others will make them look foolish or expose them as incompetent or incapable. Their internal dialogue is fearful and so loud that they have a difficult time analyzing their environment and adjusting their behavior accordingly. They tend to apologize and retreat quickly when someone disagrees with them. They avoid conflict and are easily intimidated. They tend to agree with others too easily without voicing their own opinion. When they get angry, they may strike out quietly and effectively but without fanfare. They are reluctant to tell you what they really think because they are afraid it might lead to conflict.

They tend to hide in their office or behind bureaucratic rules or the boss and often have difficulty delegating because they do not trust others to do the job. Whining and complaining about their subordinates, peers or boss is a sign of an external locus of control.

The culture does NOT TRUST this type of leader because they are quick to retreat and do not take a stand. They are seen as wishy-washy and incapable of making and sticking with a decision. Such leaders have a hard time gaining the confidence and trust needed for high performance in their organization. In a word: They are deadly to a Performance Culture.

When aggressive-defensive people stub their toe, they blame the rock. They believe the world is a hostile place and that they must strike first to get ahead. As a result, they resort to blame and fault finding. When they get angry, they tend to strike out at those nearest them. They may be hypervigilant to perceived wrongs and threats to their status or position. They have a hard time apologizing or admitting mistakes. Yelling and intimidation are extreme forms of this behavior. They deal with conflict by attacking people and tend to avoid conflict by keeping everyone else off balance. Finally, they rarely display openness and honesty unless they feel there is no other alternative.

Aggressive-defensive people are not aware of their inner processes and often say or do things that undermine their own goals. When others do not respond to them as they think they "should," they may get aggressive. They usually do not recognize when they have lost emotional control but they accuse others of losing control. They are poor listeners and often hear only what they want to hear. Their greatest fear is that others will discover their fundamental insecurity.

Anger and language that judges or implies that others are stupid or less intelligent are expressions of aggressive-defensiveness and an external locus of control. Also when a manager complains that she cannot trust or rely on her subordinates, this is another sign.

The culture does not trust aggressive-defensive people but would never say it to their face. Employees will work hard to please these persons, not to achieve or excel, but to avoid their anger and aggressive behavior. No wonder they have great difficulty getting reliable information about their performance. Aggressive-defensive people rarely trust others and few people trust them.

Cynical or sarcastic language is among the clearest signs that a leader has an external locus of control. Such leaders are judgmental and often imply that they themselves are superior or more intelligent but are victimized by others in some way.

Locus of Control and the Performance Culture

Corporate cultures display either an external or an internal locus of control. The language used by the intentional culture sets the pace. Senior managers and leaders display their locus of control by how they interact and talk with the work force. When they are defensive or not forthcoming with information, they display external locus of control. Blaming or accusatory language reflects a lack of emotional control and awareness, clear signs to the culture that the leader is not trustworthy.

The Performance Culture uses the language of internal control. Leaders model this language and insist on its use everywhere. This language includes goal focus, problem solving and self-discipline. David Spong, vice president/general manager of Boeing's Airlift and Tanker Program and 1998 Baldridge Award Winner, said before the 2000 International Conference on work teams, "Whining is OK ... occasionally, but be ready to propose a plan, find a way."[9] Similarly, Gary Henrie, CEO of South Central Behavioral Services, says, "If you come to me with a complaint, you better have a plan and be ready to work it." Both of these leaders say to the organizations, "We will not be victims. We will be proactive and control our destiny."

The Performance Culture puts far more resources in recognition and praise than in "catching people doing wrong." Communication from the leaders assumes people are doing the best they can with what they have been given. Now what can we do to help them do even better?

Blame, fault finding or finger pointing are not part of the Performance Culture. Managers who engage in this type of behavior are quickly coached in how to use the language of internal control, or let go. Top leadership does not allow inappropriate, defeatist behavior to be displayed by the most important culture carriers – middle management.

There is a transformative quality to the language of internal locus of control. As people learn it and use it, and the culture encourages it, their own beliefs begin to change. They see themselves less as victims and more as positive actors on their world. Time after time I have seen employees grow and develop as they and their team mates learn how to take action and control of themselves and their surroundings. That is a powerful part of the Performance Culture. Gossip, suspiciousness and blame all begin to melt away as people no longer feel trapped and defensive but find power in their ability to act proactively with their team mates and managers.

How Do You Create a Language of Achievement?

A language of achievement is language that shows an internal locus of control.

It encourages people to openly admit and discuss mistakes while seeking to learn and develop. The result is an environment where people make fewer mistakes and rarely repeat them – a culture where people feel they have influence or control over their world. It creates a culture that openly praises and recognizes people while encouraging active problem identification and solutions.

To create an achievement language use words or phrases that support key ideas. Keep them simple and use them often. Employees of our client companies know what a 59:59[10] meeting is and how it should be conducted. When the phrase "team business meeting" is used, everyone knows exactly what it means and what behavior is expected. Similarly, when the phrase "team goals" is used, each team member can describe what the goal is and where his or her team is in relation to it. The terms "appreciative" and "improvement" feedback are also well known. When a team member calls for a problem-solving session, everyone on the team knows what will take place at the meeting.

In developing a common team language, the organization also begins developing shared experiences, behaviors and expectations. This is the basis for the human infrastructure, which we will explore in Chapter 5.

Learning Point: To develop a Performance Culture, the language must be used by both the endemic and intentional culture in the same way and in every appropriate place and time. When the leader speaks before a group, she should use the language. When the union president talks to a team, he should use the language. Middle managers are expected to use the language every day.

Examples of a Performance Culture Language

59:59: Meetings begin and end on time along with specific rules for running meetings.

Aboutism: Gossip or criticism of others behind their back.

Huddle: A brief meeting to coordinate activities and balance workload within the team.

Shared leadership: All share in leadership in a team environment; no one may opt out of leadership responsibilities.

Real-time feedback: Individuals need and will receive information on their performance as it is happening, not a month or a year later.

Pea jobs: Work is shared on a rational basis not according to status or tenure. Tasks that are undesirable are not automatically given to the new or the least senior person.

The Language of Position

A special case in the use of language is in labeling positions people hold in the company. Labels have powerful behavioral impact. For example, the title "supervisor" comes with a lot of assumptions about the behavior expected of that position. Similarly, "manager" indicates a whole range of behaviors. These terms carry with them history and power. History, in that all employees have had previous experiences with managers and what they may or may not have done well and power; in that everyone knows that a manager has power that non-managers do not have.

Taking old terms and putting them into a new system is like putting used oil in your car. It may work but it is dirty and soon clogs up the system rather than creating a high-performance environment. At the same time, making up new words or titles while leaving the old system in place is like putting on clean clothes after a hard day working in the garden they may look nice – but the odor is bad.

To create an effective Performance Culture language, titles and labels must be changed in a way that makes them credible to the work force. It is important to change the language people use to help them escape history and preconceived notions, but major behavioral change must accompany the language change. We will discuss methods for making this change in Chapter 13.

The descriptions that are used make a big difference in how people perceive the organization. For example, many organizations call the top management group "the management team." The name may say "team," but on close inspection this group is almost always a single-leader group with little true teamwork. Most people see that what is called a team is not a team. "If management wants to pretend they are a team, then we will go along with it but they aren't fooling anyone but themselves." Such mislabeling damages the credibility of management from the very beginning of any culture change.

Many Performance Cultures downplay or even eliminate the idea of managers and, in turn, focus on leaders and leadership. Some call the group the leadership team. At the same time, the leadership is defined somewhat more broadly. At Standard Motor Products in New York City, the leadership team includes the union president. In other organizations the leadership team might include professional level people, as at Butler Manufacturing – or shop floor people, as at Harmon Industries. In these examples the idea of "leadership team" is not just a pretend idea but a reality that these organizations try to live each day.

Another example of labeling involves the line supervisor. This is generally where the most friction exists in the organization. People in this position try to walk both sides of the fence. They are subject to management's decisions but have to implement them with the work force while keeping both sides satisfied. They are often either loved or hated.

We will discuss the specifics of these positions later; for now it is important to rename this position. I use the term "team developer" since developing teams is what we want this person to do. Other organizations call the position a coach, coordinator, team leader, and so on. None of these titles describes the goal of the position or the behavior expected. However, with "team developer," we at once describe the goal of the position and the behavior. Of course there is more to changing a position than simply changing the name but in the Performance Culture, the name is important.

Training

While the training department is in no position to make cultural changes, it is a key to teaching people the requisite language. The training curriculum should use language of performance consistently and constantly, beginning with senior and middle managers. *Do not train anyone at the production level until all managers have been trained and are quite familiar with the language.*

Many a cynical word has been said about the manager who can't talk the language he is making everyone else learn. I witnessed one vice president single-handedly torpedo his own quality initiative when he stood in front of a company meeting and talked glowingly about the new quality training program. After listening to several minutes of platitudes, one of the union stewards stood up and asked, "Can you explain the term 'statistical process control' and why we have to learn it?" The VP confessed that he did not know as he had not taken the executive-level training that was required of all managers. He quickly turned the meeting over to an assistant who had not completed the training either. The laughter and ridicule from that meeting effectively undermined the local manager. No one believed the VP. The speech was a disaster.

> *Consistent with the traditional top-down model, most U.S. businesses continue to spend the majority of their training and development dollars on managers and professional employees ... of the $30 billion that business spends on employee training, only 7 percent reaches frontline employees.*
>
> **Edward Lawler III,**
> **1992, p. 234.**

You Set the Language Agenda

Anywhere people go, they generate and create language. Leaders have the choice of setting the language agenda or leaving it to the culture. Remember the vacuum we mentioned at the beginning of this chapter. Unless the leadership sets the language agenda strongly and clearly, others will fill the vacuum with language that may not match the culture you are trying to create.

Training is a critical place for setting this agenda. Frequent and repeated training keeps the language in front of the culture. The objective is to inundate the culture with the language and values of the company so that the people begin to adopt and use it as their own. When the culture voluntarily and consistently uses the language, it is a good sign that a Performance Culture is developing.

Learning Point: Much of the purpose of constant training is to make sure the leadership is setting the language agenda for the company and working toward a Performance Culture.

Team Learning

Training can strongly contribute to a positive endemic team culture by using a simple technique – team learning. Wherever possible, train the team as a whole unit at the same time. When a team learns the same language and concepts at the same time, team members tend to return to the work place and practice and reinforce the learning much more efficiently. While this may be more expensive in the short run, the skills are more likely to get transferred back to the workplace and therefore save money over time. When *individuals* are sent away for training, they return to the mountainous task of at once practicing the new skills, overcoming natural team resistance to new ideas, and trying to teach others the skills. That is too much to ask of any individual. As a result, the skills are often not effectively transferred back to the workplace.

Individual training in a team environment has a place when specialty skills are involved. But for teamwide skills, train the team together along with their manager or team developer. You will save a lot of time and money.

Learning Point: Look at the team as a single learning unit, not as a collection of individuals. This way you will be able to harness the power of teams for the learning process as well as the work.

Language and the Team

Teams develop their own words and phrases that are unique to them. Think of your own family. You have jokes, stories, and words that are unique to your family. They are part of the language of your family and that language is part of the glue that binds you together. In the same way, every team develops its own language to some degree. Our task as leaders is to guide the team to help it use positive language congruent with the values of the organization. It is easy for teams to get frustrated and begin using negative, externally focused language. They need coaching and guidance to learn new ways to deal with their frustration. Just as someone might swear like a sailor at home when they make a mistake, they don't bring that behavior to work. They learn to deal with their frustration in other ways in the work place. Teams can do this as well.

The key to positive, achievement-oriented team language is a goal focus with a strong emphasis on recognizing people when they are doing what we want and less emphasis on catching people making mistakes. As many psychologists and management authors have noted, punishing negative behavior only drives that behavior underground. The Performance Culture focuses on catching people doing good – finding people who illustrate the values of the new culture and praising and reinforcing that behavior.

Teach problem-solving and conflict management skills to give teams positive words and terms to describe their experi-

practical tip

ence and deal with the inevitable frustrations of working in a team environment. The leadership group and all managers should be actively involved in modeling the language of the intentional culture.

Controlling the Social Language

All organizations have language that describes the technical aspects of the work but they also have language to describe the social environment. This is the language that is most important to the development of the culture. It is the language people use to describe meetings they attend, decision-making processes, how they show care and concern for one another and how they view the leadership, management, and conflicts or problems.

The social language includes the way in which employees describe and deal with problems and conflicts in the organization. If you want to know what kind of culture exists in an organization, listen carefully to the social language of the group, especially the way people gossip or talk about one another.

Organizations can control and develop a positive language in the work place. Many managers have told me over the years, "You can not control gossip or negative language, it is just human nature." I emphatically disagree. Language can and is controlled in all workplaces already. Racist and sexist language once were tolerated in many work places until management and the law put a stop to it. Today not only will the manager intervene if racist language is used, but other workers will often find ways to let the person know that such language is inappropriate.

The Performance Culture controls or minimizes blaming language and other symptoms of external locus of control through a system of direct and open feedback to individuals and teams which we will discuss in Chapter 8. The more perceptions and feedback can be shared, the faster assumptions can be challenged and positive skills developed throughout the organization. The skill of feedback is arguably the single most important component of the Performance Culture. The ability of people to openly and frequently share perceptions about behavior and performance creates vast opportunities for improvement and rapid development at all levels. Most people report that just the act of participating in a Performance Culture causes them to grow and develop in ways no other work place can duplicate.

Questions

1. Who controls the idea agenda in your organization, the intentional or the endemic culture?
2. How is the leadership modeling the language and focusing on problem-solving language?
3. Can you identify specific times and places when you or your management group used blaming language?
4. What examples can you cite where training influenced language and helped a group develop?
5. If you went incognito for a week and worked alongside your employees, what language would you hear?

5

Infrastructure:
The Framework of Your Organization

I magine that you work in an organization that has the practice of changing managers every two or three years. Imagine also that when the manager changes, so does the computer system, the telephone system and the work layout. Today a new manager is appointed. She announces that all people will use XYZ word-processing software as opposed to the ABC software used under the previous manager. She also announces that the computers will be changed immediately to an entirely different type that is incompatible with all the previously used software. In what she sees as a move to make operations more efficient, she decides that the work layout will be reorganized so that all desks, work stations, and production centers will be moved to different locations over the next few weeks. In addition, one day she decrees that all wages and benefits will be reviewed with everyone getting a bonus once every three years based upon performance averaged over the last three years, but not counting any time before she came! As an employee under this manager it won't take long before you begin thinking she is crazy!

Our imaginary manager is seriously meddling with the infrastructure of the organization. What is an infrastructure?

Infrastructure Defined

Infrastructure is a commonly held resource that supports certain economic behavior.

Because infrastructure is so important and fundamental to economic well-being, we often take it for granted. Infrastructure is often invisible until it is no longer there or breaks down. For example, we take the highways and phone system for granted until one day the highway is closed for construction or the phones are knocked out by a storm. Then we quickly realize how much we rely on that supporting infrastructure to get to work or to check on our children at school. This type of infrastructure is designed, developed and maintained by someone besides ourselves.

In the work setting the infrastructure is often designed, developed, maintained, or at least controlled, by the company itself. The computer systems, the phone systems, the Intranet systems, pay systems, software systems – all these function within the control of the company and are intended to support certain economic behavior in employees and managers.

DILBERT reprinted by permission of United Feature Syndicate, Inc., Scott Adams, 1998, p. 56.

Total chaos resulted and the company at great expense had to hire an accounting firm to come in and straighten the mess up.

Most organizations recognize the importance of maintaining a solid, reliable and consistent infrastructure to support the work of employees. If managers were allowed willy-nilly to change the infrastructure, it would seriously hurt the employees' ability to do their work. It hurts by diverting enormous amounts of energy into learning how to use the new infrastructure. It also hurts because workers are not sure they can trust the new structure and may end up trying to use both the old and the new structure at the same time.

One company switched to a new accounting package. While the new package was probably better than the old, the training was expensive so the company trained only a few employees, expecting those who were trained to teach the others. When the "teachers" returned after their training, they were so swamped with the budget process that they found it easier to use the old system. Not only were they not using the new system, they only attempted to train the other employees as they found time. As a result, no training program or system was used, causing a great many errors when they finally began using the new system. People quickly learned that you could not trust the output of the new system and therefore continued to use the old system. When the deadline came to make the final switch to the new system and the old system was taken off the computers, total chaos resulted and the company at great expense had to hire an accounting firm to come in and straighten up the mess.

The Human Infrastructure

It is easy to see how much we depend on the physical infrastructure and what happens when it is not designed or managed properly. But it is not as easy to see or understand the impact of other types of infrastructure, specifically the human infrastructure, because it deals with our own behavior or cultural norms and practices. In the workplace these are so taken for granted and are so much a part of us that we often cannot recognize when they are poorly designed or ineffective.

Human Infrastructure Defined

The human infrastructure is the commonly held system of communication and interaction in an organization, including formal systems such as pay and performance reviews as well as less formal systems.

Examples of the human infrastructure include:

- The way an organization encourages or discourages communication between upper management and line employees
- The method by which managers reward, praise, punish, or ignore workers
- The method and process by which one unit communicates with another
- The method and process by which managers communicate information to employees
- The method and process by which managers involve employees in decision making
- The manner in which work groups are organized for production
- The manner in which employees are recognized, praised or corrected
- The norms and structure around which conflict is managed

Most organizations do not systematically design their human infrastructure, leaving it up to the whims of the endemic culture, including middle management and employees. Just as the manager we discussed earlier changed the computer, phone and software systems, any incoming manager can change the human infrastructure and cause great confusion and uncertainty, destabilizing the group and undermining any trust or cohesion the previous manager had developed. Since the human infrastructure is not systematically designed, it often functions counter to the goals and direction of the company.

However, when a solid physical infrastructure is established it is predictable and trustworthy. When you need to make a phone call, you simply pick up the phone and dial, expecting that the system will work. Reliability is key to an effective system. Well-designed and highly functional infrastructures allow the user to become much more efficient. For example, e-mail is faster and more convenient than either postal or fax systems.

A well-designed human infrastructure serves the same purpose by allowing people to communicate more effectively and quickly. It creates the conditions where employees can trust the communications within the system and move effectively toward a common goal. Poorly designed human infrastructure creates conflict, misunderstanding, and goal confusion.

Information Bottlenecks and Nodal Structure

Organizations are often put together in a haphazard way for the convenience of the most politically powerful in the hierarchy or bureaucracy, or were designed for an earlier time and technology. In more traditional systems the key manager or department head can be seen as a "node" of the organization, a central point through which communications must pass. Most traditionally designed organizations are full of nodal positions. For example, entire organizations may be organized around a marketing department manager or a vice president of finance. The organizational chart often does not show the full extent of the influence or power that a nodal person or department has.

The nodal organization is not efficient for the customer or the employee. It is not even efficient for management since significant numbers of managers are not part of the node; hence they are often

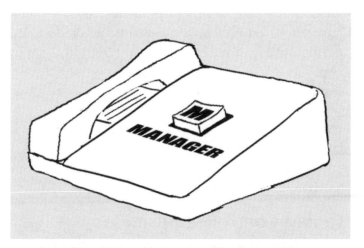

In traditional hierarchical systems the key manager or
department head can be seen as a "node" of the organization –
a central point through which communications must pass.

left out of the communication loop until the opportunity to influence decisions is long past.

Nodal forms of organization create bottlenecks in human communication by segregating areas or territories within which communication is sequestered. Within such a structure it may be seen as a betrayal of the division or department chief, for example, if one were to talk about an internal issue with another department.

A nodal infrastructure behaves something like this: The department head holds staff meetings to inform people and insists that initiatives and communication be approved through her. At the same time, the department head withholds some pieces of information from the group. Information such as budgets, finances, pay scales, market information, executive decisions and initiatives may all be withheld from the group in the name of protecting them or for some other reasons.

The excuses for withholding information always appear legitimate when viewed from an information control viewpoint, but have the net effect of keeping people in the dark about issues that affect them. Excuses for withholding information often are paternalistic or maternalistic. The manager might say, "I don't want you to worry about that kind of stuff, you have enough work to do without being told about all the finances and budget problems." Or, "I don't think you need to know about new product development until it is ready. It might distract you from focusing on our current products."

All of this assumes a "Father or Mother knows best" attitude toward the work force. It fosters a narrow focus, allows for territorial behavior, and encourages sequestering of information within organizational units as the node controls important portals of information and protects his or her own status and position in the hierarchy.

The Family-Controlled Business

The family-owned or closely held company is the quintessential nodal organization. Since a large number of corporations begin as family-owned enterprises, it is an important structure to understand. To maintain status and control of critical resources, the family often places family members or trusted associates in nodal positions, regardless of their competence. Leaders may be willing to suboptimize the larger system to ensure their own prosperity. That is, while greater profits would accrue to the system with decentralization, they maintain strong nodes so that they can closely control resources.

Families often have trouble seeing how this type of structure inhibits growth and efficiency in the family business. One plumbing company with about 50 employees had a significant turnover in the group the owner's son managed, who was widely known for his temper tantrums and arbitrary decisions. One day a particularly seasoned and well-respected journeyman plumber resigned and wrote a letter to the owner about his son's behavior. When the owner was asked why he allowed this to happen, his reply was, "I would rather lose a plumber than a son." In other words, he was willing to suboptimize the organization to avoid conflict with his son.

But many other organizations have seen the folly of this type of structure and have eliminated nodal systems and moved toward a more open infrastructure. Some family-owned businesses have recognized the problem and put in checks and balances. If family members wish to participate, they will be subjected to a higher behavioral and performance standard than others at their level. That is, family members get clear and unequivocal information about their performance and learn to be models for the organization's culture rather than hide behind their name.

The primary threat to family-owned businesses is the failure to pass on the business to the next generation. Fewer than 65% of family businesses are successfully passed on to the second generation, and only 5% survive to the third generation.[12] I suggest that a fundamental reason for this abysmal failure is the inability of the system to decentralize its information flow. Most family businesses remain closed in terms of information flow and decision making. With so much information and power concentrated in a few hands, the organization as a whole is dependent upon, and hostage to, the whims and political infighting of the family. When the intentional culture is in such conflict, the endemic culture cannot be focused on performance and achievement.

Appraisal, Compensation and the Nodal System

Nodal systems have a strong tendency to use security-enhancing approaches to behavioral control and management. That is, leaders or a bureaucracy control performance appraisals, pay, bonuses, personnel policies, and so on. While authors from Edwards Deming to Aubrey Daniels, Thomas Gilbert to Edward Lawler III and Peter Block have documented that traditional evaluation and performance, pay and personnel systems are very poor motivators of human performance, these systems persist.

No traditional performance evaluation system ever motivated a work force to achieve high performance. No traditional "merit" pay system ever made a government work force give its best year after year. No traditional discipline system ever improved labor relations or reduced grievances. These systems were never intended to motivate people, to involve employees or to ensure fairness in the workplace. Instead they were designed to maintain the illusion of control on the manager or leader's part.

Peter Block sums it up best in his book *Stewardship*:

"Everyone likes the idea of pay for performance, but most of us have rarely experienced it. We most often get paid on the basis of how our boss evaluates us. This is more accurately called pay for compliance. One human being's evaluation of another is fundamentally subjective. We try to overcome subjectivity by using numbers to rate each other. We try to be objective in what we look at and pick hard-nosed business objectives to evaluate. Still, it is very difficult to directly attribute real organizational outcomes to the actions of a single individual. Given the subjective nature of evaluations, we are as likely to be rating and paying people for compliance as we are for performance. Small wonder that when I ask groups to raise their hands if they feel they are paid for performance, 90 percent of them miss out on the chance for exercise. What we have now are pay systems based on a parent-child model and they invite disillusionment. We cannot create a feeling of ownership and responsibility with pay systems that depend on someone else's generosity."[14]

Compensation systems are also significantly different in the Performance Culture. While there may still be some focus on individual performance, there is strong emphasis on group performance. Recognizing that no one person can actually achieve high performance without a good deal of support from others, the system tends to reward both the high performer and the group who supports her.[15]

Manager as Software

In a nodal infrastructure, managers have a great deal of freedom to manage as they see fit. The traditional performance appraisal and pay systems are a major symbol of the nodal structure. It creates a dominance and dependency relationship that has very little relation to the internal or external customer. The attitude is, "Every manager should be allowed to manage in his or her own way as long as it is legal and within corporate guidelines. If they get results, then leave them alone. Everyone has their own style."

How much time and energy do employees spend adjusting to an internal political infrastructure that has nothing to do with serving the customer? Looking at it from an even broader perspective, how much time do other managers and other departments spend adjusting to changes in the infrastructure every time a new manager comes on board? Remember our examples early in this chapter about changing computers, phone systems, and software. Remember how crazy that sounded? Now look at how a change in managers does the same amount of damage to the human infrastructure. When there is no clear expectation for management behavior, the human infrastructure is subject to the whims of each different manager.

To avoid problems with new software we go to great lengths to make sure it is compatible with the old system and that users will be able to make the transition with the least amount of confusion.

We also train people carefully in the new software to minimize mistakes. We may even give people job aids, like on-line help or help lines, to get through the difficult parts of the transition and learning curve.

Think of managers as a software application program designed to help employees serve the customers. How much compatibility is there between managers, between company and manager, between manager and other departments? How user friendly is the manager? All these issues are as important as planning and implementing a software solution.

Learning Point: It is as important to manage the change in leadership as it is to manage a change in software systems.

Performance Culture Infrastructure

Structure is a key concept in the Performance Culture. It simultaneously saves time and energy and creates a platform upon which people can be creative and productive. Attention to the structure is critical. When a building, machine or social group is created there must be a framework for the process. The skyscraper has an internal skeleton of steel and supports. The struts and girders do not determine what kind of business will take place in the building, but it is certain that no business will happen if the struts and girders do not do their job. Once it is built, the walls may be changed and the furniture moved many times over the life of the building. Internal rearrangements may happen frequently but business inside the building does not change the steel infrastructure every time the business changes. The building's infrastructure often stays the same for the life of the building.

Structure creates a set of assumptions on which the group can rely. The group knows the structure and does not need to spend time and energy floundering around trying to figure out how to do things like:

- Manage conflict between team members
- Plan, schedule and execute the day's or week's work

- Cover for other teams or members who may be unavailable to the customer
- Make customer-focused decisions without management involvement
- Give performance feedback to other team members or the leader
- Communicate with another team or department

When structures are unclear, groups end up spending a lot of unnecessary time trying to figure out things like:

- "How do I tell the boss he is wrong without him getting mad at me?"
- "How do we satisfy the irate customer when we can't get a decision from the boss?"
- "How do I deal with a coworker who isn't doing her work?"
- "How do I work with another department without having to go to my boss all the time?"
- "How do I get things done when I can't get any time or guidance from the boss?"

A well-defined open infrastructure is both a time – and energy-saving device. It allows workers to spend their time productively rather than constantly having to negotiate and make one-time rules and agreements for every situation and second-guessing the boss.

Structure allows people within an organization to predict one another's behavior, which in turn allows them to trust the environment. It sets specific rules and expectations within which people can function with some level of comfort and security.

To effectively design the human infrastructure for a Performance Culture, the organization must follow basic principles of human communication and interaction. While quite simple, they are often overlooked. They include:

1. Face-to-face communication on a regular and routine basis
2. Clear and consistent focus on the specific common goals held by the group
3. A system for frequent and continuous recognition and reward for desired performance

4. Real and regular opportunity to influence decisions across levels of hierarchy

5. Regular direct opportunities for the various organizational levels to communicate their satisfaction or dissatisfaction with the organization

6. Organizational units that are small enough to facilitate communication and develop trust

7. Organizational units that are designed around a common goal

8. Direct interface and responsibility between producers and customer

9. An appraisal system that emphasizes cooperation and teamwork

10. A compensation system that measures and rewards group performance at least as much as individual performance

To the degree that these principles are followed, the organization will be able to develop a reliable infrastructure. As a result, when a person or group tries to communicate, they have a high expectation that communication will be transferred effectively through the system.

Much of the rest of this book will be devoted to understanding these elements and how they work in a Performance Culture.

Questions

1. Are performance appraisals manager-focused or do they require a wide range of input from team members, internal or external customers?

2. Does your structure systematically encourage upward feedback and information flow?

3. Does your organization have a nodal structure that creates information bottlenecks?

4. Does your compensation system actively reward teamwork?

5. Are employees dependent upon their manager for much of their information?

6. Does your communication structure encourage open and direct communication regardless of title? How would you know?

CHAPTER

6

The Leaders'
Impact on Culture

Effective leaders help make people independent and responsible. One way to do this is to create a Performance Culture that (a) fosters leadership at every level; (b) eliminates employee dependency; (c) develops self-reinforcing behavior in the teams; (d) encourages corrective feedback to leaders and team members alike; (e) develops goal focus for the entire organization, and replaces status systems with performance systems.

Aaron and the Cows

My son was about nine years old and very eager to please his great grandfather, whom we call Pappy. One morning about 10 o'clock while we were visiting at his farm, Pappy gave Aaron a long stick and told him to go get the cows and bring them in the barn so they could eat lunch. Aaron ran out, eager to do this important job. He promptly started trying to herd the cows. Running all over the pasture he would just get one going the right direction when another would bolt the opposite way. After an hour and a half Aaron was totally frustrated, worried that he had let Pappy down and afraid that the cows would not get to eat that day, and finally came crying into the farmhouse. Pappy calmed him down and asked him to follow him to the barn. Here he picked up a bucket, filled it with feed then took Aaron's stick and hit it on the bucket several times. All 20 cows came stampeding to the barn. Aaron was amazed and quite relieved that the cows would get to eat.

Getting Cooperation

The idea that people can be managed is an illusion based upon old notions of power and influence. The only way leaders get cooperation is if people want to cooperate. As a result, the leader must create conditions where people want to cooperate and want to

Just as the cows learned the stimulus that brought them to their lunch, Aaron had to learn the appropriate actions to get the desired response from the cows.

learn how to cooperate. Just as the cows learned the stimulus that brought them to their lunch, Aaron as leader had to learn the appropriate actions to get the desired response from the cows.

The most astute managers know how to get the highest level of effort from a work group using the power of the culture. These managers effectively teach members of the culture to take much of the responsibility for praise, recognition and reward. The more this happens, the closer they become to being a Performance Culture.

Fostering Leadership

The endemic culture is generally disorganized and fragmented. Nevertheless, this culture often takes root fast and is strong. The shipping department may have conflicts and disputes with manufacturing. Engineering may have difficulties with operations. Customer service may have frequent friction with marketing. Union representatives may openly criticize one another. On the surface, it appears that these groups have no single culture. But, in reality, in the normal fragmentation of an organization with a poorly formed culture, each group sees its own interests as paramount.

Left alone, the culture not only fragments but tends to be reactive. That is, little motivates it except controversy and perceived abuse by management. Unfortunately, it is far easier to focus on the negative and on what is not wanted than to define what is wanted. Those who are disaffected easily fill any leadership vacuum. To prevent this, positive leadership must be developed at every level throughout the culture.

The work force craves leadership that will help define what it wants and help it move forward. Union leaders know this well and work hard to provide leadership for the culture. Many unions give their shop stewards far more training in how to lead than companies give their supervisors and managers. In one union plant every union official has received 40 hours of training in leadership each year for the last three years. The supervisors in the same plant completed a total of 16 hours of training in the same period. It would be difficult to develop an effective intentional culture with such a lack of skills and development of the most important culture carriers – line supervisors.

The best situation is for both management and the union to develop leadership among all parts of the organization. Joint leadership training is a positive and effective way to develop leadership that has a common vision and goal.

To unite the culture around positive, goal-oriented values, the leadership must intentionally develop the leadership skills of the work force. Almost everyone can lead given the proper support and training. I have seen a shy, retiring 60-year-old lady stand up and take charge of team meetings. I have seen a painfully introverted computer programmer take a passionate lead in the team to develop a new product. And I have seen a very adversarial union steward, who had filed hundreds of grievances over the years, take a strong positive role in leading the corporate steering committee.

Leadership can come from anywhere at anytime if people are given the skills and the expectation. Gaining the involvement and commitment of the culture requires that leadership be intentionally developed in every area of the organization. The more people are involved in leading in the organization, the more influence the intentional culture will have.

Gary Henrie, executive director of South Central Behavior Services, has led a team-based organization since the early '90s. The multiservice behavioral health care agency he heads has been emphatic from the start that leadership can come from anywhere. "A leader creates an environment where people can truly chase their dreams. When you do that, you'll get creativity from people you won't believe. It will improve the organization," Gary says.

Joe Forlenza, vice president at Standard Motor Products, has been a champion of teams for more than a decade. He speaks with pride about an interview with a Wall Street Journal reporter who called to do an article on teamwork. Asked who steps forward in his organization, Forlenza's enthusiastic response was, "It is both amazing and interesting to see when someone rises to the occasion. In a team-based environment, we continue to see people making the extra effort, stepping into the limelight."

Team-based organizations thrive on the development of leadership within the teams. Therefore leadership development at every level is necessary in order to make the transition to a Performance Culture.

Employee Dependency

When I hear a manager complain about employees' lack of initiative, common sense or ability to think for themselves, I often find it a direct reflection of the way the manager treats employees.

First-line managers are generally not promoted because they are empowering, but because they get results by maintaining a strong hand on the reins and dependency in the work force.

Only 20% of the people I see in first line management positions seem to have a natural skill or proper training to lead people. While these people are great assets to the company, they cannot overcome the inertia of the other 80%. Their talents are often underutilized.

When organizations try to convert supervisors and managers – the culture carriers – into coaches, they are often set up for failure. A few training classes will not change years of poor leadership habits nor will it change the culture.

While the culture carriers can create dependency, employees often help perpetuate it. It is easier to let the manager take the responsibility than to take the risk of responsibility themselves. The endemic culture often has strong values about who should and should not have responsibility. The situation is similar to family dynamics.

When my daughter Adrienne was 12 years old, I gave her a laundry basket and told her she could now begin doing her own laundry. She had been helping me off and on for a couple of years and knew how to sort clothes, measure soap, and so on. I told her to ask if she needed help or advice but it would be her responsibility from now on.

She was not happy with the situation but she took the basket and went on her way. A week later she came stomping into my bedroom as I was getting ready for work and exclaimed, "Dad I don't have any clean clothes, when are you going to wash them?" I reminded her that it was her duty to do her laundry and asked if she needed any advice or help. She didn't like the answer and stomped back out.

Another week went by and she confronted me again. As before, I asked if she needed advice or help. She became angry and said, "Laundry is not the kid's job, it's the parent's job." I explained to her that she was mature enough to take care of many of her own things, including her clothes. Again she stomped out.

Adrienne was on strike. She was not
about to do her own laundry!

Yet another week went by, Adrienne's clothes were all piled up in
her closet and bedroom and a distinct smell was starting to emanate
from her room. She now began to borrow clothes from friends. She
was on strike! She was not about to do her own laundry.

About a week later I came home early one day. As I entered the
house through the laundry room, I met my eight-year-old son Aaron.
"You aren't supposed to be home now!" he said excitedly. Noticing
the washing machine was running and piles of clothes everywhere, I
asked him what was going on. "Adrienne is doing her laundry but
you are not supposed to know. Boy, is she going to be upset." I did
not say a word to her and she quietly began doing her own laundry.

It would have been a mistake to acquiesce and do Adrienne's
laundry for her again. Doing it for her would only perpetuate her
dependency on me and delay her independence.

Managers often perpetuate dependency behaviors because they
believe it is easier to do things themselves. When they meet

resistance, they take the easy way out rather than looking at the long-term development of the team. As a result, managers create people who learn to let them do it. When you decide to off-load a duty to someone, you have to train them well and be willing to let them make some mistakes on their own. You also have to stick to your guns until they realize that you will coach them but not do it for them. They may do a poor job, or no job, in hopes that you will back off and start doing it again.

Dependency behaviors die hard. Once people learn dependency, they feel comfortable and protected because:

- Management can make decisions.
- Management can do the scheduling.
- Management can deal with the difficult customer.
- Management can make the hard budget decisions and recommendations.
- Management can deal with the conflicts in the group.

All of these tasks require responsibility and initiative as well as a certain amount of risk. Work is a whole lot easier when management takes care of it.

In a Performance Culture, the idea is to move away from dependency – from taking care of people. Therefore, workers are expected to:

- Take as much responsibility as possible
- Learn how to take reasonable risks
- Deal with interpersonal issues constructively

It can be just as difficult for employees to learn to take responsibility as it was for my daughter to learn to take responsibility for her laundry. The initial response will be to push the responsibility back on you. But your task is to coach and assist. Make it clear that increasing responsibility is an expectation in a team-based organization. Adults who can manage their own household, raise kids, balance their checkbook, serve on community boards and deal with a host of other things are surely capable of that same level of responsibility in the work place.

Information Control and Dependency

Dependent behavior is often based on the ability to control information from a central point but that is becoming more and more difficult.

With easily available information outside of
formal sources, it is impossible to maintain traditional
discipline and dependency in the work force.

When information can flow instantly from one employee to another 1,000 miles away by e-mail, trying to control its flow through traditional channels often makes management look ignorant, malevolent or naïve. In this environment, line management feels caught in the middle between upper managers who give limited information and employees who may already know what is going on.

In the Performance Culture this situation is largely eliminated since information is widely available to anyone who wants to know.

Often line workers are involved in the meetings where major decisions are made. There are no secrets so there is no rumor mill.

After a friend of mine had applied for a job at a large company, he got online and started chatting with employees of the company. The information he received turned him off, so he decided not to take the job when it was offered. This kind of scenario will become more and more common in the future. The culture you develop inside the company will become more transparent to the outside world. The best candidates will look at your culture to decide if they want to join your company. In the future it will be more difficult to control information and maintain dependency.

Learning Point: It is hard to maintain a "party line" when the ranks can get on the Internet and find out more about your company than many of the middle managers can learn from their own CEO.

The Endemic Culture and Leadership

With large numbers of employees and smaller numbers of managers, the endemic culture has a much greater opportunity to set the tone of the workplace. If the manager is spread too thin among a large number of people, she has much less opportunity to influence the development of a strong business culture. At the same time, the fairly unskilled techniques of most line managers will be severely tested and stretched beyond usefulness.

To influence the culture the leader must use a whole new set of skills unlike those of traditional command and control skills. These skills include:

- Modeling
- Involvement skills
- Goal-setting skills
- Consensus-development skills
- Accountability skills
- Infrastructure development skills
- Teaching and training skills

The task of the leader is to help develop the endemic culture so that it is congruent with the goals and direction of the company. With large numbers of people, more leadership is required and less management. For this to work, employees must be hired and trained to be more self-directed and to be able to coordinate their own activities with others without the intervention or direction of the manager.

Teaching the Culture to Self-Reinforce

Since the leader cannot be all places at once recognizing and reinforcing the new behaviors of the Performance Culture, he must teach the culture to take on this responsibility itself.

When you are in a meeting, on a business trip, on vacation, who is praising and recognizing your group? When you are in your office all day writing a report, who is out there reinforcing and praising your group? When you are working with one subordinate, who is working with the rest of the group?

The vast majority of behavioral reinforcers in your work environment come from peers. Since employees have much more contact with peers than with the boss, peers have many more opportunities to influence behavior. How can we use this powerful force to guide people toward the goals of the company and a Performance Culture?

Leaders can teach the culture how to praise, recognize and reward positive goal-directed behavior with minimal management involvement. There are several ways to teach and reinforce this to the culture, including the following:

1. Modeling from the leadership
2. Teaching members how to recognize and praise goal-directed behavior
3. Teaching workers how to productively deal with interpersonal conflicts with minimum management involvement
4. Creating systems that encourage employees to depend more on each other than on management

5. Changing the function of the supervisor or manager to reflect a coaching/teaching model
6. Training managers and expecting them to teach and reinforce self-directed behavior

It requires the use of all these methods to create a culture that evolves into a Performance Culture.

Once you recognize that you are not the primary reinforcer in the environment, your task becomes one of influencing the culture to provide a good deal of the behavioral reinforcement needed. While leaders are powerful reinforcers, teaching workers how to recognize and reinforce will multiply the effect of what they do. The leader cannot be everywhere at once but the culture can.

The following examples illustrate how this works. At the SMP (Standard Motor Products) plant in Wilson, North Carolina, the teams are taught to regularly give behaviorally specific performance feedback to one another in a way that minimizes defensiveness. The focus is primarily on positive, goal-directed behaviors, but inappropriate behaviors can also be mentioned. The company uses various types of recognition and rewards that encourage people to support one another and other teams. The very act of recognizing someone else is often rewarded by the team developers and managers because they are trying to teach people how to recognize good performance without management involvement.

> *Relationships are the foundation on which effective rewards and recognition are built. When you have that foundation, rewards and recognition enhance other forms of reinforcement. If you don't have it, you will waste your money and your time trying to buy discretionary performance.*
> **Aubry Daniels, 2000, p. 164.**

During one particularly heavy work week the plant manager, Mark Payne, worked on the floor packing boxes for a day. The teams were impressed by his model and commitment, but more importantly, they spontaneously sent him a thank-you card for his help. This type of response indicates that the teams are learning to follow the model of praise and recognition set by the leadership.

At Human Dynamics, Inc., the company holds a luncheon meeting each Friday where employees talk about and demonstrate their work for the week. The meeting is full of praise and applause for the hard work, creativity and risks that employees take for the company. Much of the recognition comes from peers rather than management.

Harmon Industries in Riverside, CA, called a company meeting once a month where a multitude of teams and individuals were recognized. A combination of informal and formal recognition was used. Individuals or teams who had gone the extra mile were recognized. Teams who had achieved their stretch goals for the month received praise – in short praise and recognition pervaded the culture.

All participating Teaming Up® companies require their teams to learn and use self-reinforcing methods. These are practiced at least once a month by every team for the first year or until they become positive habits. At a recent visit to the SMP Kansas plant I watched as people give and receive feedback like professionals – much better than most managers. Even Kenny Lynch, the union chairperson, and Steve Doman, the team developer, received feedback like anyone else. The teams have been using this self-reinforcing process for nine years so they are very good at it by now.

The purpose of these activities is:

- To teach the culture how to praise and recognize good performance eight hours a day, not just when management is around.
- To correct behavior without need for management intervention.
- To fill the culture with so much goal-focused stimulus, it will have little or no time or energy for less constructive activities.

Congruence and the Model of the Leader

The most powerful tool a leader has is her own behavior. The work force constantly watches the model of the leader and tests that model against her words. Leader behavior that is highly congruent with the words spoken will create the conditions for trust. When a leader's words and deeds are congruent, the culture learns rapidly how to effectively interact with the leaders. If the leader says, "I expect involvement in key decisions from a wide range of people" and then proceeds to regularly gather people to discuss and decide how to implement product changes, equipment arrangement, customer requirements or hiring practices, members of the culture will soon adjust to these requirements and become very involved.

But if the words and deeds of the leader are inconsistent, confusion will result and the culture will create its own standards and direction, independent of the leader.

Congruence is the key to effective use of modeling in leadership.

Congruence Defined

Congruence refers to the degree of harmony, overlap or parallelism between a person or group's stated purpose and the observed behavior.

When a leader says "All meetings will start on time" and then proceeds to make sure the meetings start promptly 90% of the time, that is congruence. There is never perfect congruence and it may be subject to interpretation. Therefore, it is important to quantify or objectify the behavior to reduce opportunities for misinterpretation. In auditing a leader's behavior one might use a checklist like the following:

1. Do meetings start on time?
2. Does the leader ensure that 80% or more of team members participate in every meeting?

3. Does the manager solicit the team's written input before making the final decision?
4. Does the team developer get back to the team to explain his decision regardless of whether they agree or not?
5. Have 10 or more people been given special recognition this quarter based on performance?

All these questions call for answers that are observable and even measurable. In other words, they indicate whether the leader's behaviors are congruent with the organization's stated values.

Establishing congruence requires a well-developed feedback system through which the leader can gauge how well the model is working and how clear it is to those who observe it. We are generally poor judges of our own behavior and even poorer judges of our impact on others. Without a feedback system, the model soon becomes unfocused and even inappropriate. Just as a rocket launched from earth to Mars must have in-course corrections so, too, must the leader. The rocketship must have a way of measuring the congruity between its trajectory and the target. When the trajectory is off even one percent, it could mean missing Mars by a million miles.

Healthy leaders develop effective and accurate ways to measure their impact on the organization to counter the natural tendency to believe the best about themselves. Gary Henrie explains it well. "If you are a leader you are recognized because you have authority it does not mean you have power. You earn your power by treating people well, with respect. You have systems where people can give input, give feedback. People who have stayed for eight years are still here because they don't have someone over their shoulder. Leadership sees them as having value." Gary and his organization do an organizational review of their culture every 18 months. In that review each team is examined, every team developer gets feedback and the leadership gets information on its performance. The results of the review help determine the areas for continued cultural development.

How to Measure Impact and Make In-Course Corrections

When asked to assess how congruent your talk and your behaviors are, the first thing that comes to mind may be, "Just go out and ask them." But that will not get the information you seek. That's easy to see by simply turning the tables. If your boss came to the staff meeting one day and said, "I want the whole truth about how you see me and my performance. Don't hold anything back!" How truthful do you think you and your colleagues would be? How much would you hold back? Would there be any issues you would be afraid to bring up? Would you worry about repercussions if you said something critical and no one else agreed?

Getting information about your behavior must be systematic and free of intimidation. Most people will tell the boss what she wants to hear. This tendency only reinforces in the leader's mind that she is doing a good job, when the truth is that she only received the information she wanted to hear, not what she needed to hear.

Most managers have been trained in how to give feedback. They are trained in how to correct behavior and how to do performance reviews, but few managers know how to *receive feedback*. Because leaders don't accept feedback well, employees are reluctant to give it. Upward feedback is difficult to give because the boss has power over the person giving the feedback. If the manager responds defensively, or is perceived as defensive, it will cut off all future upward feedback. The manager must learn how to solicit and receive feedback non-defensively. Upward feedback is an essential ingredient of the Performance Culture.

The ability to model how to receive feedback non-defensively:

- Gets high-quality information for the manager on his or her performance
- Demonstrates how the manager expects others to act in the process of self-improvement

The most powerful model is the use of upward performance feedback from subordinates to the manager. When this process is structured properly and used on a regular basis, it creates more interaction and trust in the leader.[16] The leader at the same time has solid, unbiased information about his impact on others and has a real opportunity to make in-course corrections. At

Example is not the main thing in influencing others, it is the only thing.
Albert Schweitzer

South Central, Gary Henrie receives a performance appraisal literally from every person in the organization. Everyone is invited to complete the evaluation on Gary and submit it to the Board of Directors.

The Shadow of the Leader

To a large degree organizations are a reflection of the leader. This is called the "shadow of the leader." It is hard for many leaders to accept because it means that an organization with critical problems may be a reflection of the leader's own strengths or weaknesses.

I once worked with a major oil company on a continuous improvement project. The manager complained to me, "Six teams in my group are not working to improve their processes. They waste time in meetings, are not meeting deadlines, are over budget, working too many hours and not following through with their plans." That same day I attended his staff meeting where I observed that:

- There was no agenda.
- The meeting was scheduled to go for an hour but it went on for two hours.
- Several people asked about progress on a decision regarding a workflow analysis. The decision had been made in the last meeting, but no one remembered exactly what it was.
- An argument ensued, and two people blamed a third, who got defensive and shut up for the rest of the meeting.
- The manager became upset and told the group that they were falling far behind in their CI (continuous improvement) goals and needed to follow up on their plans.

- As the meeting adjourned, the manager designated two of the best supervisors to work with him on the workflow analysis to get it done in a hurry.

The teams were following the manager's lead very well – they were doing just what he was doing, but that is not what he wanted! He could not see how his own model was contributing to, if not causing, the problems he complained about so bitterly.

To a large degree organizations are a reflection of the leader.

In this case the manager created a situation where teamwork was almost impossible. To get through the crisis, he burdened the two best supervisors and deprived the teams of the responsibility. This may make the team more reluctant in the future, based on the attitude, "Why should we work on his continuous improvement project when he doesn't have the discipline to practice continuous improvement in his own group?"

After some testing and feedback the manager began practicing new skills, including coaching team members on how to run better meetings, running his own meetings well, giving lots of praise for the behavior he wanted and providing clear goals for the team as well as time frames for achieving them. Nine months later, the change was dramatic. Attending his group meeting the first thing I noticed was that he was not running it. Second, it started on time and ended on time. Third, he participated like a member, not a boss. In fact had I not known, I would not have been able to tell who was the "boss." Fourth, there was clear focus in the group and people seemed very proud that they were regularly achieving their goals.

After the meeting I asked a few people what had changed. Each person said that the main thing was getting a clear direction from the manager and good coaching on how to get there. They felt much more responsible for their results and appreciated his leadership.

When managers model positive leadership, following them is a lot easier. It is difficult for many leaders to see how their behavior affects the culture and that is why some type of regular structured feedback is necessary.

Goal Setting

The objective of a Performance Culture is that 90% of all employees when asked can state in measurable terms the goals of their team. I consider knowledge of goals a major part of the battle but it takes a good deal of energy, education, training and preparation before a work force is capable of this important step.

There are two important questions to ask of any work team:

1. "What are the specific measurable goals of your work group for this year?"
2. "How are you doing toward reaching that goal to date?"

The answers to these questions tell a great deal about how close the organization is to a Performance Culture. In many companies, almost no one can answer these questions! NO ONE. Even middle and senior managers may have only a vague idea.

How can a manager model goal-focused behavior if she does not know what the goal is? *To get a sense of your organization's goal focus, walk around your workplace and ask each person you encounter, "What are the specific measurable goals of your work group?"*

If you get answers like the following, you have a well-focused organization.

- "Achieve 95% on-time delivery this quarter with an average of 98% for the year by the fourth quarter."
- "Complete 75% of our cross-training plan by the end of the second quarter."
- "Maintain a 99.3% reliability check on the first test for three months in a row."
- "Decrease customer response time from eight hours to two hours by July 31 and maintain a two-hour average for the last six months of the year."
- "Maintain a 20% profit margin on each project while increasing measured customer satisfaction by 10%."
- "Maintain 70% billable hours and a 95% on-time delivery for all projects."

Goals structure and prioritize the work by providing a framework on which leadership can model goal-focused behavior. Teams with clear and unambiguous goals waste less time and accomplish more than groups without clear goals. The first step in achieving a goal-focused, team-based system is to ensure that the leadership group has clearly defined goals so the teams can develop goals like those listed above.

> *Too many goals are useless. You should only have two or, at most, three goals over the course of a year. What's important is to make sure each goal encompasses five or six things right ... You don't have to tell people to get the parts in on time if you can get them to concentrate on getting the tractors out.*
> **Jack Stack, 1992, p. 50.**

In helping leadership groups define goals, I find that they often have goals but no one outside of the leadership group seems to know what they are. At the same time they might say, "We have goals but things change so much that it is impossible to stay focused on them." This can be an indicator of disjointed leadership – one in which focus and direction are lacking. Look under this leadership group's organization, and you will find a disjointed and confused work force as well.

Goal focus gets results and that is the model leadership must show. To ensure that the culture sees this model, non-managers must be involved regularly in meetings where goals are discussed. The culture must see and understand the importance of goals by watching the leadership model this behavior constantly. Much more will be said about goals and goal setting in Chapter 9.

Rental Mentality

When I was growing up my father owned some rental property. As the renters came and left, I was expected to help clean up for the new renters. I was appalled to see how some renters treated my father's property. They seemed to have no respect for the home. This was my first encounter with a "renter mentality." That is, someone who rents something often does not care for that property as well as if they owned it. The same principle applies to organizations at all levels.

When a rental mentality creeps into management behavior and attitudes, managers (a) treat people as if they were dispensable, (b) say or act out the attitude, "If you don't like this job go find another one," (c) show disrespect for people, and (d) fail to listen or forget to involve people in decisions. The message in the work force is often heard as, "We just rent you to work here, it is not worth my time to deal with you as a permanent and valuable part of our organization." This has always been a problem, especially in autocratic organizations and it has taken on new meaning with the increased use of temporary employees in recent years. Temporary employees literally are rented, and management and others often treat them that way.

The rental mentality can be seen in management's reluctance to train or develop employees. Managers often say, "If we train them, they will just go to work somewhere else. Why should we develop

The rental mentality can be seen in management's
reluctance to train or develop employees.

someone else's work force?" In other words, "We just rent them,
why should we put anything into their development or maintenance?" People are not seen as assets and may be treated as liabili-
ties. Just as my father's renters would not repair the holes in the
wall, paint the kitchen, or clean the crayon marks on the wall,
"rental" managers see no reason to invest in or maintain their
employees. Paul Heacock, president of Human Dynamics, Inc.,
looks at it from a different viewpoint, "What if we don't train them
and they stay?"

How do employees respond to a rental mentality? Not surprisingly, when people feel "rented," they often act that way. They show
little commitment to the organization and even less respect for the
work they do. They take poor care of the organization's property
and may work well below their capacity. This is especially true in
union organizations. Treating the union as an inconvenience or

afterthought in decision making sends the signal that they are not important owners and partners in the organization.

The leadership of the entire organization sets this "rental mentality" by creating rules and restrictions on middle managers with respect to employee development. The clearest signal is sent when the organization puts few resources into training and development of people or fails to involve them in decisions for which they have key knowledge. You do not invest in people whom you rent. Managers only invest in people whom they see as a permanent and integral to the organization. When only certain groups get training and development, it sends the signal "everyone else is rented."

> *Ways of valuing assets reflect underlying nonrational value systems, such as the fact that machines are considered assets while people are not. Hardware is less uncertain than software.*
> **Geert Hofstede, 1997, p. 158.**

In one organization, the company was quite generous with training and continuing education for the engineers but had few or no resources for training and development of the technicians who supported the engineers or the manufacturing employees who made the engineered products. In this way the intentional culture conferred an "ownership" status on the engineers and a "rental" status on everyone else. This was clearly seen in the attitudes and behavior of each group. Engineers were constantly complaining about the laziness of the "rented" employees and the employees were angry about the way the "owner" engineers treated them as second-class citizens in their own company.

Rental Mentality and Management Mobility

Managers come and go. They generally have shallow roots in the community and may be relocated. The workers know that the leader is not tied to the community and that she may have little knowledge or interest in it. But, they themselves are often tied to the local culture. The shop floor worker, the receptionist or computer analyst are very likely products of the local schools and religious organizations or at least have some strong connections. Through churches, synagogues, schools, clubs, and so forth, they have a network that reaches deep into the local culture. It is very difficult for these people to trust a leader who does not share their commitment to the community.

Every time a leader changes, the trust between the intentional and endemic culture drops dramatically with the potential for productivity, labor, morale, or quality problems. These problems may not show up for some time, but once they do, they are hard to repair. In a Performance Culture, the leadership works to ensure that the handoff between departing and incoming leaders is smooth. Incoming leaders work to show that they and the company are committed to the culture and the community, no matter who is currently at the helm.

To achieve a smooth transition the incoming leader must be well versed in the norms and processes of the Performance Culture. As a representative of the intentional culture, how she treats the culture is a sign of how committed the company is to the local facility. Workers can deal with leadership changes if they trust that the intentional culture will remain consistent in the development of the Performance Culture. Inconsistent, self-absorbed, or fast-track managers are easily spotted and do not engender trust and high performance.

Status and Culture

Status is a powerful force in the human psyche and historically it has played an important role in the way companies were organized. All cultures include indicators of status with rules about how that status is shown.

Desire for status comes from two sources:

- A basic need to be esteemed by society and the group with which you identify (your company, church, social club, neighborhood, work group, etc.)
- The need to order the social relationships of the group

If the organization is hierarchically based, it relies heavily on status and status symbols for structure.

Organizations recognize this strong drive in people and sometimes take advantage of it. For example, have you ever seen people receive promotions with more responsibility and a title but little or no salary increase? Have you ever been in a situation as a manager or supervisor where you actually earned less money than someone below you because they could earn overtime and you couldn't? What would cause someone to accept a position where she might be expected to do more work but get paid less? The answer is often status. Status is important to many people who wish to feel they have a special place in the order of things, that they are not just a worker, but have a valued skill or talent.

Status and Managers

In certain corporate cultures only persons of manager status wear neckties at work, or only senior VPs get company cars, and only department heads and above get reserved parking spots. I once witnessed a manager get taken to task because he had a credenza in his office and credenzas were reserved for managers at a higher level. To gain loyalty and ensure proper chain of command many organizations manipulate these status symbols. Consequently, to violate the symbol is seen as a direct affront to the system.

Sometimes there are unwritten rules about status. Anyone below the level of director who drives a BMW, Lexus or similar type car might be seen as stepping outside of their status, as perhaps being too ambitious. More senior people might see a director who lives in the "wrong" part of town as not promotable.

Visible signs of status and the rules associated with it help the nodal system order itself. Symbols confirm a person's status and ensure that those of lower status give proper deference to the higher-status person. In a large organization where people often do not know each other, symbols create a shorthand by which people instantly know how to behave around a person because her status is clearly marked.

Status and Non-Managers

Status is also important to those who are not managers. For example, on the manufacturing shop floor there are clear lines of status. The highest status are the skilled trades, with the specialists like tool and die and electrician. Next comes the general maintenance person, followed by the shop leads, then the machine operator and the support person. Within each of these levels there is also seniority status. Similar levels of status are found in office environments with the professionals being the highest status, nonprofessional degreed people next, nondegreed technicians or paraprofessionals next and then support people. These status levels and the struggle to achieve them can cause conflict. Conflict over status is often more vicious at this level than in the management ranks. People vie for even the smallest sign of status.

One department in an insurance company experienced major turmoil when the manager gave new computers to some newer employees working on a special project. The more tenured employees were irate that they did not get the computers. The manager tried to explain that the new equipment was ordered because the new hires could not complete their project without it. But this argument fell on deaf ears. Productivity fell and petty conflicts flared into major fights between the groups. Such stories are played out in many organizations because they reward and recognize status independent of any business plan.

While status can be an effective motivator, it can also create bottlenecks in productivity and learning. Because of status differences, some competent people may be prevented from learning new tasks or performing certain duties.

Once people buy into the status system, it becomes an important part of the culture and any violation of the system will create conflict and confusion. For example, if a person does not get the large desk or corner office with his promotion, he may feel cheated out of his status symbols. This can lead to demotivation and morale problems.

I once worked with an organization where a rather extensive list of furniture was associated with every managerial level. Everything was measured, down to the size of office and size desk allowed for each management level. When one upper manager retired, the decision was made not to replace him, which left an empty office in an already crowded work area. When the vice president decided to move one of the lower managers into the vacant office, it caused a virtual soap opera of conflict and disruption. What corporate saw as a good temporary use of the space the other managers and supervisors felt was a major violation of their rights. "I don't think the conflict would have been any bigger if the manager had taken 10% of everyone's pay. This was huge to them," the vice president told me. The poor manager who moved into the office soon asked if she could move back to her old office.

Language and Status

Historically, in most societies specific customs of speech define or defer to status. For example, in England in the 1600s the pronouns "thee" and "thou" were reserved for people of higher status while "you" was reserved for people of lower or equal status.

Even though many leaders do not like it, we still have status customs that require people of lower status to refer to high-status people as Ms., Sir, or Mister, while higher-status people may use first names for those of equal or lower status. When the president of the company walks through, most people refer to her as Ms. Jones, not Margaret. Her equals or those just below her might work with her on a first-name basis, but in front of others of lower status they invariably refer to her as Ms. Jones and she refers to her vice president as Mr. Arnold.

Such customs are neither right nor wrong, they simply reflect the way hierarchical organizations and societies have organized themselves for thousands of years. They serve an important function to keep the society orderly and organized with clear channels of power and deference.

The high-status person has daily evidence that
he is in control by virtue of the deference he receives.

Status Distance

Status distance refers to the psychological distance between two people of different status. The greater the status distance, the more inhibited a person of lower status is to speak his mind or tell the truth if it could get him in trouble. Status distance has nothing to do with rank or how high one is in the organization. Instead it is the perceived distance between two people that inhibits the person of lower status.

For example, a line worker might feel freer to speak frankly with the president of the company than with her immediate supervisor. In this case the supervisor, who has more direct and visible power over the employee, has greater status distance than the president with respect to the line employee. On many occasions I have seen people in small groups speak frankly in a skip-level meeting with the president or vice president but say absolutely nothing in a regular staff meeting with their supervisor.

Status distance is designed to maintain control. The high-status person has daily evidence that he is in control by virtue of the deference he receives. Deference in any system is a sign that power is respected and often means that people perceive danger if deference is not given.

Status distance creates major bottlenecks in communication. Generally speaking, the high-status person has access to more information than the low-status person. It is assumed that higher status means greater and more accurate knowledge. But due to high speed and wide access communication, this assumption is often false. Frequently the lower-status person has more and better information than the high-status "boss."

Emphasis on status inhibits information sharing and can create major blind spots for the leader. People have a learned reluctance to approach and communicate frankly with a person of higher status.

Classification Systems

Classification systems are often methods of solidifying status in the organization. Based on such things as the number of people supervised or the span of responsibility and control, employees or managers receive compensation and perks according to their level in the system. The system was very popular for many years because it gave organizations a way to order status relationships within an organization. Performance or ability to lead and direct was not necessarily part of the equation.

Union and government classification systems function in similar ways. Classifications can proliferate in response to a powerful individual or group's need for status, including pay. Early in my career I worked as personnel manager in a state institution. Often when a powerful group wanted a pay raise, they found it easier to go through the system and get a higher classification than to get the system to raise the pay of their current position. I saw many examples of people whose rank was changed to give them higher pay even though their duties did not change. The trick was in writing the upgrade proposal to convince the central office that the job really did require a higher classification.

In one case, a classification change evoked an uproar in another group who saw it as a direct threat to its status. So the second group petitioned for an upgrade as well. In the ensuing debate the leader of the group said to the board chairman, "Even if you do not increase our pay, we still want our classification to be raised." Clearly, the group felt that its status was under attack.

Pay itself is a strong status symbol. I once saw an entire department brought to its knees because a new classification system gave some of the union members a 5¢ increase ($2.00 per week) over their compatriots. The ensuing conflict was not about money, but about who now had higher status in the group. No one felt that 5¢ was the issue.

Classification does not work well in Performance Cultures. Job levels or rank categories should be few and clearly justified in business terms. Fewer classifications allow for more fluid job sharing and load balancing and less wasted time as when perfectly qualified people cannot work outside their classification. I strongly encourage client companies to reduce the number wherever possible. Often this is done by collapsing several into one higher classification with the clear understanding that while everybody will receive increased pay, they will be assigned increased responsibility with higher performance expectations.

How to Confer Status

Since status can be a powerful motivator and symbol of belonging and acceptance, it should be used to enhance performance not position. How can this be done? There are other ways to depict status than as a permanent condition or position.

In the 1980s when I first suggested this concept, somebody accused me of being a communist. Today, the advent of high-participation work environments has led to a deemphasis on status and the increased popularity of business casual as the dress mode in North America. High-participation work environments cannot function effectively if there are many status barriers between people at different levels. To some degree we have learned to reduce dress as a measure of status and to get on with the work.

To use status as a tool for performance, we first need to eliminate the idea that status is a finite resource. Status is limited only by our cultural habits and customs. The idea that only a few people can have status in a group or organization leads us to hoard it, as if it were money or a scarce resource.

Status comes from three sources:

1. It can be bestowed by a person of higher status – *superior-based status*. The Queen of England does this when she knights a person.
2. It can come from people of equal or lower status – *peer-based status*. The high school ritual of voting on the homecoming king and queen is an example.
3. It can come from performance or knowledge – *performance/knowledge-based* status. An Olympic champion or the World Cup champions are examples of performance-based status.

To influence the culture, both superior and peer-based status should be minimized unless they are clearly tied to performance. For example, no one would contest the Olympic champion's right to high status, but many might argue that the high school homecoming king and queen did little to achieve their status. Every year, this argument is made over the Academy Awards, for example. Did the best actor or picture win, or was it just the most popular and politically connected?

Superior and peer status have major shortcomings because they are so easily based on something other than performance. In a traditional environment, superior status is more frequently used than peer-based status. In a Performance Culture, the focus is on performance status.

In a Performance Culture, status is a temporary focus on a group or individual for a certain performance. The Quarterly Triple Crown Award for consistent goal achievement over three months confers status to every team that meets the criteria at SMP in Long Island City. The Most Improved Team of the quarter goes to the single team that has shown the most improvement, not necessarily the

THE LEADERS' IMPACT ON CULTURE **109**

top performing team. The "110% Award" goes to the team that provides the most help to other teams while still maintaining its own performance standards at Harmon Industries.

These awards spotlight the behavior the organization desires, by conferring status on those who exemplify the behavior. If this sounds like simple recognition, just watch what happens when a team does not achieve the status again the next quarter. Teams want the status of achievement. Leadership can give it by recognizing clearly defined achievements as worthy of status. With this type of status, anyone who achieves the goal gains the status. In other words, status is not limited.

In a Performance Culture, it is not uncommon for teams to give recognition to other teams or to a manager. This is appropriate and encouraged. Peer-level status is productive as long as it is goal-focused and based on specific behaviors. On occasion such recognition can turn into popularity contests or mutual admiration societies. But it is usually not a problem. It is best to err on the side of too much recognition. It is better that teams be totally involved in recognizing one another than in criticizing or becoming jealous or envious.

Teams do not spontaneously recognize others. Like most managers, they believe that status is limited. "If we recognize them, they may think they are better than we are." Or "If we recognize them, we might not get recognized for the hard work we have done." Teams have to be coached and must see a model from you, the leader. When another team helps one of your teams, it is appropriate for you to ask, "What do you think we should do for them to show our appreciation?" Then let the team discuss and decide. You can model this behavior by simply writing a thank-you note to a team or team member who helps you. Your note confers status to the individual or team, just as the team can confer status to another team. The objective is to get teams involved in conferring status on one another with less dependence on superior-based status.

Most important in conferring status and giving recognition is: DO NOT COMPARE TEAMS OR INDIVIDUALS! This always implies a difference in status. People hate to be compared to somebody else. As a child how did you like being compared to your little brother or big sister, cousin or neighbor? Adults don't like it any better. When giving recognition, focus on the actual goal achievement and the behavior that made the difference. Make no comment about other teams or last quarter's winners.

After a very positive and motivating awards ceremony, one insurance vice president effectively undermined his whole message when he concluded with the following remark: "Thank you for coming today I hope you will all take the example you see in these two teams and try to be like them next quarter!"

The anger in the room after that statement was palpable. Afterwards as people filed out, there was little excitement or enthusiasm but plenty of grumbling about being compared to the two teams. In effect the manager had taken the spotlight off the two award-winning teams and placed it squarely on those who did not win. Keep the spotlight on what you want, NOT on what you do not want.

Status Within the Performance Culture

Performance Cultures diminish hierarchy and reduce status structures. This is one of the reasons why it is so difficult to develop Performance Cultures within an existing organizational structure. All the fine nuances of status from the top to the bottom and within each group are eliminated or greatly reduced. Many of the larger, not-so-fine nuances are eliminated as well. Although there still may be some levels of status, a true Performance Culture tends to minimize them, or create status based on business need or goals rather than hierarchy.

Status systems are often counter to the best interest of the business. For example, Performance Cultures place a heavy emphasis on cross-training. In the beginning this evokes a good deal of fear from some people, especially the higher-status employees, who see their skills as unique and special. They may be the only one who has the skills. Low-status workers are often discouraged from learning "higher-status skills." Many pay structures, work rules and reward systems are designed to maintain knowledge and skill monopolies in certain areas without regard to efficiency or effectiveness. Governments and union shops are infamous for this approach to skills, but it occurs in virtually all hierarchically based organizations. Through cross-training many companies make strong productivity gains. By having multiple people training to do critical tasks, there is never a time when the customer suffers because the person with the skills called in sick or went on vacation.

Cross-training also posses a threat to the first-line supervisor. One of the informal rewards the supervisor often uses is assignment of new roles and responsibilities along with training and skills. In this way the supervisor can control the workflow and reward people with new challenges or responsibilities. These special responsibilities often create a level of status within the group that is coveted. In the Performance Culture cross-training is mandated for all, and much of the responsibility for assignment and completion is put on the team, not the manager. This can be seen as a direct blow to the traditional manager's discretionary authority and to the status of those who once exclusively performed these duties.

In one client organization three people were the "month-end" group for the accounting department. They had done month-end and year-end together for over 10 years. They guarded this job jealously, but at the same time often complained that it meant they could never take off at the end of the month or year. Before the team implementation, attempts to get people cross-trained to help them met with hostility. They felt no one could do it as well as they could and did not want the responsibility of cleaning up the mess of less competent people afterwards. The irony was that there were many degreed accounting people in the department, yet none of these three people had any formal training in accounting. Month-end was for them a symbol of their status and importance to the department. In their own words, "Even the new college graduates can't do what we do every month." Never mind that they were not about to train anyone.

With the advent of the team process, certain expectations and plans were made with mandates for the team to complete cross-training. A schedule was developed with everyone's participation and goals. At the same time, these three employees were required to learn some new skills outside their narrow areas. Initially they expressed a good deal of resentment and anger with covert resistance. But with some coaching and the reassignment of one person to another special project, the cross-training got underway. It took about three months. The immediate outcome was a much greater understanding of the process by the whole team and some process improvements that cut the time required for the month-end and year-end tasks from three days and three people to two days and two people. In addition, more people could help so no one was denied vacation time just because it was month-end.

One person was so bitter about the change that she took early retirement. The other two found their skill development rewarding and became valuable to the team. While they had less education, they had been at the company much longer than many of the degreed employees and were likely to be there long after the college-educated people had moved on.

In this example, what appeared to be an efficient and dedicated group of people was actually a dedicated but inefficient group, very concerned about their status.

Recognition and Esteem in the Performance Culture

Shifting from a hierarchical structure to a Performance Culture disrupts the old status system. At the same time there needs to be a new system to take its place to satisfy the deep human need for support and recognition. Generally, team status systems, while not hierarchical, can meet this need better than the old system, as they give workers a more genuine feeling of confidence and a mastery of skills.

One important key to helping employees make the transition is to train them in what is required and then ask them to help develop the plan for the transition. Dan May, a team developer in Butler Manufacturing Engineering Division, said it best: "We are not asking anyone to step down, but are asking everyone to step up." With this approach everyone will see that they are no longer stuck in narrowly focused skill areas but are allowed to learn many new and interesting things. They also find that in learning about new areas they can offer suggestions and insights, which may improve the process. Having a wide range of people cross-trained takes pressure off of a few and allows the team to allocate resources better than a manager or supervisor ever could.

Performance Cultures create opportunities for people to gain status as a result of skill development and creativity in the group setting. Contribution to the group and its goals gains recognition and status within the team and in the organization. Status helps meet the need to be accepted and esteemed by one's group. But it is not the only way to achieve this goal.

In a Performance Culture, team members find that a well-run team with clear goals and productivity measures, along with well-designed recognition, quickly replaces the old status system. People find satisfaction and reward in working productively together. They understand the destructive nature of status symbols that often undermine productivity and good communications.

Status may be gained by skill certification systems or by designating particularly skilled people as trainers in the team. But unlike traditional award systems, this type of status is skill or performance-based and allows employees to feel pride and a sense of accomplishment. The military takes full advantage of this in its system of medals and awards. These recognize and give status to people based upon their training and proficiency in certain skills or performance in combat or other endeavors. You don't get the productivity payouts without some important costs. One cost is the need for management to do much more in terms of recognition and cheerleading. There is also a significant need for well-structured and designed training to ensure people have the skills to take on much greater responsibility.

Recognition systems are as unique as each company but they are essential in the Performance Culture. Some of the recognition ideas I have seen include:

practical tips

- The Blue Ribbon Team Award: Quarterly awards for top-performing teams and most improved teams. Several teams can win the award.
- Extra lunch time for hitting monthly goals.
- Pizza party for meeting quarterly team goals.
- The Triple Crown Award in the plastics department of the SMP New York plant given for meeting the three most critical goals each month for an entire quarter.
- Pink Flamingo Award at Butler Manufacturing given to a team for some performance achievement. The award is voted on by all the teams.
- Dumbest Mistake Award for $25 at Harmon Industries given to the person who owns up to a mistake and can show how to prevent it in the future. According to Jeff Utterback, plant manager, "It's worth $25 for the whole plant to learn from one person's mistake."
- The 110% Award at Harmon given to any team that loans a team member to another team for at least 10% of their time while still achieving their own productivity goals.
- The Brownie Points Award at Butler Manufacturing, Annville, Pennsylvania, given to a team or team member who is nominated by any team or team member. The "Brownie Points" are given to the team member but can only be spent by the entire team. Jeff Feaster, engineering manager, says, "After almost five years, people still want to recognize each other with Brownie Points. It is a good way to ensure we are recognizing each other's good work. When they accumulate so many points they can cash them in as a team for some gourmet brownies."[18]

These are only a few of the things you can do to recognize teams and highlight the kind of performance that helps everyone achieve goals.

Most Performance Cultures have dozens of team recognitions a year. From Most Improved Team to the Dumbest Mistake Award, a Performance Culture means you are serious about recognizing good performance and having fun doing it. According to Tom Short, team developer at Harmon Industries, "We had more fun and produced more than we ever could have without teams." Paul

DILBERT reprinted by permission of United Feature Syndicate, Inc., 2000, p. 27.

What if Alice had been asked to help decide what might motivate her?

Heacock, president of HDI, says, "Having fun is a critical part of working here." He has even put it in the company mission. Team-based companies work hard at having fun, and recognition is a major part of that fun.

Think of recognition systems as a spotlight within your organization. The spotlight shines on specific behaviors to help everyone see and understand what kinds of performance are desirable.

Recognition systems need to be well thought out in terms of the goals and the desired behaviors. A haphazard approach to recognition could actually reward or recognize the wrong behavior. In the Dilbert cartoon above, Alice hits the boss with a "Motivational Rock." The $1,000 rock had the opposite effect on Alice than expected. To her it was an insult. Improperly thought out recognition can actually be insulting to the individual and the culture as a whole. What if Alice had been asked to help decide what might motivate her?

One vice president in a call center was fond of giving a monthly team award to the team that had the highest phone time average. His goal was to make sure that teams were answering phones and talking to customers, but the unfortunate effect was an increase in customer complaints about poor service. While teams were competing hard to stay on the phones, they were not completing the paperwork from one call before they took another. As a result many things got lost or were improperly resolved.

practical tip

It is important to think through what you want and how to recognize that behavior. Exemplary behavior comes in many forms from many people. A recognition system should spotlight many different teams and people. It is difficult to show *too much* recognition but very easy to show too little. If you make an error, err on the side of too much recognition. The purpose is to permeate the culture with recognition for the desired behavior to such a degree that other competing, less productive, behaviors never get a chance to take hold.

Poor habits and attitudes develop when the leadership does not model the desired behavior and/or fails to provide adequate reinforcement for the appropriate behaviors.

Recognition Within Teams

Teams have a major advantage over more traditional systems by their ability to involve everyone in the rewards and recognition system, not just the manager. Having everyone flooding the culture with recognition and praise creates a positive and motivating environment. No single manager could ever provide such high levels of motivation.

The Wilson SMP plant has created a process where a pool of money is set aside for charitable gifts. The money is distributed at the end of the year to all teams according to their goal performance. The team then gives the money to a charity of their choice in the team name! According to Eric Sills, plant manager, "It has given the teams a chance to look outside of themselves and to help the company as a whole be a good corporate citizen. The teams seem to like it and it ties the team and company goals to something bigger than any of us." You might not think of this as a recognition system, but the teams are very interested in how much money they will be able to give to their charity. They see their goal achievement as something that also helps their community.

Self-Reinforcement and the Performance Culture

The majority of recognition and reinforcement comes from peers in the workgroup, not the manager. Since employees have much more contact with peers than with the boss, peers have many more opportunities to influence behavior. How can we use this powerful force to guide people toward the goals of the company?

Without attention to the reinforcement of team members by team members, teams produce relatively few improvements and never achieve their potential. Often teams stay together but are a team in name only.
Aubry Daniels, 2000, p. 61.

Leaders can teach the coworkers how to praise, recognize and reward positive goal-directed behavior with minimal management involvement using the techniques listed earlier in this chapter. It requires the use of all these methods to create a culture that evolves into a Performance Culture.

You are not the primary reinforcer in the environment, your task is to teach the culture to provide most of the behavioral reinforcement needed for high performance. While leaders are powerful reinforcers, their ability to teach members of the culture how to recognize and reinforce will multiply their effect. The leader cannot be everywhere at once but the culture can.

The following examples illustrate how this works. At Butler Manufacturing the engineering teams are taught to praise other teams and individuals. One day a team received a some significant help from another team. The team leader asked the team, "What special thing can we do to show our appreciation?" No one could come up with anything until a member said, "I have a pink flamingo yard decoration in my car that my wife asked me to throw away." The team got the pink flamingo and held an impromptu award ceremony – giving the pink flamingo as a token of their appreciation. The other team thought it was hilarious and proudly displayed it for several weeks. Later they decided to give it to another team who had done an outstanding job of achieving their goals for the quarter. In this manner the pink flamingo was passed around for over a year. This was totally spontaneous goal-focused recognition. It clearly illustrates that the teams have taken on much of the responsibility for praise and recognition following the leadership's strong model.

At Human Dynamics, Inc., the company holds a luncheon meeting each Friday where employees talk about and demonstrate their work for the week. The meeting is full of praise and applause for the hard work, creativity and risks that employees take for the company.

Harmon, Riverside, called a company meeting once a month where a multitude of teams and individuals were recognized. A combination of informal and formal recognition was used. Individuals or teams who had gone the extra mile were recognized. Teams who had achieved their stretch goals for the month received praise – in short praise and recognition pervaded the culture.

The purpose of these activities is:

- To teach the culture how to praise and recognize good performance eight hours a day, not just when management is around.
- To fill the culture with so much goal focused stimulus it will have little or no time or energy for less constructive activities.

The objective is to get the whole team involved in recognizing and praising one another so they can achieve their goals. When the culture engages in this type of behavior spontaneously it is a good sign that the two cultures are merged.

Questions

1. How do you know if your leadership model is appropriate for what you want out of the organization?
2. How do you know if people recognize and respond to your model? For example, if you are punctual and efficient in running your meetings, do others follow your example in their meetings?
3. Does your system flood the environment with recognition and praise for desired behavior?
4. How do you get people on your teams involved in praising and recognizing one another?
5. What status symbols does your organization use that might impede efficient work?
6. Are the symbols of status in your organization focused on performance or on position?

THE ELEMENTS OF A PERFORMANCE CULTURE

Boundaries:
Defining Cultural Direction

To create a Performance Culture, the endemic culture needs a clear structure that easily interfaces with the intentional culture. The team developer helps set boundaries for the team while also teaching the skills needed when the boundaries expand. Teams mature faster when boundaries are effectively managed.

Boundaries Defined

Boundaries are the predetermined limits of acceptable behavior for the level of training, experience and responsibility of a particular organizational unit and its individuals.

We know and understand boundary management with our children. For example, we must actively manage the boundaries of a three-year-old to prevent disaster or bad habits from developing. The child may only play outside under an adult's supervision. She may only eat one piece of candy, not the whole box. She must pick up all toys and put them away before going outside to play, and so forth. For an older child we would set wider boundaries. For example, an eight-year-old can play outside but must stay in the yard unless she asks permission. She may ride her bike on the sidewalk but not on the street. She must finish her homework before watching her favorite TV show, be home before the street lights come on, and so on. All these represent boundaries that are wider and show a growing level of responsibility for the child.

When managers complain that their people are not able to accept responsibility, they are really saying, "We have not taught and coached them on the proper boundaries and expectations for their level of maturity."

Depending upon the culture and the effectiveness of the indoctrination process, it usually takes a few years of systematic effort to teach employees to assume high levels of responsibility toward a Performance Culture. It cannot be done with a training course or a memo from the boss, especially with employees who carry with them well-learned dependency behaviors from past management practices. Workers must mature into responsibility, both as individuals and as groups.

In a Performance Culture the speed with which workers can take on responsibility is greatly accelerated compared to traditional organizations. Because the Performance Culture has a unified structure for managing boundaries, there are much clearer messages about boundaries. A Performance Culture involves the entire organization, including every team member, in managing boundaries. When someone violates boundaries, team members are just as likely to give feedback as a manager. Further, Performance Cultures are just as quick to give boundary feedback to managers as to employees.

To find out how well some boundaries are followed, try violating one and see if anyone calls you on it. In a manufacturing plant, try going onto the shop floor without proper safety gear and see if anyone asks you to go back and put on the proper gear. If you are a manager walking around in violation of safety procedures and three different people correct your behavior, you know that your organization has done a good job of teaching appropriate boundaries around safety.

In an office environment, go to a meeting that you do not normally attend without advance warning. Observe how prepared participants are and how well the meeting is run. Observe how well they document decisions and follow up from previous meetings. This will tell you how well your organization has taught boundaries about business meeting behavior.

I once worked with an insurance company that adhered to a standard that the phone will not ring more than three times before it is answered – *a boundary*. As I was touring with the unit's manager, a phone started ringing on the desk of someone who was temporarily away. All others in the group were on the phone, so on the third ring the manager excused himself and answered the phone. He took a message and laid it on the person's desk. We then resumed the conversation. Shortly afterwards the person returned to her desk, found the message, and promptly thanked the manager. The manager did not make a big deal out of it and we walked on.

Later I was able to interview some of the people in the group and asked about this incident. They seemed quite casual about the whole issue. They were not surprised that the manager had answered the phone and said nothing else. They all had the attitude that customer service is #1, so if the manager is the only person in a position to provide that service, he should do it. At the same time, the manager said in his words later, and in his deeds at the time, "We do not spy on people, I don't care where that person was when the phone rang. I trust that she was doing something important or if she wasn't, I trust the team to correct her behavior if it is out of line. We have set the boundaries clearly. If I have to get into reprimanding or spying on people for such a little thing, when will I get my work done? Our teams meet their goals and we keep close tabs on the three telephone ring rule, if we see problems we let the team know and they can take care of it."

This manager was in fact telling me, "I have a mature team that is capable and trustworthy because we have taught the boundaries and how to self-enforce those boundaries. As a manager I don't have to worry about it, which frees me to do more important things." Looking behind this example we would find a very well-developed orientation and indoctrination process for all new employees. We would also see clear management modeling of expected behaviors. In addition, we would see a good deal of training in teamwork and a lot of emphasis on accountability and responsibility. Every team and every team member is expected to give feedback and appraise their fellow team members at least twice a year. New employees get monthly feedback from the team. It took this company two years to achieve this level of maturity in the team process. As a company progresses in its ability to indoctrinate and teach people, the boundaries become less restrictive.

Learning point: Managing boundaries begins with the understanding that boundaries are moving targets, changing with the maturity of the team and the culture.

Most companies think of boundaries in terms of policies and procedures. While these are intended to serve as boundaries, they are only as effective as the leadership that models them. Policy and procedure manuals are one way to influence and direct the culture, but they are not the most effective. If you need a big manual to govern behavior, chances are you are not doing very well influencing the culture or teaching boundaries. Organizations with large policy and procedure manuals are trying to control human behavior in ways that show a profound lack of trust in the employee. Workers who are properly trained and indoctrinated into a system know what behaviors are appropriate, they don't need a thick policy manual to tell them.

Policy manuals are not a substitute for training or good indoctrination into the corporate values and behaviors. As a general rule, the larger the policy manual, the less the employees are trusted. Bureaucracies and large corporations are notorious for preferring this method of control – not a Performance Culture.

The Roadmap to Empowerment

Boundaries are the key to empowerment. Well-defined boundaries allow people to learn how to function effectively without the danger of major mistakes. As employees learn how to function within a set of boundaries, the boundaries should be widened to offer more autonomy and self-direction. This increases the team's ability to self-discipline, allowing leaders to focus more of their energy on growing the business and less on internal boundary issues.

Good boundary management includes four components:

1. Behavioral modeling by the leadership
2. Effective orientation of new employees into the system
3. A system of praise and recognition for the desired behaviors
4. A well-designed disciplinary system

Employee empowerment and teamwork require a systematic approach. People do not become empowered easily. Teaching people how to function as a team requires a roadmap that both man-

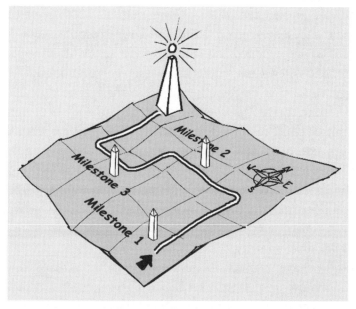

Teaching people how to function as a team requires
a roadmap that both management and teams can follow.

agement and teams can follow. I call this roadmap "the levels of empowerment." It is a concept based on the idea that teams are a developmental project over an extended period of time, much like raising a child. I do not intend to imply that team members are children or immature, but that the group is immature before it is well established.

I first developed this idea back in the 1980s while working to implement self-directed work teams at Monogram Retailers, a GE Capital company. I noticed that teams have a strong tendency to think they are fully empowered as soon as they are trained. Like an adolescent[19] who thinks he should be able to drive a car at 14 and stay out until 1:00 a.m. any night of the week, teams tend to think they have a higher level of skill and competence than they actually do. Defining the boundaries allows teams to safely learn team skills within given boundaries before progressing to higher levels of skill and competence.

practical tip

At each developmental stage the team needs a different type of guidance and training. In the beginning, clear and unambiguous boundaries are needed. But as teams mature, boundaries can be widened and teams given more and more responsibility. If the boundaries are widened too fast, however, teams flounder, fail to mature, and often cause more harm than good. If boundaries are too rigid or narrow, on the other hand, teams will become frustrated and fail to mature moving back into dependency behaviors.

Think of child rearing. The child who has unclear boundaries becomes confused and acts out her anxieties. Children whose boundaries are not expanded as they mature, become depressed or rebellious, spending more time and energy fighting the boundaries than on maturing and becoming a responsible adult. Effective parents constantly work to define boundaries appropriate to their child's age and maturity.

Teams behave in much the same way. While the team members may be mature adults, the new team is an infant. Team skills are not common in the work force. Team skills are something that must be learned, just as children need to learn to share their toys and resolve conflicts. Very few people, including managers, have effective team skills. To treat people as capable of true team behavior without proper guidance and training is like giving a six-year-old the keys to your car.

The team's developmental stages must be respected. Proper and specific boundaries must be set at each stage and the team must be clearly trained and cognizant of those boundaries from the beginning. In setting boundaries for a child, he is clearly told that he cannot go to the neighbor's and play without specific permission and a time to return. A team's boundaries might be that the team can set its own work schedule but that it must be approved by the manager. Other boundaries could meet specific criteria for customer coverage, production scheduling and personnel policies around attendance and overtime. As the team learns to set its own schedules with the help and training of the manager, the boundaries can be gradually widened.

Boundaries and the Performance Culture

Boundaries cannot be set for a team in a vacuum and must be similar or the same for all teams in the environment. Just as a family might say, "All children in this family must be 16 before dating," the organization may mandate that all teams demonstrate certain competencies before expanding the boundaries.

While attending a party about 20 years ago, I met a former Wal-Mart store manager who told me a story about Sam Walton that illustrates the enforcement of boundaries. At the store managers' annual meeting, Sam Walton talked about the importance of the return policy as a cornerstone of the Wal-Mart quality guarantee. He then held up a pair of soiled children's underwear commenting "The manager who refused to take these back is now an assistant manager." He added nothing else! He simply demonstrated in unequivocal terms that the boundaries would be enforced. My friend went on to say that about a year later the manager was promoted back to a store manager – lesson learned.

Through this one act, Sam Walton was enforcing the boundaries, not only for that one store and that individual manager, but for the whole organization.

Successful organizations find ways to delineate the boundaries within which teams are to function. Within such clear boundaries, employees feel safer because they know the rules and trust that they won't be changed at the whim of the manager. They also feel more empowered to enforce those rules with their team members.

When boundaries are not clear or the team is allowed to do things that it is not properly trained for or mature enough to handle, conflict and major mistakes arise. As a result, the manager will have to "ride to the rescue" and clean up the team's mess. Every time a rescue is made, it is tempting to take back the reins of control and stop the team development. This is why proper boundary management is important. Boundary management supports the growth of teams as they learn to take on more responsibility. It also helps the manager know when to step in and when to stay out of the team's business.

Levels of Empowerment

I have used the concept of levels of empowerment to help companies develop a roadmap toward fully functioning, self-directed work teams. The levels of empowerment are actually designed by the company itself to match their needs and the level from where they are starting. A knowledge-based business such as an engineering firm will have a different roadmap than a manufacturing plant. Educational level, type of work and level of training in management ranks are all considered in developing the roadmap.

Once decided, the roadmap is known by all and is followed by every team under the supervision of the steering committee and the unit leadership team. (The steering committee and leadership team will be thoroughly discussed in Chapter 12.) Each level has specific requirements that must be met before the team is allowed to move to the next level. At each level the team has to complete certain developmental tasks that help gain self-confidence and technical skills.

This structured developmental approach makes sense to most people because they can see the progression of skills and self-direction in the roadmap. As with any roadmap, the teams can tell if they are getting closer to the destination or not. Directions are measurable and definable. Achievement at the different levels gives both the steering committee and management a major opportunity to recognize and praise the teams. Levels of empowerment are really process goals for the team.

It is important to recognize that this process is a TEAM process, not an individual process. Only teams can move up on the levels of empowerment, NOT individuals. It is not a competitive system in which individuals rise above other individuals, but a system whereby the whole team rises far above its former level and often above even its highest performing individual.

Most companies include four or five levels in the empowerment roadmap.

Level I – this is nothing more than an orientation and basic skills development, which may last from four to six months.

Level II – this is where new technical and interpersonal skills are learned. Much cross-training takes place at this stage. Forms of self-management are taught, such as basic scheduling, performance coaching, group leadership skills, safety, goal setting and so on. This level may last from 8-12 months.

Level III – here teams begin to put it all together. As skills in scheduling, feedback, goal setting, safety, and so forth, have been mastered at a minimum level, the team is ready to begin directing itself more completely. Level III may last a year or more while the team demonstrates higher and higher levels of self-direction.

Level IV – once a team reaches Level IV it is functioning at the highest level of authority allowed by the company and is very self-directed.

Boundaries and the New Employee

While many companies claim they have high-performance teams or work systems, don't be fooled; very few do. When you hire new employees, chances are that they do not have the skills required to succeed in your Performance Culture. That is why it is essential for all new employees to be carefully enculturated into your organization.

New employees bring the attitudes and behaviors they learned in their previous employment. Most new employees have no idea of how to behave or perform in a true team environment so they cannot be blamed for using skills they learned in their previous job.

With clearly established boundaries and expectations, new employees integrate into the team process rapidly. They are malleable and want to learn so they will fit in and be accepted by the group. It is at this crucial time that the organization can create a very effective team player.

Teaching Teams Boundaries

In the 1980s, I developed the concept of team developer because I was not satisfied with the terms "facilitator" or "coach." A team developer (TD) is NOT a supervisor or manager but does help maintain boundaries for teams. We will discuss the role of the TD more specifically in Chapter 13. For now, the team developer is defined as a specially trained person who is assigned to work with one or more teams. A TD may play two roles – a TD **and** a manager. Although this is not recommended, in some cases it is unavoidable – if the organization is small with only one manager in the first place.

As the TD begins to develop teams, the major challenge will be to manage the teams' boundaries. Early in the process TDs are tempted to say, "They are a team so they don't need me anymore." TDs who back off too quickly create a vacuum. In trying to fill the vacuum, teams will quickly get in over their heads and cause major problems. Developing a team infrastructure is a major step toward a Performance Culture. People and teams must be developed carefully at this stage to ensure the culture takes hold as quickly and efficiently as possible.

The TD should do a number of activities with the team to help members understand the TD's role. For example, it is important that the team and the TD discuss and know how the TD will behave.

Without such an open discussion, the team may feel that the TD is acting strangely or has too much or too little involvement with the team. The team developer should explain what he sees as boundaries and what the goal for development of the team should be in the coming months. An example might be as follows:

"As we begin developing the team, I will be working closely with various people to accomplish some important team-development tasks. I will work with the team trainer to help get a cross-training plan in place. I will work with the team leader to ensure that goals are set and meetings are running efficiently. I will not run the meetings, but I will meet with the leader each week to coach him or her on how to run meetings and stay goal focused. I will work with the scheduler on how to do scheduling with the goal of turning the basic schedule over to the team within six months. If there is conflict on the team, you may come to me but I will probably call the other person in immediately so we can talk about it in a three-way meeting. I expect the team to learn how to deal with most of its own conflicts without my help. To that end I will act as a facilitator rather than arbitrator. In the first few weeks I would like the team to discuss and set a goal for itself to present to the steering committee for Level II. We have a lot to do in Level I empowerment so we need to look at our workload and see how soon we want to try to move to Level II. Most teams take six months or more to get to Level II. Our primary goal is to learn how to run our team like a business with real bottom-line results for our efforts.

"I will also be involved in most of the decisions to ensure that we follow company policy and that we consider all aspects of the business. For example, as we discuss holiday scheduling I may ask the team to show exactly how its schedule will meet the weekend coverage requirement. If we are not meeting our weekly production goals, I may call a special team business meeting to discuss and problem solve. I will avoid imposing decisions on the team, but occasionally this may be necessary especially in the beginning when we are all learning how to run our part of the business.

"It is important that we follow company policies and consider the goals of the company in all our decisions. Since we are all new at this, I will stay close to you and try to teach you what I know. At the same time, we can ask the manager to come in and explain things we may not understand. Other TDs may occasionally sit in on our team business meetings in my absence. All the TDs are a team, responsible for helping all teams in our area, so while I am the main TD for your team, all TDs are available to help.

"Finally, we need to remember that the reason we are doing all this is so we can develop a Performance Culture where everyone knows what the score is and how to do what it takes to meet the goals while supporting one another and having fun doing it."

In this way the team developer sets the pace and shows clearly that much of the responsibility will be on the team, with the TD in a facilitator role. At the same time, the TD will not hesitate to manage boundaries.

Jumping Boundaries

Boundaries set off areas that are outside the team's competence or control. In the early stages of development teams have a strong tendency to want to jump boundaries and get involved with areas outside their control, while ignoring things clearly within their control. Young teams almost always have an external locus of control (see Chapter 4). For example, many manufacturing teams spend inordinate amounts of time and energy trying to change the way engineering works with the shop floor. While this may be a problem for the future, there are many quality and production problems right in front of the team that they are ignoring.

Boundary Jumping Defined

Boundary jumping means working on problems outside of the team to avoid dealing with important problems inside the team.

In an insurance company new teams, in the initial stages of development, became concerned with the way the field agents completed their paperwork and wanted to create a major task force to get the agents to perform better. At the same time the teams were actively ignoring their own errors and mistakes. Upon further examination the teams' mistakes were more costly than the agents', but it was easier to boundary jump and work on the agents than on themselves.

Psychological Reasons for Boundary Jumping

The psychological reasons for boundary jumping are grounded in conflict avoidance. In working on internal problems and mistakes, conflict may arise if someone gets defensive, denies a mistake or refuses to accept feedback on his performance. Conflict is scary to a young team, so it will do almost anything to avoid it, including ignoring obvious problems.

In many organizations, the culture and the culture carriers place great value on conflict avoidance. Harmony and the appearance of peace may be far more important than business goals. The culture says, "Avoid conflict, do not hurt people's feelings, do not tell management about a coworker's mistakes, because that person may become angry and defensive and, 'pay you back' in some way." The idea of paybacks in the workplace is a powerful way to keep people in line within the culture.

The idea that the group might stop inviting you to lunch, fail to help at a crucial time, or do something to make you look bad in front of the boss, terrifies many people. Nothing that the manager or team developer can say or do will overcome such a powerful social sanction. We have all seen or heard of a work group that made a person's life miserable when the person refused to go along with the group, or when he or she violated a norm of the group.

Because team members perceive internal team conflict as dangerous, the temptation to boundary jump is almost irresistible. Teams must learn how to deal with their internal issues in a mature manner before they are competent to deal with issues outside of the team. Managers or team developers must determine that the team can and will take care of internal business, to ensure that an external problem is not a ruse to hide or avoid an internal one.

By learning effective conflict management teams move closer to a Performance Culture that says, "Get conflict in the open and resolve it so that it does not hurt performance, efficiency or profitability."

Working from the Inside Out

A key in helping teams stay within their boundaries is to work from the inside out. In other words, we want to teach the team an internal locus of control. This means that the team should spend the majority of its time learning and practicing conflict management, problem solving and process improvement, thereby focusing on those things that clearly are within its control. As these issues are brought under control, the team can slowly work to the next level, which may involve problem solving with another team or department.

For the first year or so, the team must be focused on internal issues and strongly monitor and help correct any boundary-jumping behavior. Until the team has fully learned how to identify problems, measure them, deal with conflict and stay in the problem frame, it is not likely to have sufficient skills to constructively engage any other team or department in positive nonblaming problem solving. Premature work on problems that fall outside the team's level of skill or competence leads to poor decisions, frustration and unresolved conflict.

Keeping a team focused on internal issues helps it gain confidence in its problem- solving and conflict management skills, while also maturing faster. When the day comes to work on outside problems, the team will be much better equipped and the probability of success will be much greater.

Mick Schneider, manager of Butler Manufacturing's central region engineering, uses the metaphor of a river. "The team is like a river. If the river's banks are not clearly defined, the river tends to meander all over. If the river's banks are clearly defined, the river runs straighter and faster. The TD's job is to make sure the banks of the river are well defined and that the team stays inside those banks. As a result the team will mature much faster and actually accomplish much more with fewer distractions and side tracks."

Is It Worth It?

What we have described here sounds like a lot of work. Why would any leader want to do all this work to achieve a Performance Culture? Using the child-rearing metaphor, we might just as well ask, "Why would a parent want to do all that work to develop a child?" The answer is that a poorly developed child is a spoiled, or an angry and misbehaving child, who will remain dependent on the parent too long. Similarly, an immature culture is a product of poor development on the part of leaders who create a dependency, or worse, an entitlement mentality.

A child who moves out of the house, gets further education or a good job and learns to support himself and his family is a point of pride for his parents and himself. He has become a productive citizen who creates value for society. Similarly, a culture that is properly developed becomes highly productive, creating value for the company and its people. Its members feel great pride and motivation with less need for supervision.

Is it worth the effort? The answer depends on how important it is for the company to reduce levels of dependency and entitlement. If the company plans to reduce layers of management and supervisors, foremen or leads, it needs to learn how to develop and empower employees so they become capable of functioning largely without traditional supervision.

In most environments, it is difficult to empower individuals without also empowering the group. The culture is strong and capable of preventing an individual from doing his or her best. Unless the endemic culture is aligned with the intentional culture, efforts at empowerment may force well-intentioned people to swim against the current of the endemic culture.

It is for this reason that teams are the most logical way to empower a work force. They provide a structure that can weave the endemic and intentional cultures together. Efforts to empower without this structure generally fail.

Questions

1. Do your teams tend to ignore important problems inside the team while complaining about other teams or departments?
2. What would happen if you violated a safety or procedural rule? Can you be sure someone in your organization would call it to your attention?
3. How do you teach boundaries and boundary management to your teams? What roadmap do you use to systematically widen those boundaries as the teams mature?
4. How thick is your policy manual? How many policies do you have that are designed to control or manage people? What do these policies say about the development or dependency of the culture in your organization?
5. How do you ensure that new employees learn team skills quickly? How do you ensure that new employees do not bring in behaviors and attitudes that undermine your culture?
6. How do you hold teams accountable for managing internal conflict and staying within their boundaries?
7. Does your culture encourage or discourage positive conflict management? How would you know?
8. Have you tried to reduce management or supervisory personnel without providing the structure to empower people?

Self-Discipline:
The Key to Organizational Effectiveness

D iscipline and accountability are important concepts in a Performance Culture. Sound organizational discipline begins at the top and includes five components designed to gradually allow workers and teams to become self-disciplined. As a part of the Performance Culture, corrective action follows a process that involves the teams at some level. The emphasis is on helping people improve, not on termination or punishment.

Discipline in the Performance Culture

Discipline is a powerful element in shaping behavior when it utilizes a set of standards, boundaries, rules and expectations within which all agree to participate. A well-focused, disciplined team can accomplish far more than a chaotic, scattered work group. In this sense, discipline is absolutely necessary to effectively accomplish a task.

The Performance Culture views discipline quite differently from traditional corporate cultures. Discipline is seen primarily as something one imposes on oneself not on others. As a result, self-discipline is taught, encouraged and valued by the culture and its leaders.

There are three levels of self-discipline in a Performance Culture:
1. Organizational self-discipline
2. Team self-discipline
3. Personal self-discipline

Each of these levels has specific practices and requirements, and each impacts the others. Generally speaking, organizational self-discipline has the most impact on the performance of the entire organization, with team-level discipline having less impact and personal the least. This runs counter to what you might think, but the key to a disciplined organization starts at the top, not the bottom.

Organizational Self-Discipline

Five disciplines help support the Performance Culture across an entire enterprise. The organizational disciplines should be implemented by the steering committee and leadership team (see Chapter 12). A well-developed work system that uses the five disciplines will create the conditions to support the organization at the team level.

1. The Discipline of Communication and Recognition

Leadership in a Performance Culture involves specific, regular and trustworthy information exchange between all levels. Effective communication processes do more to create trust and organizational confidence than any other single aspect of leadership.

All too often leadership treats communication in a hit-or-miss fashion.

- "If we have time, we will have a quarterly meeting."
- "If the vice president does not get called out of town, we will go over the quarterly results with the union."

So often, "ifs" get in the way of effective regular communication. What teams need is a reliable way to find out what is going on. Just as important, they need a way to express their concerns to management and to participate in making the business more competitive. Communication is the fabric in which the intentional and endemic cultures are woven together to make a Performance Culture.

Leadership teams need to structure a communication system that ensures information flows freely and efficiently throughout the organization – between those who do the work and those who create the market strategies and execute the plans.

The following specific aspects of a communication discipline help make the process more manageable and understandable:

- Communication must be regular.
- Communication must be reliable and trustworthy.
- Communication from the leadership must be nondefensive.
- Communication must be two-way.

We will now discuss each of these requirements in more detail.

Communication must be regular

Many team-based companies have regular communication meetings that include quarterly business results where financial results are shared along with market conditions and the company's strategic moves. In addition, monthly department meetings are held that include non-managers. Many companies also send out regular newsletters that highlight the team process and various aspects of problem solving and success stories.[20] The key is to ensure that these forums are regular and that they become an important part of the organizational routine.

Communication must be reliable and trustworthy

Honesty is the most important component in communication. Effective leaders do not hem and haw. They tell it like it is. Even if workers do not like what they hear, they will come to recognize when the leadership's word is trustworthy.

While employees do not like to get bad news, they do respect leaders who do not try to protect them from it. On two occasions in the last 10 years Standard Motor Products in Kansas has gone through tough times. Rather than hold back, they shared all the news with the union and its members and then worked together on a transition plan.

Communication must be nondefensive

When leaders talk in front of groups or answer questions, it's remarkable how often they look and sound defensive. Defensiveness creates suspicion and mistrust. Leaders often have no idea that they sound or look defensive. I work closely with leaders to help them identify defensive styles and coach them to communicate more directly. Defensive leaders undermine their own effectiveness. Good communication is open and straightforward, does not avoid hard questions, and is quick to say, "I don't know all the answers but we will work this out together." When leaders are perceived as giving poor or evasive answers, arguing with people, or changing the subject when hard questions are asked, it undermines trust in the leadership.

Communication must be two-way

Skip-level meetings between senior managers and the work force are important to ensure that communication goes up as well as down. Open meetings are also important so that the endemic culture can hear and see things for themselves rather than relying on middle managers for all their information. Many leaders forget that the upward form of communication is critical for knowing how the organization is actually performing. Employee surveys may also be a part of two-way communication, but are no substitute for regular face-to-face information gathering on the part of management.

Employee surveys are a common method of gathering information from the culture. In addition to ensuring that you are using a valid and reliable instrument, the manner in which the information is used is very important. Many companies conduct annual surveys but do not effectively communicate the results back to the teams. Further, they fail to involve employees in the action planning and goal setting for improving the organization based upon the findings of the survey.

Many companies conduct annual surveys but do not
effectively communicate the results back to the teams.

Once again, Dilbert is not far from the truth as many employees
see it. The perception comes from poor follow-through on the part
of management. Survey results should be carefully and completely
debriefed to the whole organization. When organizations report
declining enthusiasm and involvement, the cause is often found in
a lack of feedback to employees. When people do not receive the
results in a timely and comprehensive manner, they are less inclined
to give their best effort the next time. It is not good enough to post
the results on a bulletin board. Each area should be a debriefed by
a key person. It is best if the debriefing is done by someone who is
well trained in the process and not a part of the group they are talking to. Local managers have a tendency to gloss over the problem
areas, especially those that might be unflattering to them.

Well-developed surveys can tell a lot about an organization.
Most of all, they can spot areas where middle management may
need help and coaching in the team process. Surveys should be
designed so that the responses can be broken down to at least the
department level, if not the team level. This enables management
to see where further training or coaching is needed and where the
strengths of the organization lie.[21]

2. The Discipline of Involvement

The essence of employee empowerment is involvement. To the
degree that you want teams to take on high levels of responsibility,
they must be involved at the first and second level of management

above the teams. Such involvement may take many forms. I recommend team involvement at the department and business unit level. In some cases involvement is appropriate at even higher levels. When the endemic culture is locked out of important meetings and planning sessions, it often creates a Dilbert effect on the work force. Secrecy in meetings breeds paranoia and mistrust of leadership. Butler Manufacturing routinely involves their engineering teams in the corporate annual operating plan.

DILBERT reprinted by permission of United Feature Syndicate, Inc., 1996, p. 313.

What difference would it make if Dilbert were involved
in the meeting or could obtain reliable information about it?
Would he be updating his resume?

Involvement is not an option or a "nice" thing to do – it is a way of doing business in the Performance Culture by ensuring strong commitment to the goals. It reduces non-value-added activities as fewer people actively resist or misunderstand decisions. Further, involvement increases job satisfaction as people feel a direct link to decisions that are made and a stronger focus on goals.

Part of the discipline of involvement is knowing who to involve and learning how to move effectively while involving people. Involvement does not mean everyone has to sign off on a decision. But it does mean that those most affected by a decision must be able to provide input. Such input may come from an individual representative or from a whole team. Effective, team-based organizations are good at getting people together, moving through the decision-making process and implementing. They develop a rhythm and a sense of urgency that helps avoid the "decision by committee syndrome."

3. The Discipline of Goals

Goals are the key component of any team-based organization. We will discuss them in detail in Chapter 9. The discipline of goals means that every unit of business – team, department, business unit and indeed the entire organization – has specific written goals. To be effective and useful, goals must be posted in a public place and reported every month. This discipline forces teams and organizations to be clear about what they do and how it will be measured. Fuzzy thinking and sloppy workflow are incompatible with well-structured goals. As performance-based organizations become more and more goal-focused, they learn how to measure their work in both business terms and human terms.

4. The Discipline of Accountability

Performance Culture accountability is quite different from that used in a hierarchical system. Organizations require a good deal of training and development to make the process effective. With a well-structured accountability system, teams respond to goals and help individual members do their best. Without such a system, they are often dragged down to the level of their lowest performer. It is difficult to motivate or develop a team that feels little or no accountability for its goals and processes.

There are two levels of accountability: individual accountability to the team and team accountability to the organization. Policies and procedures for team member evaluation, feedback, self-development and goal achievement are all part of individual accountability to the team. On the other hand, audits, goal reporting, budgeting, and so on, are parts of team accountability to the organization.

5. The Discipline of Training

It is unreasonable, unfair and "un-team" to ask someone to do something if you are not willing to train them properly. Continuous improvement means constant improvement – most often accomplished through training of the team and the individual. Training consists of two types – classroom or formal training and on-the-job training. While classroom training is important, on-the-job training in this context is far more important because that is where "the rubber meets the road." Performance Cultures have well-organized and structured on-the-job training systems that require the teams themselves to do much of the training. Teams do almost all of the cross-training and arrange and coordinate much of the skill development training for the team. Classroom training may account for 20-35% of the training hours of any individual. On-the-job training takes up the rest.

Classroom training is essential for developing the team's technical and social skills. Training should be seen as a team activity, wherein the whole team learns. Teams learn and reinforce learning on the job better than an individual skills program. Think of the team as a single organism. The whole organism learns together in order to make the learning a part of everyday work for all members.

The discipline of training has to do with ensuring that people always have the skills to do what is asked of them. To this end, monitoring, evaluating and developing skills is a continual process that involves a good deal of work at the team and team developer level.

Team Self-Discipline

Teams also need to practice discipline. The following five disciplines ensure that teams learn to function well within a Performance Culture.

1. The Discipline of Conflict Management

Teams can learn to manage most of conflict that was formerly ignored or dealt with by management. During the formative stages, the leadership must teach teams the necessary skills and give them opportunity to practice conflict management on a regular basis. Early emphasis on conflict management skills leads to faster team maturation. The sooner teams learn how to deal with this critical issue, the faster they will show real business results.

2. The Discipline of Problem Solving

Regardless of which problem-solving process you use, it should be used consistently throughout the organization. When there is no system or when multiple systems exist at the same time, confusion often reigns and no problem solving gets done. Problem solving should be a regular agenda item in team meetings. Frequent practice helps build the discipline so that it eventually becomes a habit.

3. The Discipline of Team Business Meetings

At the beginning of its implementation, a Performance Culture must also learn the discipline of meetings. All teams are taught and expected to use a system for governing meetings. This is important for managers since they are the ones having the most meetings and experiencing the most non-value-added time in meetings.

practical tip
I encourage the use of the term "team business meeting" to help focus the team. Each team is a small business and should run itself in a business-like manner. Well-run business meetings help everyone get the most out of the meeting and feel good about the time invested.

In a Performance Culture, meetings are the heart and soul of the team's coordination efforts. They are an investment that should bring a positive return. Regular weekly team business meetings should be well-organized, task-and goal-focused. When this important discipline is followed consistently, teams get a tremendous amount of work done in a single hour-long meeting. They find that the focus and discipline of a well-structured meeting makes them more enthusiastic about their everyday work. People feel good about going to the meeting because they can see it serves a useful purpose.

On the other hand, when the discipline of meetings is poorly followed, the result is frustration and a steady erosion of the team's effectiveness. All too often management finds that the team business meetings are ineffective and unproductive, and cut them back to half an hour, or to once every two weeks, or even once a month.

This is a vicious cycle because with each cutback, the meetings become less effective and eventually teams stop meeting altogether.

Unfortunately, it is easier for managers and teams to cut down or eliminate team business meetings than to create a discipline and structure for making them effective. Failure to properly structure team business meetings is the death knell of the Performance Culture. If an organization is having trouble with the simple discipline of meetings, it is probably having much greater trouble with most of the other disciplines. The first place to look for a lack of discipline is in the leadership itself. Most of the time, poor meeting discipline in the teams starts with poor models at the top.

4. The Discipline of Goals

"Without goals that can be measured, there can be no team."[22] The discipline of goals is the single most important team discipline because goals and goal achievement are what gives people a sense of purpose and meaning in their work. With unambiguous, measurable goals, the need for all the other disciplines becomes crystal clear. Goal achievement requires efficient meetings, effective conflict resolution, and focused problem solving.

The discipline of goals begins with the leadership team. The discipline is simply this: every team will have measurable goals that are displayed in public and that are reviewed weekly. Goals are posted on a public board in the team's work area. Every team is expected to document its goal progress and report it monthly to the leadership team.

The leadership team publicly displays its goals and measures and reports on its progress to the entire organization monthly. Many organizations have a quarterly report as well. This may take the form of an all-facility meeting where the leadership team briefs everyone at the same time about goal progress.

5. The Discipline of Performance Feedback

In Performance Cultures performance feedback is different from that of the single-leader work group. In fact, one of the key ways of determining if an organization is truly performance-based is to look at the level of team involvement in giving performance feedback. Organizations where teams regularly give performance feedback to their members, their coaches and managers are clearly performance-based. However, organizations that rely upon managers, coaches, coordinators or supervisors to give most of the feedback to the teams are single-leader work groups, regardless of what they call themselves.

Learning Point: In a Performance Culture, open and honest feedback is practiced at all levels.

In a Performance Culture, multiple sources of information about performance are used, each of them important for helping people improve performance. For team members there are four sources of information: teammates, managers, customers, and the members themselves.

As mentioned earlier, new teams do not deal well with performance feedback. It requires training and lots of practice for teams to become proficient at this important skill. There are three levels in achieving proficiency in performance feedback:

1. Direct verbal feedback
2. Team performance coaching
3. Team performance feedback

Direct verbal feedback is the lowest level. The team must learn the simplest form first, since these skills will be used in the two higher levels as well. Second, after six months or more, teams learn how to do performance coaching within their team with the input of both managers and team developers. Third, after about 18-24 months, the team learns how to do its own performance feedback with little involvement outside the team.

As teams learn performance feedback skills, they become more emotionally mature and capable of dealing with specific issues without management intervention. It takes two to three years for teams to reach a proficient level of performance feedback. But becoming self-corrective and achievement oriented is the hallmark of a Performance Culture. Teams become skilled at solving problems, recognizing and praising, integrating new members, correcting behavior, and setting challenging goals.

As Paul Heacock, president of Human Dynamics, Inc., has noted, "The process begins to take on a life of its own where I can pull back and focus on other things like growing the business." Or as Steve Doman, team developer at Standard Motor Products, once said, "I don't have to worry if the teams will do the right thing. They do more right things than I would do as a supervisor. The few mistakes they make are just good learning opportunities for all of us. They know a lot more about their work than I do."

Team self-discipline DOES NOT mean writing people up, putting them on probation, firing or "disciplining" in the misguided belief that discipline and punishment are synonymous. While these actions may be required with a poor performer, if the team does a good job of self-discipline, negative types of discipline are far less common than in a hierarchical organization. Problems are often dealt with by the teams long before they become major issues. In this way people develop faster and do not learn bad habits that can get them in trouble later.

While there will always be a need for negative forms of discipline, the more they are used the less effective they become. Negative forms of discipline and sanctions should be reserved for only the most destructive problems in the workplace. Indeed, the more focus there is on poor performers, the less time management gives to recognizing those who are good performers. The net result is that those performing badly get a lot of management attention, while those performing well are generally ignored until they make a mistake or get so frustrated that they act out or leave.

The Performance Culture keeps the spotlight on the desired behavior. Consistent praise and recognition of many people across the whole enterprise is a constant reminder and model for everyone about what is needed to achieve the goals and develop the culture of performance.

Personal Self-Discipline

There is no single way to teach personal self-discipline. However, Steven Covey's *Seven Habits of Highly Effective People* [23] is one of the more effective methods I have seen. Some of the elements that must be present in personal discipline are:

- individual accountability
- ability to accept personal feedback on performance
- cooperative and interpersonal skills
- willingness to learn and teach new skills to others
- basic technical skills

I strongly recommend some kind of personal skills training for every employee, including managers, within the first year of implementation of teams. In this manner everyone will learn the same terms and speak a common language related to individual discipline. Although the content should be the same, the manager version may be more intense and in-depth, since managers will be expected to model the behaviors.

Many employees have never been taught personal discipline. Yet people are interested in, even grateful for, learning personal disciplines, recognizing that it not only helps them work better but improves their personal lives as well.

Unfortunately up to 10% of a typical work force cannot, or will not, learn and use personal discipline and cooperative skills. There are many reasons for this, from psychological difficulties, poor interpersonal skills, or personality problems, to simply doing better in a very individualistic environment. Regardless of the reasons, it is important to recognize when there is a mismatch and then help the employee learn to adjust or to find other work inside or outside of the organization. This issue should be handled in a nonjudgmental but direct manner. It is no crime not to like the environment of the Performance Culture, but it does create major problems for the organization and the teams.

Accountability and Corrective Action Procedures

So far we have looked at discipline from a fairly nontraditional point of view, allowing teams and individuals a high degree of empowerment. The following discussion will help the manager or team developer deal with teams or individuals who are having performance problems and need corrective action.

Coaching

Coaching is the first and most important component of accountability. I use a coaching form, which the TD and team work on together. It is used two to four times a year for each team member and for the TD. It is a simple form that is developed by each organization.[24] The form is NOT the process, however. Too many companies get hung up on the form and forget that the form is a tool in the process of coaching.

practical tip The process works in the following way. The team is given a brief training session in how to carry out the coaching process. A facilitator from outside the team guides the first session to show the team how it works. The first person to receive a coaching form is the team's TD. The team developer leaves the room. The facilitator goes through the coaching form asking the team to evaluate the TD on each item. Specific behavioral examples are required. This is a coaching form – you cannot coach someone if there are no specific behavioral examples.

The facilitator goes through the form with the team, soliciting ideas and examples. As much emphasis is placed on what the person being coached does well as on what needs improvement. The facilitator tries to gain consensus on the items and to write down *specific behavioral* examples. This part of the meeting should take

15-20 minutes but the first few times will take longer. The TD or manager is then called back into the room, and 10 minutes are spent giving feedback and asking questions. No arguing or debating is allowed. The total coaching session should not last more than 30 minutes. As teams get better, the time will decrease to as little as 15 minutes. Team members know at least a week in advance who is next and everyone is expected to come prepared to give their observations.

This process continues for the first 18-24 months until the team is comfortable with the process and shows the ability to objectively coach teammates. Once a team has shown strong competence in coaching, the process may be done every six months, except for new team members or a team member who has performance problems. For these individuals, the process should continue quarterly, if not monthly.

Proper use of the coaching process greatly reduces or eliminates major performance problems long before they become critical. Most people respond well to coaching by their own team and want to improve to help themselves and the team.

What happens when someone does not respond to coaching?

In answering this question, we are assuming that the organization practices the disciplines of a Performance Culture and that most workers want to do a good job, if given the tools, skills and recognition. When somebody does not respond to couching as expected, it is easy for managers and teams to get into a "punishment" mode. But effective teams are able to analyze the situation and ensure the team member is properly trained and supported to do the assignment.

In a Performance Culture corrective action is nonjudgmental without punishment and anger. Coaching is the main skill required. Although coaching may lead to termination, just as a basketball coach may cut a player from the team, there should be no punitive intent, only improvement and development.

The object is to retain people and help them improve. It is important to begin by determining if there is a proper match between the person and the job. It is no shame to be mismatched in a job. It happens quite frequently. If there is a poor match, see if there is another position that would be better. If not, termination may be necessary.

At one client company, two individuals were consistently poor performers in a highly detailed and tedious task that required close attention. After several efforts at training and coaching, performance skill still did not improve. The manager then began to look for other causes. In one case another team member noted a pattern of mistakes that was consistent with possible eyesight problems. The target team member was asked to get an eye exam which revealed that he needed a new prescription. Performance improved immediately. For the second team member, a discussion revealed that she did not have the concentration skills needed for the work. She had transferred to the position for a pay increase from a job in which she had always excelled. With some counseling from the manager and human resources, she agreed to go back to her previous position in another work area where she once again performed well.

The Poor Performer

Despite all the efforts of the team or the TD, there will still be an occasional team member who does not perform satisfactorily. Such employees are sometimes even destructive or disruptive to the team. Ignoring their behavior or pretending that it is not harmful can have major negative consequences for the organization.

As mentioned earlier, as much as 10% of the general population has trouble working cooperatively with others. Either their interpersonal skills are underdeveloped or they do not have the emotional capacity to accept information about their performance and make the necessary adjustments.

Sometimes these people are high performers in a system that does not require high levels of cooperation. DO NOT expect high performers in a hierarchical system to be the high performers in a

Performance Culture. The skills required in the two systems are very different. I have seen many examples of poor performers in traditional systems becoming star performers in Performance Cultures. However, some star performers in traditional systems become disruptive and unproductive in a Performance Culture. This is not totally surprising as the rules and skills have changed. We would not expect a star in golf to be a star basketball player. Individual performers do well in golf-type jobs but not in basketball-type jobs where cooperative skills are important. Some are able to adjust and become stars in the team system, others are not.

This is true of management as well. Up to 30% of incumbent managers, supervisors, shop leads, and so forth, do not perform well in the Performance Culture. Interpersonal skills, cooperative skills and involvement skills are simply not important to them. They succeeded in the hierarchical system using a different set of skills. The best supervisors in a traditional environment may not be not be the best team developers.

Learning Point: It is important to recognize that no matter what type of work system you choose, there will be managers and employees who do not perform well.

From my observations, traditional systems have a higher rate of poor performers than team-based systems. This is largely because traditional systems are poor at coaching people and helping them improve. Employees can be forgotten or ignored until their performance problems and bad habits lead to termination. Poor performance is more easily ignored or overlooked in an organization where managers move frequently or where there is a high turnover in the management ranks. In such situations, no single manager ever feels responsible enough to do something about a problem. If an action plan is made, the next manager may drop the ball.

In a Performance Culture, on the other hand, people are hired, trained, coached and evaluated on their technical and cooperative skills with continual team input. Therefore it is far less likely that a poor performer is ignored. Further, in a Performance Culture, the constant is not the manager but performance, which allows careful documentation of coaching, development and performance goal setting. No matter who the manager is, the process goes on. It would be difficult for an employee to remain a poor performer for long in a system that gives performance feedback from the team every three to six months.

Corrective Action

Poor performers can drag the whole team down. Even other teams can be affected. If nothing is done to help them, other team members soon begin to say to themselves, "Management doesn't do anything about Sam's poor performance so why should I bust my butt to cover his performance problems?" The ultimate result of ignoring poor performance is mediocrity on the whole team. It is very discouraging for a team to work hard while one of it's members has a "free ride."

When the TD or manager determines that an employee is not responding to coaching from the team, a formal corrective action process is started. This is an infrequent procedure that may need to be used with as little as 1-3% of the employees in any given year. Frequent use of formal corrective action may say more about the system than the individual team member. Nevertheless, corrective action is occasionally necessary and we need to be prepared to use it properly and effectively.

I strongly recommend Dick Grote's book *Discipline Without Punishment*,[25] an excellent model for corrective action. However, it needs to be modified to work in a Performance Culture.

Once the problem has progressed to the point where the manager and TD have determined they need to take direct action, the process moves outside the team's control. We call this going "off-line." When going "off-line," the team developer and the manager work together with the team member and are present at every step in the process and at every meeting. This is not the traditional "going to the woodshed" meeting with the boss. Concern for the person is as important as improved performance. This process carries a strong message and is generally taken much more to heart by the employee. He or she can see that it is not just a matter of "The boss doesn't like me." The procedure shows a real concern for the employee and his performance.

Step 1: Once the TD and manager have determined that corrective action is required, the first step is to have a private talk with the employee. The manager and team developer meet with the team member and outline the issues as well as expectations for change and development.

Step 2: The employee is asked to think about the issues and return in two days with a written plan of action for performance improvement and specific time frames. If the employee has problems writing this down, someone other than the manager or TD may be assigned to help him write the plan of action.

Step 3: The plan is reviewed by the TD and manager. If it is acceptable, they all sign it and go to step 4. If it is not acceptable, further discussion takes place and modifications are made until the manager and TD are satisfied or until it becomes obvious that the employee is not willing to create an action plan; if so, the process moves to Step 3a.

Step 3a: If the plan is not acceptable, further action may be required, such as suspension or termination.

Step 3b: If the plan of action is acceptable, go to Step 4.

Learning Point: It is critical that the action plan comes from the employee. Performance improvement, change and planning are fully the responsibility of the employee, not the manager or TD.

Off-Line Process

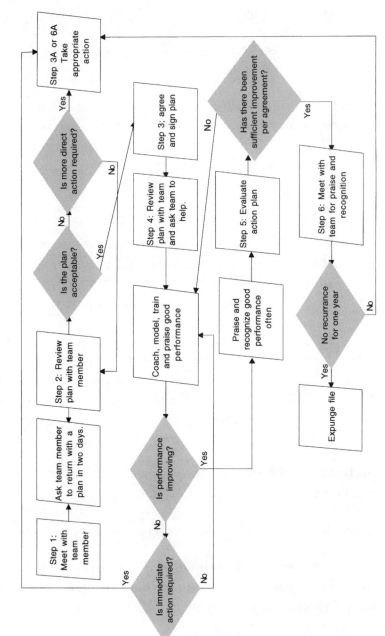

Step 4: A special meeting is held to go over the action plan with the entire team. The TD and manager are present at this meeting. The purpose of the meeting is to inform the team of the issues and to ask for everyone's help in correcting the problem. Team members are told that they are free to coach or help the person in any way they can, but management is responsible for making the final decision about the team member's employment status.

A note on confidentiality: Step 4 goes against all the instincts and training of the traditional manager. However, a problem as serious as this is obvious to the entire team. Traditional systems pretend that such an issue does not affect or concern the team and therefore try to handle it confidentially. Treating it confidentially leaves the most valuable resource out of the loop, fellow workers. Coworkers usually know more about how an employee is performing than any manager or supervisor. In a Performance Culture the team is a critical part of the improvement process. The object is not to terminate the person, but to correct the problems that are hurting the team's ability to perform it's mission. Therefore, the team needs to be involved.

Step 5: The action plan is evaluated by the TD and the manager weekly. Praise for improved performance should be given at every opportunity. Focus on the positive as much as possible until the criteria for performance have been met. Then go to Step 6. If performance does not improve to meet the minimum criteria, or if it is determined that the team member is not willing or capable of making the necessary changes, go to Step 5a.

Step 5a: The team member is terminated or other appropriate action is taken.

Step 6: A special meeting is held with the team member, manager and the TD to inform the team that the team member has demonstrated satisfactory improvement. Praise the team member and the team for helping him. Tell the team that all the documentation on the problem will remain in the employee's file for one year. If the problem does not recur, all the related documents will be expunged. Ask the team to continue to help and coach the coworker so he can continue to improve. Praise both the team and the individual for successful completion of the process.

It is important that all meetings with the team member include the manager and the team developer. Two people have a much greater impact than one and help prevent misunderstandings. If appropriate, a representative of human resources may also be a part of the process.

Issues that can appropriately be dealt with using this process include problems related to task performance, attendance, and cooperative behavior with the team or other teams. However, some issues should NOT be handled in this manner even in a Performance Culture. These include sexual harassment, workplace violence, drug use, discrimination, and so on.

Corrective Action Rules

To ensure the integrity of the process it is important that certain rules are followed with respect to team members who are involved in corrective action.

1. A person who is involved in corrective action of any kind is not eligible for increase in status, specifically increases in pay, promotions, or transfers. Voluntary demotions may be appropriate but the corrective action plan may still be appropriate even after a demotion.

2. No person involved in corrective action may transfer or be transferred to another team until the problem has been resolved, or the receiving manager has full knowledge of the problem and agrees to carry out the action plan. Do not let teams or managers dump their problems onto other teams or managers.

3. All managers AND teams must be trained in the process so there are no surprises when the "off-line" process is used.

This process is very powerful. In fact, the very act of using this process reduces the need for it in the future. Once a few teams have seen the process in action, they quickly learn how to help coworkers correct their performance problems before formal corrective action becomes necessary. Finally, the openness of the process takes away the suspicion of unfairness. With the charade of confidentiality eliminated, all can see that the process is designed to help people improve, not to terminate people.

This has not been a conclusive discussion of the "off-line" process. Each company should design its own process in conjunction with other best practices. The all-important common denominators are the involvement of the team and the issue of confidentiality.

Team Accountability

In a hierarchical organization, accountability flows through the manager up through the ranks. Within a Performance Culture, each team is seen as a small business unit with responsibility for specific goals and is therefore accountable to the organization for achieving those goals.

This is a difficult concept for traditionally trained managers to understand but it is a critical distinction for successful implementation of teams. With fewer managers, more teams and team members, it is physically impossible for any manager to hold individuals accountable. Therefore, the manager must be able to rely upon the teams to do most of the low-level behavioral adjustments. Teams cannot be expected to exhibit self-correcting behavior if they have not been trained properly and if there is no system to support their own low-level behavioral adjustments.

To begin to understand team accountability, let's look at Dick Jarman's approach to working with the Butler Manufacturing engineering teams. Dick is president of the buildings division. In the past, when Dick visited the various regional offices for their annual review, he met primarily with the managers who briefed him on various aspects of the business. As a traditionally organized company, the managers were accountable to Dick.

But when the engineering division became team-based, Dick changed his approach to emphasize team accountability as well as manager accountability. In his speech to the Teaming-Up® Conference, here is what he said:

practical tip "Every team meets with me at least once a year, face to face in a small conference room to review their performance against their goals and to talk about their needs and their priorities. I'm always energized by the focus and enthusiasm of the teams and by all that they are doing. They, in turn, know that I am interested in what they are doing and that I hold them accountable for their results. For the first time ever, everyone is in touch with the goals and priorities of the business … so what did our engineering self-directed work team effort do for Butler and its shareholders, and its customers?

- Three consecutive years of record volume, with a 39% increase in engineering output.
- Three consecutive years of record earnings.
- An 18% improvement in engineering productivity.
- A 40% improvement in on-time reliability.
- Much happier dealers and customers.
- Much happier and more involved employees, with a much lower turnover rate than most companies."[26]

It is clear from Dick's speech that the teams are directly responsible to him and that he sees firsthand what they are doing, unfiltered by layers of management. This has had a large impact on the culture by shedding a whole new light on the concept of accountability. Dick wants the teams to understand that they are a part of a larger company, that what they do has a direct impact on how well manufacturing and marketing do their respective jobs. He is concerned that they see the big picture and not simply see themselves as one region among many.

At Harmon Industries, teams were expected to make regular presentations to the steering committee. These presentations dealt with the teams' goals, process improvements and future plans for improvement. Jeff Utterback worked hard to show the teams how their behavior affects the whole company. He, too, wants the teams to see a bigger picture and feel accountable for the results of the whole plant, not just their team.

These are a few of the ways in which organizations try to break down the old notion of manager accountability to help teams see themselves as accountable to a larger part of the organization. Teams need to see how their behavior helps or hurts others.

Load Balancing

Harmon instituted something called the 110% Rule, where teams were encouraged and recognized for sharing resources when other teams needed help. Sometimes teams become self-focused and forget that they are part of a larger organization. The 110% Rule was intended to encourage teams that finished their work early to share their extra time and people. In a traditional organization the manager is the one who does the load balancing, which means that single-leader work groups might wait around until the manager or supervisor tells them what to do. But in a Performance Culture the team can do load balancing, often much more quickly and efficiently than a manager can. The manager may not even know there is a workflow problem while the team knows immediately because the teams talk to each other constantly and generally know within minutes if extra help is going to be needed in some area.

At Baptist Health Systems in Little Rock, Arkansas, the child-care facility under Mo Jones is organized into self-directed work teams. Part of the team's job is to ensure that the facility is adequately staffed. Mo taught the staff how to evaluate staffing needs and empowered them to make the proper adjustments. Often a manager is not involved when someone needs to fill in for someone, or when staff needs to be shifted to meet an unexpected emergency.

Celestia Ramm, team developer at Baptist Health Systems, and her teams have devised excellent load balancing methods for coverage of the hospital phones 24 hours a day and in times of emergencies. Teams have been carefully trained and cross-trained and are responsible for ensuring all positions are covered for any emergency. They also coordinate all holiday leave. The first year they tried scheduling people to work two hours on each holiday. Celestia did not feel this was a good solution but she let them try it anyway. The result was that they soon changed to rotate holidays over the entire year so people could go out of town. Celestia said, "They learned a lot about self organizing and trusting one another by figuring it out themselves."

Load Balancing: The Performance Advantage

In Performance Cultures the team does the load balancing; in traditional companies supervisors do it.

The "Floating Palates" at Human Dynamics, Inc.

The "Floating Palates" are a semicross-functional team. They are heavily involved in product development for clients using on-line software assistance and training aids. At the beginning of each day the team meets for five minutes to discuss the day's workload. There are generally no managers present as the team discusses the workload. If someone wants a day off or wishes to leave early she may ask the team at that time. The team distributes work among members and briefly discusses the previous day's performance and the goals it is working toward. If anyone needs help, they ask at this time. If someone has free time that day, they let everyone know they are available.

The Schedulers at Standard Motor Products

The Schedulers are a group of six people representing about 90 warehouse team members. These six rotate into the position from their teams every three months. Each day they meet for 15-20 minutes to discuss the day's orders and shipping schedule, often with no manager present. The group determines the amount of work to be done and the staff available to do it. They decide if overtime will be required to complete the work or if there are too many people for the workload. If there are excess people, team members are given the option of leaving work early according to a predetermined formula or working in another part of the plant.

In both these examples the teams see themselves as accountable to the organization. "Accountability" for them means making sure the human resources are properly distributed to take maximum advantage of time and people resources.

Load balancing is an important function of teams, which are far more efficient at balancing than managers. Given the right tools and information, teams know much sooner what the work load will be and what needs to be done to accommodate it. This leaves the manager free to do higher-level work.

When Teams Have Problems

In many cases when a team is having difficulty achieving its goals, one of the following is involved:

1. One or more members in the group are having performance problems and the team has not addressed the issues through coaching or performance feedback.

   Cause: The problem often comes from a team's conflict-avoidance tendencies due to poor training or lack of guidance. It can also result from an intimidating or dysfunctional team member.

   Solution: The team developer can use a series of structured feedback exercises, both written and verbal, to help the team get back on track and face the issues.

2. One or more members of the group are having performance problems that the team has unsuccessfully tried to address.

   Cause: The team may not be effectively coaching the person or skill deficiencies are involved that are too difficult for the team to handle.

   Solution: The team developer should observe the team and give them coaching and guidance on how to help the coworker. If this does not succeed you may need to go "off-line" with the individual.

3. An individual in the group is in need of corrective action that exceeds the team's ability and the team developer has not identified the problem or begun the process.

    Cause: The team may not have brought the problem to the attention of the team developer or the TD is avoiding the issue. This often happens when a team is having difficulty meeting its goals and the TD is uncertain what to do and tends to withdraw from the team.

    Solution: Withdrawal will only increase the problem. The TD should meet with the team and do some problem solving and root cause analysis. If you stay close to the team issues often surface quickly. If the problem cannot be identified, the TD should work more closely with the team for the next few weeks. The problem will surface over time. Coach the individual(s) or move to higher levels of intervention if necessary.

    Note: If it is a matter of TD avoidance, the team may need to go directly to the team developer and discuss what they have done to help the individual and ask for help from the manager or team developer.

4. The team's goals are not appropriately matched to the team's skills or tools.

    Cause: This problem often occurs when highly skilled team members leave the team or there are unexpected equipment or software problems.

    Solution: The TD reexamines the goals of the team as well as the skills and resources and looks at the method by which the goals were set and then revisits the goals with the team. Develop a plan for gaining the skills or resources as soon as possible. Don't change the goal itself until you are certain that the team cannot possibly obtain the resources or skills in time to achieve the goal.

Accountability vs. Rescue

How can the TD hold teams accountable while not rescuing? The role of the team developer is to *guide* the team through the process, *not to do it for them*. In order to guide a team the TD must follow some basic rules.

practical tip

1. No changes in status may be given any member of the team (transfers or promotions) until the team has resolved the issues and made substantial progress toward achieving its goals. While changes in team membership may be beneficial at times, those same changes can enable destructive behavior. Be careful about allowing people to leave teams before they have resolved their problems or conflicts.

2. A third party, such as a steering committee or leadership team member, must be involved in the accountability procedure in addition to the team developer and unit manager. Until they are willing to "sign off" that the team has satisfactorily resolved its issues, the team remains on accountability status.

3. An outside facilitator may be helpful as well, since it is possible that team developer or management behavior is a part of the problem. The key is to make sure the process does not center on one person such as the manager or the team developer. Both are responsible for helping the team work out its problem.

All too often a team will avoid conflict and leave difficulties unresolved while eliminating one of its members. As a result, the team learns how to avoid problems rather than growing by solving problems. For example, in the early stages of a team's growth, it often tries to get the team developer to take on the tough interpersonal problems. The net result is that the team loses an opportunity to mature and instead becomes more dependent on the TD. Even more devastating, the team will start expecting the TD to come to its rescue rather than facilitate learning. The more often a TD rescues a team, the less likely the team is to mature. This is a vicious cycle called "learned helplessness." The more helpless the team acts, the more management rescues and the more helpless the team becomes.

Once a team has worked through a difficult time, it is generally stronger and more capable. After graduate school I worked as a psychologist with families and adolescents and also did marriage counseling. I found that many of the dynamics in marriages and families parallel those of teams. Like a family, when teams go through tough times they either become stronger or fall apart. If family members will not work through their problems together, if they tend to avoid problems or conflict, it is difficult for the family to survive.

When parents rescue children from the consequences of their own actions, they actually teach inappropriate behavior. A parent I once knew bailed his daughter out every time she got in trouble with school or the law. The more the youngster was rescued, the more she got into trouble. Eventually the pattern led to jail – then the parent could not bail her out.

This is not a parent-child pattern; it is a human relationship pattern that is the same whether the group is a family or a company. I have witnessed organizations that have attempted to establish a team process several times. Each time the team or the organization gets to a conflict stage, management rescues the team or pulls the plug on the process. If they can ever get through to the other side, they invariably see great results with positive changes in the attitude of the work force.

Managers find it difficult making it through the emotionally challenging early stages of team development. The temptation is to rescue the team or stop the process. Each time there is a false start, people learn many poor lessons. They learn that when conflict gets heavy, management will rescue rather than facilitate and teach. People learn that their high level of commitment to the process can be destroyed by a single manager who is unskilled or easily frightened by this natural process. *Most of all, they learn that they are not accountable for their own actions.* Managers are accountable for the team's actions and teams are more than happy to let management take the heat so they won't have to answer for their own behavior.

Dr. Dan Dana, author of *Conflict Resolution*,[27] has studied this problem extensively. He finds that people tend to engage in "guerilla" conflict resolution tactics. That is, they negatively engage each other until the situation gets too hot, then they run away. This pattern recurs over and over, but they never stay engaged long enough to resolve the conflict. As a result, the conflict becomes entrenched and more difficult to resolve.

As this pattern is repeated, teams learn how to avoid the hard work of conflict resolution and push problems onto the team developer or manager. But accountability as practiced in a Performance Culture means holding the teams responsible for resolving conflicts appropriately, given support and facilitation where needed.

Questions

1. How well do you and the leadership model the five organizational disciplines?
2. Does your organization practice the five team disciplines?
3. How involved are teams in the coaching and feedback process?
4. How is corrective action in a Performance Culture different from that of a traditionally organized system?
5. Can you identify examples where you might have rescued a team rather than facilitated its resolution of a problem?
6. When have you seen a team in your organization work through some difficult issues successfully? What was the long-term effect on the team?

CHAPTER

Goals:
The Glue of the Performance Culture

G oals are the essential ingredient in any Performance Culture. Understanding and using the concepts of task and process goals will help the leadership stay focused on what is important and resist the temptation to push task goals at the expense of process goals for short-term gain. Recognition and celebration are the key management behaviors that support increasing goal focus and continuous improvement.

Learning Point: A team without goals is not a team.

The Role of Goals

Humans are goal-focused creatures. Each person who comes to work in your organization has personal goals. The goal may be to get a new bass boat, to pay off the mortgage early, to send a child to college, to retire early, to become president of the church board, or to raise the bowling average by 10 points. All these are goals that motivate and make life meaningful.

Goals are important for basic mental health. They give us a reason for living and make our lives worthwhile. When goals are clear, we find it easier to work regularly toward them. It is difficult for people lacking goals to become motivated; they have nothing to work toward, no focus for their energies. It is equally true in work as in private life, goals motivate and focus people. Without goals, people may even develop signs of depression.

Goal Defined

A goal is something that motivates a person to plan ahead, whether for a few hours, a day, or even years.

The direction and focus that goals provide to the Performance Culture is described as the key to success by many who lead team-based organizations. "Until the goals are set and we can hold the teams accountable there is no leverage ... without the goals and accountability, you just have social change," says Dick Jarman, executive vice president of Butler Manufacturing, the world leader in pre-engineered metal buildings.

Jeff Feaster, builder services manager at Butler, literally puts the goals in employees' hands. Each month, teams receive packets of information on their team's goals and how they were met, or not met. For example, numbers of error claims steadily decreased when teams were given monthly updates on performance as measured in the context of their goals. "I saw the shift in ownership of goals and performance measures," Feaster reported, "I can't argue with their performance as we have improved every year."

Over the 10 years Standard Motor Products has been pursuing self-directed work teams, Thom Norbury, general manager of the Wire & Cable Business Unit, believes a great strength of his organization's successes is that they have developed both effective goals and goal reporting. The audits I have done periodically over the last 10 years have verified this sentiment.

Eric Sills managed SMP's Oxygen Sensor Unit for the first two years after it opened. Sills says the employees were screened when hired for how well they could be expected to make the transition to teams. "There was a big emphasis on goals. I knew we needed a system for our goals. We always placed an emphasis on measurement, on asking, 'How are we doing?'

In the early stages, before the teams were formally introduced, Sills held monthly meetings where he would ask for responses on goals and measures. Mostly he got blank stares, spacing out, and the feeling that he was not communicating well. He then started posting graphs everywhere that explained the measures and also began to hand out prizes to those who knew the answers. This led an ambitious minority to look for the answers prior to the meetings to collect their prize. They had little competition. As Sills said, 90% were still ignoring what he saw as crucial to effective operations of the teams and the work of this unit.

Sills learned that his attempts to communicate companywide goals was falling on mostly tuned-out ears. A breakthrough occurred after the teams were formed and they began dealing with goals at their level. Sills and the steering committee set goals and rewards. As the teams saw how the goals related to their specific job functions, they became more goal focused. According to Sills, this new team-centered focus on goals was the most dramatic example he has seen of the adage, "Think globally – act locally!" Into their third year and under Mark Payne, the new and equally goal-focused plant manager, the plant is functioning extremely well.

As Dick Jarman, Eric Sills, Thom Norbury and Jeff Feaster have told us, the task of leaders in a Performance Culture is to help workers take our inherent goal focus and learn to use it in the workplace.

Goals and Organizational Health

Traditional organizations do not ask the line worker to participate in goal setting or goal measurement. As a result, employees feel no ownership for the goals of the organization and do not understand many management decisions that are based on those goals.

Well-formed goals are important for the health of a team-based organization just as they are for the mental health of the individual. Goals keep everyone focused on what is important and help prevent the wasted energy caused by infighting and conflict related to poor goal focus.

The city of West Palm Beach waste-water treatment facility found the power of team goals when the city considered privitization. Lou Haddad, employee relations manager, was charged by the city and the Public Utility Department to trim the facility's budget. A consultant reported that it seemed realistic to trim the $7 million annual budget by $700,000 in five years. With the goal of reducing costs and the promise that the teams and the union would be responsible for operating the plant, in October of 1998 the transition was made. The result was astounding! By the end of the first year the savings were already at $740,000 and each worker received an $8,000 bonus. In the second year, they met their goals again with another significant bonus. These goals were achieved despite problems and resistance from many sectors.

> *The power of a clear goal is that it provides a focal point for our attention and energy, thus helping us move toward it ... When we focus our energy on the obstacles in our path, we spend time and energy dealing with those obstacles rather than on getting where we want to go.*
> **Ed Oakley and Doug Krug,**
> **1994, p. 77–78.**

Haddad commented, "The most important thing I did was structure on the front end the basic belief that they could achieve the goals in the consultant's report and that the city would stand behind this activity." The results speak for themselves and three years later the teams continue to outperform the privatization estimates.

Harnessing the energy of everyone requires well-formed goals. In this case the city developed well-formed goals and enlisted the help of the teams and the union to achieve those goals.

Six Characteristics of Well-Formed Team Goals

Well-formed goals bring everything together in the Performance Culture. People with well-formed goals are motivated to work together effectively and to learn cooperative skills.

Well-formed goals share the following characteristics:

1. They are clearly measurable and time-based.
2. They are publicly known and displayed for all to see.
3. Team members understand how goals will affect the company's performance.
4. Team members participate in setting the goals and feel they are realistic.
5. They are supported by a plan with milestones so the team can map its way.
6. There is a system for celebrating goal accomplishment at every level.

We will now discuss each of these characteristics in detail.

1. Goals are clearly measurable and time-based.

While this characteristic may seem obvious, our examination of numerous organizations has shown that many corporate measurement systems are useless for helping teams measure their goals. Information systems are set up for accounting, forecasting, organizational productivity, and so forth, but information is not available to help people at the team level measure their work. In many cases, a good deal of work must be done to give teams the information they need to determine if they are performing well. Performance Cultures MUST develop reliable information feedback at the team level. Unreliable metrics are fatal.

This speaks directly to the infrastructure required to support true teams. With a well-designed measurement infrastructure, teams can take on a great deal of responsibility for their work.

The goals of the team must be so clear that they can be easily charted, easily tracked. In working with a performance-based organization my own goal is that 90% of the people will be able to say what their team's goals are and where they stand toward meeting those goals at any given time within nine months after the start of the journey to a Performance Culture.

Well-formed goals allow everyone to understand what tasks are required, what to plan for and how to anticipate problems. Most people are competitive in some way. They may not be competitive toward others, but they do feel a desire to compete with themselves. Clear, measurable goals allow workers and their teams to measure their progress and compete to improve themselves.

2. Goals are publicly known and displayed for all to see.

To be effective, goals must be public. Employees must be able to see on a daily basis how they are performing toward their goals. Measures need to be talked about and discussed at every team business meeting. It is hard to keep people motivated toward goals that are invisible to them. Out of sight, out of mind.

In the Teaming Up®[28] process, goals must be one of the key agenda items at every team business meeting. Teams have large white or cork boards called "huddle boards" where all measures are charted by the team. Most teams meet briefly at the beginning of the workday in front of the huddle board to discuss the goals for the day, as well as their performance yesterday, and any expected changes for tomorrow. This heavy emphasis on goals is essential for success in a Performance Culture.

3. Team members understand how the goals will affect the company's performance.

Team goals should be nested within the goals of the department, the division, and the company. Teams should know the goals of these other levels and set their overall goals accordingly. Teams need to know how their goal achievement contributes to the company's success.

To make this possible, management must have clear goals, which are then discussed with the teams before they set their goals for the year. Butler Manufacturing begins its corporate goal setting in August, with meetings in September and October. These meetings include both management and nonmanagement people. Once the goals are set, the teams go about setting their goals for the year.

4. Team members participate in setting the goals and feel they are realistic.

Having various levels of management and nonmanagement involved in the corporate goal discussion brings commitment and understanding, which in turn helps ensure that team goals match corporate goals. Some other group, such as a leadership team or a steering committee, must approve all team goals to ensure teams don't set unrealistically high goals, goals that are too easy, or goals that do not match those of the company.

Goal levels should be encouraged to allow teams to shoot higher than they might otherwise. Too often we have seen teams meet their goals by the tenth month and then cut back, when they could have far exceeded the goal. Teams can set two or three levels of goals. First the basic performance goal; then, the stretch goal; and perhaps a "blow-away" goal. By using this approach, if the team meets the basic performance goal, it still has something important to work toward. Since management has approved the goals and the team had a say in setting them, both are ready to go to work.

5. The goals are supported by a plan with milestones whereby the team can map its way.

Planning skills are often a weak point in the goal system. Most people are not good at developing long-term goals and a plan to implement them. Short-term or daily goals come more easily. Even managers often have poor planning skills and easily get distracted by routine interruptions. Therefore, it is important to teach both managers and teams how to plan and set milestones for progress towards the agreed-upon goals.

While plans need not be elaborate, they must be well articulated and clear to everyone. Depending upon the type of work or project involved, some goals require more planning than others. The trick is to know when the plan is good enough and then get on with the work. Overplanning leads to unnecessary complexity, which can hinder goal achievement.

The best plan is simple and leaves discretion to the team on many issues. It also includes clear milestones that help the team and management assess progress. Leadership can teach planning skills by taking teams through planning sessions and letting team members attend management planning sessions. A companywide planning structure should be followed that is known and understood by all. This planning system becomes a part of the team infrastructure that all use.

There are many approaches to planning. The specific approach is not as important as ensuring that the whole team-based organization learn and use the same planning process. Such a process makes it easier to blend plans at different levels of the organization and to understand the plans in terms of the organization's direction and focus.

6. There is a system for celebrating goal accomplishment at every level.

practical tip Without celebration and recognition, or even a small reward when a goal is achieved, employees soon feel that the only reward for achieving a goal is more work. Therefore the best companies are constantly recognizing people for goal achievement and celebrating achievements. Celebrations should not wait until the entire goal is achieved but must take place at each milestone along the way. Teams that celebrate goal achievement are motivated to move on to higher levels after the celebration is over. However, teams that are not recognized or celebrated tend to hold back and give only enough to make the goal by the deadline. This is a tremendous waste of the power and potential of teamwork.

The most important part of celebrating is making sure the right people are celebrating. Is it the team or the manager? I once attended a team celebration with Pete Worth, vice president of a Leader National Insurance regional office. During the celebration, Pete said almost nothing but encouraged the team to recount how it had eliminated a major backlog in applications in record time. He simply asked, "How did you do that?" or, "Who came up with that idea?" Pete's purpose was not to talk, but to listen and reinforce the achievement in the minds of the team. Too often managers think they must lead the recognition and celebration. This can be a big mistake. The managers were not there, they don't know the details and in opening their mouth they are certain to get something wrong, which will detract from the team members' sense of pride and achievement.

The primary objective for the manager is to help employees capture the moment and remember how they achieved the result so they can do it again. No manager can tell them that. The manager can help them imbed firmly in their minds the behaviors that got them there. Be especially careful NOT to name names or cite specific individuals who contributed, unless you know personally and specifically what they did. Too often the manager ends up praising the wrong person, which undermines his credibility.

I once watched an entire design team get angry and leave a celebration in disgust after the plant manager stood up and praised two team members effusively. I had worked closely with the team and knew that these two team members had been a constant source of resistance and argument throughout the process. In fact, the team had come close to voting them out at one point. The plant manager was unaware of any of this and as a result turned a positive celebration into a disaster.

Never let goal achievement go unrecognized or uncelebrated. When management ignores hard work and achievement, teams soon feel that their extraordinary efforts to achieve the goal were unappreciated. As a result, the effort soon becomes less extraordinary. Look for milestones and small achievements to recognize every week or month, or as often as possible. Each time a team or an individual gains recognition for a small achievement, they are motivated to move to the next level of achievement.

Leadership's Role in Recognizing Goal Achievement

Teams work hardest to meet goals when they see the leadership rewarding, recognizing and supporting the goals. Mick Schneider, Butler Buildings builder services manager, sums up what many leaders have said over the years, "It is important that leaders lead by example. They must 'walk the walk'." Schneider and many others insist that if leaders do not support teams and the team approach literally at every turn, employees will react by saying some version of "... if not them, then why should I?" If leaders do not live the importance of the goals set for the organization, no one else is likely to head toward those goals.

As Dick Jarman said, "Goals are what hold each team; therefore the entire organization, accountable for the work." Each of the six characteristics of a well-formed, goal helps build the message about how work will be structured, approached and accomplished in an organization. When goals are not well stated, people do not know where to focus their activity – how to best accomplish their work.

When a team makes its goals, it should be celebrated with gusto. After all, it has fulfilled a promise. One of our clients gives an extra paid day off to their teams to be taken in the next quarter if they make their stretch goals. Windsor Insurance let teams have a two-hour party on the last Friday of every month when the teams met their goals. The plastics division of Standard Motor Products has a Triple Crown Award that can be won by every team that meets its quarterly goals. Along with the award comes a free lunch and a celebration.

In all these examples the recognition and reinforcement for achieving comes as soon as possible after the goal is achieved. These companies do not wait a year or until the next appraisal to celebrate achievements. Further, they have structured their recognition and rewards systems so that anyone who reaches the goal is a winner. *Teams compete against the goal not against each another.*

Compensation and Goal Achievement

While extra compensation is useful in some situations, great caution should be exercised. Compensation may make people feel good today but it is not as strong a motivator as recognition and celebration along the way. If compensation were the answer, the highest paid sports team would win the championship every year. But, there are many years when the highest paid teams end up in the cellar.

Too many managers use compensation as a substitute for being a good coach. There is no substitute for good coaching. Better to put the money into tangible recognition than into compensation, which is fleeting. This assumes you are paying market value or more to your employees. If you are not paying market rate, other rewards and recognition may not have the desired effect.

Harmon holds monthly business meetings in the cafeteria, attended by the entire plant of 250. The business results are discussed along with company goals. A good deal of time is also spent giving certificates of achievement for: Team Goal Achievement, Most Improved Performance of the Month, Most Cross-Training Skills Learned, Most Helpful to Other Teams When Under Schedule Pressures, and so on. Harmon works hard to let employees know what behavior is appropriate in their organization by recognizing and praising that very behavior.

Recognition is far better at modifying and teaching behavior than punishment. Joe Forlenza, VP of SMP in Long Island City, spends more than half his time traveling around to the various locations of his company to participate in meetings at which recognition is always on the agenda.

Jeff Feaster said ownership of goals is "Number One!" In addition, Feaster has found a technique for recognition that helps tie goals to behavior when he literally hands out Brownie Points.

The system works like this: When a team or individual sees behavior from another team or individual that in some small way helps achieve a goal, they can ask the manager to give that person or team a "Brownie Point." In this way the goal focus is reinforced by the teams and individuals, the recognition is almost immediate, and the whole team benefits. "Brownie Points" (BPs) may only be cashed in by the whole team.

According to Bill Herzog, a technician who has watched and used the process, "Brownie Points" resemble a wooden nickel with the Butler company logo on it. When a team has earned 50 BPs, it goes to lunch on the company at a local restaurant. This is an opportunity for the team to receive a group reward off-site, which is a public display of recognition for continued good work.

Feaster says he is most pleased when people advocate for BPs to go to someone who has done something that was helpful to them. Simple to some, even silly on the face of it, Feaster and Herzog agree that this technique is a strong support of the goals and team-work Butler has come to value. Jeff Feaster has been using the system for over five years and continues to feel it is one of the best things he has found for recognizing and reinforcing goal-focused behavior among his engineering teams. Ironically, when he first told me about it, I cautioned him that the motivational value might not last more than a few months! Five years later, Jeff likes to remind me that my advice was wrong.

It is obviously not in the BPs themselves but how Jeff handles the process that works. There is no substitute for a good coach, and a good coach does a lot of recognition and praise – and recognition as well as correction.

Two Types of Goals

Your car has two important but very different compo-nents. The "hardware": engine, transmission, steering column, wheels, tires and drive train; and the "software": oil, gas, water and antifreeze. You need both components to run your car. With only the hardware, you would go nowhere or the car would overheat from friction and lack of cooling. With only software, you cannot control the energy in the gasoline, and the water, oil and antifreeze are useless for transportation.

practical tip

Teams have two types of goals that serve much the same purpose. Teams drive the car but to do so they need both hardware and software. The hardware is the task of the team – *task goals*. The software is the skill development, cross-training, goal setting, recognition, conflict management, and so on, the – *process goals*.

Every team in a Performance Culture should have both of these types of goals written out and publicly displayed, and the steering committee or the leadership team should hold teams accountable for them.

Task Goals

It is obvious why task goals are important – they are what gets the work done. Task goals are the type of goals that most managers are familiar with. They measure tasks.

Examples include:

- We will process an average of 25 insurance claims per day, with all claims processed within three working days. No more than 5% of claims will be deferred over three working days and 100% of those will be completed within seven working days.
- The team will check 100% of the circuit boards within three hours after final assembly. Rejects will have a completed form and failure report back to the assembling team within one working day.

Process Goals

Process goals are somewhat more difficult to understand because they do not seem to relate directly to the tasks at hand. Instead they maintain or improve team skills and readiness, and increase morale and motivation. For that reason management is often tempted to put them on the back burner or ignore them altogether. Failure to have systematically structured process goals is like running your car month after month harder and harder while never changing the oil or antifreeze.

Examples include:

- Each person on the team will complete his or her cross-training skill certification within nine months using the team cross-training plan.
- The team will receive an hour or more of team building or skills training each month directed at improving conflict management, project planning, performance feedback, or other skills directly related to the team's mission.
- The team will improve throughput on engineering processes by 15% this fiscal year while reducing error claims 50%.

While its important for each team to work toward process goals, it is just as important for the entire organization to map out its process goals. Process goals at the organizational level deal with issues related to the skills of the work force and processes that supersede any one team. Process improvement at the team level is of little use if the systems at the organizational level (infrastructure) do not allow for timely information sharing and feedback. Process goals also include improving and refining reward and compensation systems. These processes must be continually improved to meet the needs of the teams.

How to Avoid the Two-Year Slump

A common problem happens when the organization has one or two good years and the Performance Culture is starting to take hold. Inevitably, a downturn occurs and the teams lose steam. To stick with the car metaphor, at this time, management pushes harder on the gas pedal, while passing up the gas station. In their anxiety to produce more or keep the productivity increasing, they fail to maintain the processes that got them there in the first place. Continuous improvement in processes, which includes cross-training and skill building, for example, are just as important as production numbers. Without these goals, teams soon stop improving themselves and their processes.

The most important thing managers forget at the two-year slump is to recognize and reinforce goal achievement. They begin taking teams for granted. Emphasis on celebration decreases and funds for recognition or reward are reduced or even eliminated. Teams soon learn that achievement and extra effort are ignored or given too little recognition. This essentially cuts off the very life blood of the team process, quickly starving the teams into mediocre performance.

Thom Norbury, general manager of the SMP Kansas plant, reports being in a rut at SMP as the steering committee had grown too large and goals were not being set. "We lost our focus, our ability to monitor teams and provide leadership. After a two-day retreat and a good hard look at ourselves, we decided to redesign the steering committee and develop a new performance-monitoring system based on the coaching model." Soon, they began to leave their rut behind. "The challenge over the long haul is to keep things fresh," Thom says "It takes leadership to keep continuous improvement going." That means knowing what the goal is and continuously recognizing and reinforcing behavior that leads to it.

The two-year slump, or some equivalent thereof, seems to happen in all organizations. In the excitement and energy that comes from first implementing there is a strong drive and goal focus. A great deal of work gets done and people demonstrate a well-deserved sense of pride. But as soon as the system begins to relax, it starts to lose focus and often falls back into old habits.

While this is predictable, it does not have to happen. A regular checkup where the organization is brutally honest with itself about processes and goals will help keep it on focus and on track. The two-year slump actually seems to happen every two years, not just the first two years. This up-and-down, sawtooth pattern can be reduced as the organization moves closer to becoming a true Performance Culture.

It is somewhat like baseball. While the Yankees may have a roster full of professionals who have played baseball all their lives, spring training often takes these professionals back to the basics — hitting, catching, fielding, running. Every two years or so an organization needs to go back to the basics and relearn the skills and attitudes that got it where it is. This "back to the basics" forces the whole organization to look at itself, make adjustments and ensure that time and energy are not being wasted with poor habits that undermine the Performance Culture.

In the Teaming Up® process we hold a follow-up retreat with the organization every two years to assess its progress and help it make in-course corrections. We have found that if the organization goes more than two years without a checkup, the process begins to break down. When that happens, it requires a great deal of energy and time to rebuild. It is like moving a freight train, it takes a lot more energy to take it from zero to 55 miles an hour several times than to keep it moving steadily between 45 and 55. Starting and stopping the team process eliminates the value advantage of teams and impedes the development of a Performance Culture.

Using Process Goals to Increase the Sustainability of the Performance Culture

The manager who makes the decision to eliminate critical team processes usually does so in the name of productivity. In the worst-case scenario the manager who scuttles these processes is long gone – promoted or transferred – before the damage is recognized. Regardless, often the system has sustained permanent and irreversible damage.

Teams that have been asked to do more without proper tools, skills or infrastructure support soon become bitter and resentful. Earlier in this chapter Lou Haddad reported the success at the wastewater plant in West Palm Beach. This happened in great part because he worked hard before and during the transition period to support the goals for the project. And with support, the employees' performance vastly exceeded the goals that were set and supported.

But Lou tells another story about the crew in charge of maintaining the parks. "Their attempt at self-directed team structure failed due to lack of infrastructure and support. There was no precise data available about work performance, no set-up to regulate the work, and too many disconnects in the process of how this work would be planned and funded. Without the ability to segregate administrative costs from capital expenditures and control the work according to specific goals, this team fell short of expectations. Whereas the wastewater plant had clear goals and the tools to work toward them, the park maintenance crew had no effective performance standards – or clear and useful goals." So, according to Haddad, what could have been successful wasn't. His success at the wastewater plant gives credibility to this opinion!

All too often it is the teams that get blamed for the problems. One organization we worked with years ago had great success in their team-based system through two vice presidents, both of whom were highly committed to the team system. When a third vice president with no knowledge or training in the system took over, he was able to get immediate improvements in productivity along with increased sales. But in the process he quickly violated most of the basic structures, including the training and process improvement systems that were in place.

He only stayed two years and the wheels fell off soon after he moved on. A bitter work force remained who resented his heavy-handed approach. With his autocratic management style teams soon reverted back to dependency behaviors, relying on managers to make all decisions and refusing to participate in process-improvement initiatives. Talk of unionization became common, turnover increased, and quality problems began to creep in. The teams no longer trusted corporate headquarters or believed their many statements supporting the team process. A corporate employee survey documented the dramatic decline in morale but the damage was done. The division never recovered and eventually was closed down.

I call this the Bungee manager after the Dilbert cartoon. The Bungee manager jumps in, gets some short-term results and a quick promotion. He never has to deal with the damage caused to the organization. This is possible because the organization has no way to gauge how well a manager is attending to the process goals as well as the task goals. Bungee managers focus far too much on task goals to the exclusion of process goals. They may pay lip service to the need for process goals like training, recognition, process improvement, and so on, but when push comes to shove, they slight these goals.

DILBERT reprinted by permission of United Feature Syndicate, Inc., 1997, p. 203.

According to Scott Adams, "This strip was so popular that the phrase 'Bungee Boss' has entered the vocabulary at some companies."

Stewardship of Company Resources and Process Goals

A manager is the steward of the human resources within his division. Morale and skill development as well as quality and productivity are his responsibility. Managers who steward human resources are continually adding value and capabilities to the company and to the work force. An effective steward helps foster an ownership mentality in everyone.

Process goals are one important way to ensure that the people resources are properly stewarded by management,[29] as they help keep management focused on developing people. People who are being actively developed do not feel rented. They see the company investing in them and respond with feelings of ownership or partnership in the company.

A Performance Culture values process goals and rewards teams and managers for achieving them. Using this approach there is less danger that a single manager will undermine the system with a rental mentality since the system expects and evaluates the manager in part on how well he maintains the skills and motivation of the work force. Managers are expected to leave a "clean house" when they move to another position. Since no one knows when a manager might have to move, it is best to keep the house clean all the time. If a manager depletes the motivation and skills of the work force to get quick improvements, he will be held accountable for that abuse of company resources.

The manager who is a good steward can make claims similar to one I once worked with whose resume read in part: "During my two-year tenure, productivity improved by 31% while quality measures increased by 54%. The work force increased its problem-solving skills so that 20% fewer managers were required to manage the work force while grievances went down 85%, and morale improved significantly as measured by a standard company survey. On-time delivery improved from 69% to 98%. Teams were in place to deal with virtually every major issue and much more management time was devoted to planning and product development than to conflict resolution and supervisory duties."

This statement demonstrates that this manager knew the value of both task and process goals. He left the place in better shape than he found it.

Questions

1. Does your organization have specific measurable goals at the team level?
2. Does the team have process goals at both the organizational level and the team level?
3. Do the goals meet the six characteristics of well-formed goals?
4. Is the team primarily responsible for the data collection, measurement and display of their goals?
5. Are the goals reviewed by the leadership team?
6. How effective are you at celebrating goal achievement with the teams?
7. Are leaders expected to be good stewards of the human resources as well as the physical ones? Does the culture value leaders who constantly improve the interpersonal as well as the technical skills of the organization?

SECTION III

WORKING IN THE PERFORMANCE CULTURE

CHAPTER

10

What Does a
Performance Culture
Look Like?

I n this chapter we will visit two teams to experience the personal and interpersonal dynamics that shape good teamwork toward a Performance Culture. In subsequent chapters we will return to these teams to illustrate issues of teams, leadership and the Performance Culture.

In visiting the two teams – one an insurance application and underwriting team, the other a manufacturing team working in a cellular manufacturing system – we will look at their day-to-day activities to see the unique characteristics of a Performance Culture at the "floor" level. While the situations and issues are real, names have been changed to protect confidentiality.

Two Days in the Life of the NE1KAN Team at ABC Insurance

Cynthia, the daily huddle leader, meets the visitor and we move toward the pod that is the working home of NE1KAN, an insurance applications team. The team works in a pod of cubicles arranged in a horseshoe shape. A large low-slung file cabinet occupies the center, several items are arranged on top of it. Most notable is a stuffed lion with a note attached. Before being asked, Cynthia explains that the lion and the attached note are congratulating the team for a performance achievement. "He's sort of our mascot ... and he belongs to all of us," she says with obvious pride. Cynthia goes on to describe some of the group pictures with quick descriptions of the events in the team's life that led to the photos. The common themes seem to be that they were having a good time while celebrating goal achievement and milestones in the life of the NE1KAN team.

The huddle is done early in the day or shift. It is a rapid-fire meeting of no more than 10 minutes. It is always done standing up so no one gets too comfortable.

Anticipating the next question, Cynthia explains that the room was designed with team performance in mind. "Everyone's seat is turned from the center, but by simply turning around they can see or talk to anyone else in the pod. Each person has a computer at his or her desk and the way we turn determines easily if we need to work together or on our own." The desks and surrounding spaces are decorated with family pictures and personal artifacts. The shelves hold manuals and work materials.

As it gets closer to 8:00 a.m., team members arrive. Introductions, greetings and salutations are offered while everyone's first attention at their desks is to check their e-mail and in-box. Mixed with the sounds of greetings are comments and remarks that foretell of quick assessments of what needs to get done that day. The huddle leader, Cynthia calls the daily huddle at 8:15. She has a short list of items to discuss:

- The vice president is visiting next week; we need two volunteers to meet with him in a skip-level meeting.
- Production figures for last week were down 10% from goal, partly because of vacations; we need to try and make up some this week. (Cynthia points to a white board with graphs and charts and talks briefly about the numbers from the previous week.)
- Jerry's birthday is Thursday (the next day) and the team is going to celebrate over lunch; bring something to share.

Each person quickly reports on any meetings or other times when they anticipate being absent from their work station during the day. The meeting lasts only 10 minutes and it is impressive to see at how quickly yet professionally information is shared. No manager is present. The manager attends the huddle about once a month, or if there is a specific emergency issue she needs to address. The team developer used to attend two or three times a week but now comes only about once a week. The team has developed well so it dosen't need much input from the TD.

This team has been together for over two years. In that time, three of its eight members have changed. One transferred into the claims department, one took a position as a team developer and the third left the company when her husband was transferred.

Watching the team throughout the day an obvious routine is noticeable. In talking with team members one learns that most routine duties rotate among team members so no one gets stuck doing the drudge work or the work no one else wants to do. On each cubicle is a sign with a different time. At Sally's desk the sign reads "2:00-3:00." She notices our attention to this simple sign and explains that each day at that time she can transfer her phone to another team member and have one hour of uninterrupted time to get work done. "During that time no one will interrupt me unless it is a true emergency. The team found that most of us can get two or three times as much work done in that hour. We value that time and find that it helps us stay focused and sane in the middle of an otherwise busy day. No one is required to do this but the team decided about a year ago that everyone had the right to this uninterrupted time. We saw a 10% productivity increase almost immediately. All but one of our team members use the hour. Our newest member is still learning and he has so many questions that the hour would not be a good idea for him." Finished with her explanation, Sally returns to some paperwork on her desk.

Moving back around the outside edge of the pod, we notice a white board/cork board combination. It has a wheel diagram with the names and the duties of each team member outlined. The board also includes a set of graphs and charts that are labeled with the team's goals. Each chart shows the goals of the team in that area and current performance levels. Most of the charts seem to show the team being at or above goal except in one area, which says "Agent Timeliness." I make myself a note to ask about this at the team business meeting the next day.

Suddenly, but quietly and calmly, Sally signals to two other team members and the three quickly form a small huddle. An agent has called Sally to request some underwriting work on a particularly good client and Sally does not hesitate to collaborate. The group looks over some documents and talks briefly. Jennifer takes charge and tells Sally to do several things. Mark makes some suggestions and the ad hoc meeting breaks up in less than five minutes. When asked, Jennifer says of her "take-charge" behavior, "Three of us are fully cross-trained in underwriting; Mark, myself and Azulia. I am the one with the most experience but we are in the process of training Sally. She hopes to take her underwriting exam in a couple of months. Mark generally keeps me in control since I can come across pretty hard. The team has given me feedback that I am too directive and don't allow them to think for themselves and learn. We all agreed that it would be good for Mark to jump in and work with me whenever we have a potential problem. That way I get to see how Mark maintains his low-key approach to helping people and he gets to see how I analyze problems and come up with solutions. So far it has been good for both of us."

At 10:00 someone says "break time," but only two people leave their work stations. Azulia notices our puzzled look and realizes that an explanation is necessary, "We can't just leave the phones so we have a rotation worked out. Two or three people may break at once if the phones aren't too busy. We have gotten so we don't really need to negotiate on break times. We just look around and quickly decide who goes first. Some people like an early break, others like to take it late ... so it generally works out pretty well. But that wasn't the case a couple of years ago when we first started. We had several major battles over who could go on break and when! Before we went to teams, Sally and Jennifer always went on break together. The supervisor would tell people who could and could not go. Since Sally and Jennifer had been around the longest, the supervisor always let them go when they wanted. The rest of us didn't like it but what could we do about it? When our team formed, Sally and Jennifer assumed they would still have the privilege and the team did not challenge them. But one day it all came to a head when they got up and left while the phones were going crazy. The rest of us were left trying to deal with the situation. When they got back, we were so busy that none of us got a break that day. At lunchtime Sally and Jennifer got up and started to leave when Mark stopped them and called a emergency team business meeting. Mark did not like being the bad guy. You can see right off he is the low-keyed one in the group. But he could also see how the rest of the team was getting the shaft with this arrangement."

Cynthia joins in the conversation and interrupts to say, "Mark used the FBI method that we learned in training. It has nothing to do with the government." They laughed, "It's just a technique we use to ensure good communication around emotionally thorny issues."

"Anyway," Azulia continues, "Sally and Jennifer repeated what they heard using the FBI method. Several on the team said they agreed with Mark and he asked to have the issue put on the team agenda for the next team business meeting. For the next two days, until our team business meeting, the atmosphere was cold as ice around here. People were not talking to each other and we did not get a lot of work done. That was the beginning of a long conflict stage for our team."

"It took about three different meetings over a couple of months to iron out this issue. It came up in feedback several times and was put on both Sally and Jennifer's quarterly coaching forms. I would say that was the beginning of the biggest time of conflict for our team. A lot anger and frustration came out. Our team developer – Valorie – tried to help us do some problem solving around it, but initially it did not work. We would come to a team agreement but then something would happen and all hell would break loose. Like it so often happens, there was a simple explanation. Jennifer and Sally were afraid we were trying to break up their friendship and we were afraid they were using their friendship to avoid work or responsibility for the team."

Cynthia comments, "That was the first of several major problems we faced as we tried to figure out how to assign work without a supervisor telling us what to do. We had real problems the first Christmas/New Year's holiday. Everyone wanted off and no one was willing to give in. The supervisor used to do all the scheduling and while we did not like it – sometimes we had no choice. Now we had a choice and we didn't like that either! As the holiday season came closer, Valorie met with us and said that one of the boundaries she had to enforce was proper coverage during the holidays. Since the team had not come up with a solution, she was bound to schedule everyone for every work day during the holidays. She told us to be prepared to work accordingly, unless we could come up with a schedule which at least seven out of the eight of us could agree upon."

"That hit us like a ton of bricks." Azulia says, "We started negotiating and compromising. We came up with a schedule that no one was happy with but we all signed off on. That was one unhappy holiday season. We did not even do anything as a team for the holidays! It was pretty bad, but all through it Valorie worked with us. She never told us what to do but she knew how to draw the line so that the customer was protected and the team learned to deal with problems. She taught us several problem-solving skills and facilitated our coaching sessions very well. When there was a problem, she was always ready to meet with us and work on it. If we complained to her about someone, she was quick to take us right to the source and work out the issues immediately. One thing about Valorie, she won't listen to gossip! If you have a complaint about someone you'd better be ready to have her walk with you straight to that person to get it ironed out."

"While we work very smoothly together now, we had to go through tough times to get where we are. This lasted for over eight months. It is not easy learning how to be responsible for yourself. It is a lot easier to let a supervisor make all the hard decisions and then complain about it afterwards. At this time, we make most of the hard decisions without anyone's help. Valorie just sits back and watches unless we ask her opinion. We realize what the requirements are and we know that Valorie can enforce the boundaries when she needs to. That is something Valorie takes very seriously – boundaries and expectations."

"You may be wondering how we do holidays now." Cynthia says, "We have gotten a lot better at negotiating and working with each other. As it is now, I think most of us feel we have a lot more control over our personal schedules than we did with a supervisor. On the other hand, we know we have to be here for the customer so we make sure of that. Valorie talked a lot about boundaries and expectations, especially when we were a young team. We thought that being a team meant we were free to make our own independent decisions. But she quickly set us straight on that one. We are a team within certain boundaries. As we have gotten better, Valorie has widened the boundaries. What happened with Carl and Wednesdays is a good example."

Cynthia tells the story of just a few months after the team structure was implemented when the team agreed to let Carl off early each Wednesday so he could pick up his child from day care. Valorie quickly stepped in and asked her famous question, repeated here by Cynthia, who makes a friendly attempt to imitate Valorie's deeper voice, "Is that best for the customer?" Cynthia's smile disappears as she talks about the real anger team members felt toward Valorie for her intervention. Carl thought she was trying to hurt him personally. She insisted that we think the issue through and come up with an approach to the problem of how we decide to let someone – anyone – off work early.

"It took a couple of weeks to think it through but we came up with a team policy and tried it for a month," explains Cynthia. "True to form Valorie insisted that we evaluate how well the policy was working. In that case we gave everyone a secret ballot and let them vote on how satisfied they were. Six out of eight were satisfied, so we had a discussion and found some problems with our policy. We modified it and tried it again. That was almost two years ago and we have not had to change the policy since. By the way, Carl has been able to get off early most Wednesdays with some exceptions for coverage when we have a heavy work load or people are on vacation. On those few days he can't make it, he knows it's because the burden on the rest of us is too much. We simply had not thought about all the problems that could happen to the team, or the customer, with a simple decision to let Carl off early."

In discussions with all the team members their descriptions of Valorie's job as TD are remarkably similar. Her emphasis on what best serves customers is mentioned by each team member at the outset. Each one says Valorie has done a good job of teaching the team how to take care of the customer. What Mark said is a good reflection of team agreement on this crucial point. "We have found that most of the time when we think things through it not only serves the customer better but serves us better as well. We have a lot more flexibility than we used to have under a supervisor." Valorie is adamant about the customer. Whenever we get stuck or can't make a decision, she asks, "What does the customer want?" Or "If we do it that way will it improve our service to the customer?"

Team members also describe how Valorie has taught them to measure their work and how effectively it is being done. Beckey said, "When we make a major decision, she also insists that we have some way to measure its effectiveness. She is a stickler for proving that something is working better. If we can't prove it, then she doesn't believe it. She insists on quantifiable measures. If we can't come up with a measurement, then she will tell the team to table it until a measure is decided upon."

Several team members repeat verbatim one of Valorie's mantras: "The kindest thing I can do for you is teach you how to fight out your differences without killing each other." She believes being a successful team developer lies in learning to communicate as adults face to face. With training in listening skills and the FBI process, her job is to point out when team members are not using those skills. Team members admit that it is easy to "... open your mouth before you really understand what the other person is saying." They also describe how Valorie has reinforced the techniques in getting them to step back and listen better, partly by her own example. All team members agree Valorie is a good listener herself.

They also agree that Valorie has had an impressive impact on all of them. They have learned hers, and the Performance Culture's, emphasis on recognition. Sally tells the story: "Two months ago, on Valorie's company anniversary celebration, we gave her the Devil TD Award. She uses the phrase the 'Devil is in the details' when she is trying to get us to think through a problem. It was around Halloween, so we had several team members dress up like devils and goblins and give her the award. The certificate said, 'For the most devilish TD in the company.' We all joked about how she never lets you do anything fun; no gossiping, no whining, no complaining. And to top it off we had a devil's food cake decorated with a little demon."

Sally is not the only one to mention this story. And in the telling, you can hear the respect and appreciation shared for what Valorie has taught the team about how they can get their work done effectively and efficiently.

The next day the team business meeting begins at 11:00 a.m. Valorie explains at the outset that it is by design that no one is on the phone as the meeting begins. The whole team is in the conference room because it shares phone duties with two other teams. Team members forward their phone to somebody on another team who can answer many of the routine questions or take messages. The favor is returned when the other teams have their meetings.

The meeting is called to order by Beckey who is team leader for the present quarter. (The wheel on the white board keeps track of team members' assignments.) She passes out the agenda and asks Sally to give a quality and production report. The report is brief, with an emphasis on the phone timeliness problem, which was noted at the graphs on the board. Sally, who is the quality leader for the quarter, states, "A problem-solving group was appointed by the team to look at our phone timeliness and this is what they concluded:"

"Agent timeliness deals with the average amount of time it takes to respond to an agent request. When Jill left and Jason came on board, we suffered a decline in performance. While Jason is doing much better, we still don't have the problem solved. We can't blame it all on Jason. Jill was very efficient and her numbers brought some of the rest of us up a bit. We looked at the records from before Jill left, and it is clear that we were meeting goal largely because she was so good. We relied on her to answer a lot of the more complex questions because she was so experienced and efficient. Now we know we have a weak spot in our team and need to improve. The committee recommended that we begin tracking individual agent timeliness. Sally will make herself available to coach anyone who is below the optimum level. If she is unavailable, Valorie will back her up. Team members will get their individual statistics every Friday. Anyone who is below optimum should make an appointment with Sally to see what he or she can do to improve. We will continue to track individual performance until the team reaches and maintains goal for one month."

The team adopts the report and recommendation and then goes on to Mark's report. Mark is training coordinator for the quarter. "We have met 70% of our cross-training goals for the year," he reports. "Sally is scheduled to take her underwriting exam in two months and if she passes it, we will be ahead of plan. The training plan calls for six out of eight team members to complete level I certification and four to complete level II in this calendar year. We will begin working to get another person ready for level II certification at the end of the month when the class begins. Jason has completed five of eight modules in level I and probably will be eligible for certification in two months."

Next comes a discussion of the team's level of empowerment. Valorie has been quiet but she is on the agenda for this issue. She passes out a sheet listing the levels of empowerment criteria. She has done a preliminary assessment with the team leader. The team quickly comes to agreement on the areas where she thinks they are doing well. She notes five areas that need attention before the team applies for level IV of empowerment. At level IV the team is eligible to participate in the highest level of team sharing as long as it meets or exceeds all goals in every quarter of the year. Team sharing last year for all level IV teams was an average of $1,200 per person. She notes that team sharing is based upon profits, so it usually changes from year to year. She asks the team when they want to apply for level IV. After some discussion, all agree that the team could be ready by the beginning of the next quarter. The team leader asks for consensus and then tells the team that she will notify the steering committee that they would like to make a presentation to go to level IV in two months.

Last on the agenda is a short team-building activity led by Azulia. She has found a case study in a book, which she reads to the team. It deals with a performance problem a team is having with one of its members. Azulia asks team members several questions about the case and then concludes, "How should we deal with this type of problem if we ever have it on our team?" The team is hesitant at first but Azulia is able to get a few ideas started. After about 15 minutes the team has recorded several ideas it would try if it saw this problem. The ideas are written down in the team book for reference later if needed.

As Azulia's activity winds down, Beckey calls for an evaluation of the meeting. Each person makes a quick comment and at exactly one hour after the meeting started, Beckey adjourns the group. The consensus seems to be that it has been an efficient meeting run proficiently and professionally by Beckey. A number of topics were covered and decisions were made without any argument or debating. The team is clearly focused and able to direct its own activities with almost no help from the team developer.

The group adjourns to the cafeteria where a small party has already begun in one corner. It's Jerry's birthday. We get our food and move over to the party where we learn that Jerry is a former member of the team who is now a team developer. Jerry's old team and the teams he now works with are all there to celebrate his 29th birthday – for the 10th time! A good deal of laughter and joking is evident as the group enjoys cake and assorted goodies. Once the party is winding down, we approach Jerry to ask him what it has been like moving from team member to team developer.

"It was really hard at first," he says, "Before the team concept I was like the lead person in our group. I had a lot of supervisory duties although they did not call me supervisor. When the team concept began, I had to learn how to work with the team without being in charge. Now as a TD, I have to learn how to guide and coach several teams without taking over."

Jerry continues, "Many times I know the answer to a problem but it is not my job to tell them; it is my job to help them find out for themselves. I tried giving them the answers when I first began but soon found they were asking me for more and more answers. Before I knew it, I was right back acting like a lead person. The other team developers saw this, and in one of our regular team developer coaching sessions I got some feedback that I was encouraging dependency behavior in my teams. That really hurt. I thought I was doing a great job by helping them all I could. But what I learned was that I was actually hindering my teams. I needed to teach them problem-solving skills and where to find information on their own. There were times when they would not work because they did not know the answer and could not find me! Often it was as simple as picking up the phone and asking an agent or looking in a manual but I had not given them those skills. Valorie and some of the other TDs worked with me to become a coach and not an answer man. Valorie led my team in completing a coaching form on me. I got a lot of good feedback from the team on how they viewed me. They liked the fact that I gave them the answers but they also realized that it wasn't helping them to become a better team."

To conclude the visit, we asked Valorie, "How do you view this team?"

Valorie paused and then responded, "They had their difficulties and they still have some friction, but it is far better than before and much better than when we had a supervisor. They are pretty goal-oriented and know how to use the problem-solving skills methods. When they get in trouble, they have learned how to call for help. A couple of months ago two members asked me for a three-way meeting on an issue they could not resolve. That showed a lot of maturity on their part. I conducted the three-way conflict mediation process I had learned in team developer training and we came out with a plan. So far they have followed it pretty well. I would give them a B+ overall. They have done some good things, especially in meeting their production goals. They still have to work on their interpersonal skills but I know they will mature more in the next year. After all, as a team they are only two years old!"

The Hustlers at Middle America Manufacturing

The second team we will visit is a second-shift manufacturing team. Mickey serves as a team developer for several teams in the plant and acts as guide for the visit. We go to a team business meeting room to get a briefing on the plant and the teams. In the room we notice a number of white boards and flip charts that are being used to deal with current issues. When asked about the charts

Mickey says, "Every team is required to be actively involved in problem solving of some kind all the time. We take continuous improvement very seriously. Every team member has been trained in basic problem-solving skills and we are constantly putting people on problem-solving teams to work out issues. It is important to keep people on their toes and thinking. In most traditional manufacturing operations employees just put in their time. We don't want that. We want people thinking, using their brains as well as their muscle. If you don't keep people thinking, they get complacent real fast. We made that mistake early in our implementation of teams. As soon as we achieved some initial success, we backed off and stopped challenging the teams. But we soon noticed that production was slipping, along with safety and other areas. A hard-nosed self-analysis revealed that we were not following our own system. Things were slipping back rapidly. It was hard to get people remotivated once we let them get stagnant."

Mickey has been team developer with this team for about a year. He describes the team and some of its history:

"This is a 10-person team in a manufacturing operation. The team is divided into two cells but that really does not make much difference since people constantly rotate into different positions between the cells. The team is about four years old and has long since completed all cross-training. In the work design of this team, everyone can do everything except the maintenance person, who is assigned to this team and two other teams. It is his job to make sure all the equipment is running properly and to teach the teams how to do as much preventive maintenance as possible."

We ask Mickey how much turnover there is in manufacturing in general, and second shift specifically, and what effect it has on the teams.

"Turnover is always a problem on second shift because many people want to go to first shift, no matter how well things run! Seniority transfers to first shift have taken a steady stream of people away from this team since the beginning. About one person every five or six months gets a chance to bid on a first-shift job. Despite this handicap the team has done pretty well. They have reduced scrap by 98% and reduced work in process (WIP) by 95% with a goal of no WIP in the entire last quarter. Safety used to be a major problem throughout the plant but has improved so much that people are having a hard time finding anything to improve. The leadership team, which includes shop floor representatives, have pushed a process whereby all near-accidents are reported. No longer do the safety leaders on each team simply report accidents; the report now includes close calls or potential problems. Safety is aggressively addressed. The plant manager calls it the FAA approach – airlines are not just concerned with accidents but with any near-accident. This aggressive approach has given the teams a new way to look at safety."

When we ask him to explain more about the team that named itself the Hustlers, Mickey notes that as a team they have won an All Plant Award twice over the last two years, being the most improved team or the top-performing team in some key area. The plant not only recognizes the best teams but tries hard to recognize teams that are showing significant improvement. This approach has allowed many teams to gain recognition for strong positive results, regardless of how they compare to others. The leadership team tries to deemphasize competition between teams where it is unhealthy. Instead, they want teams to look at themselves and compete against their own performance goals. The general manager is fond of saying, "It is not enough that you beat another team. If you cut them down or hurt their performance in the process – you are hurting everyone."

Mickey continues his explanation, "When teams first began, this plant had a major problem with competition between first and second shift (there is no third shift). First shift would max out its numbers to make goal each day while leaving a mess with lots of rework and scrap for second shift. As a result, second shift had a hard time making its goals. This hit the Hustler team particularly hard since they were in a key production area. It took several meetings and some tough discussions before a plan was worked out to solve the problem. Essentially, the plan called for each shift to be responsible for its materials and to account for everything before they leave shift. Any scrap or messes that were left for second shift counted against first shift goals. With a few refinements the system began to work with a reduction in rework and scrap as well as less hostility across shifts. Some areas have quarterly cross-shift meetings to look at problems. All areas measure and track any issues that could cause cross-shift problems."

At 3:30 p.m. as the shift is beginning, the Hustlers gather around two large white boards. With all 10 team members assembled and standing, one leads the group in a brief huddle. The huddle leader, Mahamet, points to the production numbers and graphs from first shift and numbers from the night before on second shift and compares them to the production schedule. From the graphs we can see that the Hustlers have been routinely hitting their production goals. Then Mahamet reminds the team of the plan for tonight. Several first-shift team members were in Statistical Process Control training today and production fell behind. With advanced warning, the second shift had prepared itself to increase their production to make up some time on the schedule. During the huddle we learn that two members came in early to pull materials and set up an extra testing machine not generally used on second shift. In addition, one team member was borrowed for the evening from a team that did not have a heavy schedule. The borrowed team member is in cross-training for some of the skills in the Hustler area, so this will give him an opportunity to practice new skills.

The huddle lasts only 10 minutes, then everyone goes to work. As the huddle is breaking up, we approach Mahamet and ask how they arrived at the plan he described. "Our communications person on the team was alerted to the potential production problem last week in our weekly production meeting. All teams have a representative in that meeting so we know what the schedule is going to be. We try to anticipate problems and plan for them."

When asked where the plan came from, Mahamet replies, "It came from a the communications leader and the team leader. They put together some ideas and proposed them to us in our last team business meeting. We had a few suggestions. Carol suggested we borrow someone from another team and I mentioned that there was a testing machine we could use. We all agreed, and everyone said they would be sure to be at work. We also told everyone to take extra vitamins so no one would be sick tonight!"

Watching the Hustlers work looks like a ballet, with each person moving in well-defined areas not wasting any steps. The area is remarkably clean. As people get to work some are talking and joking while others get down to business. About every two hours the team does a major shift with people moving to different areas and doing new work.

When asked, Jean smiles and says she will explain the shifting. "It keeps the job interesting and reduces the possibility of repetitive injuries to our team members." She keeps right on working even as she carries on a pleasant conversation over the moderately loud noise of the machines. "I have only been here six months but I have never worked in a place where they work so hard and have so much fun at the same time. When I first came, I was pretty intimidated. I put my application in and then they made me go through three different interviews and some testing. The final interview was with this team. Three of the team members did the interview and they really grilled me. They were very hard-headed about their team being the best and let me know that they were looking for good team players. After I was hired, they made out a cross-training schedule and began teaching me all the skills I would need. I went to basic training the day I was hired and did some team training about two weeks later. I was surprised to the team members in the plant carrying out a lot of the training. It means a lot to see people from the shop floor doing the training. Where I worked before, the trainers were all 'suits,' who did not know what it was like to work on the floor."

Queried about her cross-training status, Jean responds, "I graduated from level I last month and will probably be finished with my level II training in a couple of months, but I can do about everything already. My main goal is to learn how to do the testing and then to loan out to some other teams to learn some of the skills in their areas."

practical tip

About 9:00 p.m. Mickey drops by to see how the team is doing on its plan. The quality leader, Vicki, runs to the computer and punches in some numbers and comes back with a one-page print-out. "Looks like we are going to make it with room to spare. If we keep it up we could easily make up for all the lost production on first and maybe 4-5% more."

Mickey says, "Great, when you go on break I want all of you to come in the break room for some pizza – it's on me." Yells and laughter echo accross the team as people hear the news.

At break time no machines are shut down. A yellow light flashing above the team's huddle board brings two people out of the break room. They move right into the team spots, replacing people who are leaving for break. One of these replacements explains to us what is taking place. Her name is Maria, she is from Ecuador and speaks with a strong Spanish accent.

Maria says, "We all trade and back up each other. I have been here 10 years and before teams we all shut down the machines before we went to break. The whole plant would shut down. When we came back it would take us 10 minutes to get everything going again. When the leadership team looked at this it seemed very wasteful. I was on leadership team at the time and we came up with a plan to keep the machines running by sharing people across teams who did not have constantly running equipment. I am from an assembly team. We can lay our work down on the bench any time and come back. It's no trouble for me, and it gives me a break from my regular work. At first, many seemed to think it was the stupidest idea. Most of them did not want to miss breaks with their friends. Some also were used to taking a little longer on breaks and they could see that our plan would mean they would have to get back in 15 minutes."

Maria pauses, sighs, then continues. "It was hard at first ... no one wanted to loan anyone for fear it would hurt their goals. Others felt it was beneath them to do manufacturing jobs when they had graduated to assemblers years ago. My team took the lead and started sharing with a production team. We could quickly see how much more effective it was. Our goal charts showed up to 5% improvement on the production floor. It did hurt my own production at first, until we worked out a system inside the team and started cross-training people to do more tasks. It took us about a year to work out the details like the yellow light and which teams would back other teams. Now it is pretty routine and people seem to like being able to move around and see other people. I like this Hustler team because they always have so much fun and seem happy to see me when I come over."

Vicki interrupts to say, "Maria, did you hear we are going to make production goal and Mickey's buying pizza? Do you want me to grab a piece for you when I go on break?"

"Sure," Maria replies. She turns back to us smiling broadly and says, "They really look out for you here. It was a good company before teams, but it is even better now. We do a lot of our own planning, and as long as production is covered, we have a lot of control over what days we can take off."

At the end of the shift Mickey introduces Sandra to us. He explains that more than anyone else she can describe the team's early stages. He explains, "This team really works well despite the fact that they regularly lose members to first shift. I work with three teams and I am in charge of production planning for this area as well. That is a lot, but production planning is so much easier than it used to be without the teams. As you can see, they take a lot of responsibility for production goals and planning. They can pull their own numbers from the computer and they always have a representative at the production meetings. With this kind of help, everything goes much smoother. Over the last three years we have been able to show quite a bit of improvement. It also helps that the team developers work together very well."

Sandra interrupts Mickey, "We see ourselves as a team of developers with responsibility to support all the teams in our area. The leadership team has us rotate every couple years to work with other teams. It keeps us on our toes and ensures that neither we nor our teams become complacent. I think complacency is the biggest enemy of the team concept. It is hard work to keep challenging people. But if you think about it, we are out to win the Super Bowl every year. In our competitive market we cannot afford to come in last place or be middle of the pack."

When asked how he views the Hustlers now, Mickey says, "The Hustlers are just like their name, they hustle – but that was not the way they began. Four years ago when we first started the teams in the plant, this team virtually threatened to go on strike! I wasn't their team developer, thank goodness. Sandra was. They really struggled and gave Sandra major headaches. Maybe you could talk about that part, Sandra."

"The main problem was cross-training," Sandra begins. "Everyone had their ideas about what work they would not do. As a result, work stations would set idle because the person was on lunch break and felt like it was his personal property so no else could work there. We had a heck of a time getting people to teach each other even simple things. The most senior people were adamant that they were not going to waste their time training some new guy just to see him mess things up. It got pretty bad. The worst thing that would happen was when a senior person would bid out to first shift and leave only one person poorly trained to do the job. We would have to start over getting someone up to speed."

"The first time this happened was with Juan. He had been with the company about five years and we knew he would soon bid on a first-shift position so we set up a training schedule between him and three other people. We had plenty of time to get the training done, but he virtually refused to cross-train two of the three people. He simply chose the person he liked best and trained him. It was not the process the leadership team had prescribed but that was the way it had always been done and Juan was not going to change."

Sandra continues, "Since training and cross-training are essential to the team process, the leadership team mandated that no one could transfer to another shift or team if they had not completed their training duties. That caused a big conflict and Juan stopped training altogether. I had several meetings with him but made little progress. We weren't very skilled in the coaching process at that time and I probably came off too heavy-handed. Unfortunately,

Juan appealed it to the leadership team and they relented, letting him go to first shift without training anyone."

Mickey interrupts, "That was a big mistake and the leadership team learned a hard lesson – don't mess with the boundaries. Soon after Juan transferred to first shift, he was called upon to do exactly the same kind of training with his new team, and again he refused. This went on for over a year. But much worse, since the leadership team had broken its own requirement, no one took the training mandate seriously. From then on, when people were asked to cross-train a less senior team member, they would resist and mention Juan as their reason."

"The leadership team lost credibility over that one," Sandra chimes back in. "It took a long time to recover from that mistake. Unfortunately, Juan quit the company. Looking back, we can now see how afraid he was of losing status. Status was everything to him. If we had to deal with Juan now, I think we would handle it a whole lot differently and much better. We know how to give people a sense of status in the team system and make them feel valuable and important to the process. Back then we did not have a clue. I would bet Juan would still be here and doing very well if we had the skills then that we have today."

Mickey comments, "The team developers were a part of the problem because we did not understand how much we needed to work as a team to help support each other and the other teams. We pretty much left Sandra out to dry. With no help, backup or support she got frustrated and made some mistakes that made things even worse. About the time it looked like Sandra was going to get taken out of the TD role, or even be fired, we realized that none of us could have dealt with the team any better."

"Fired!" Sandra exclaimed, "I already had my resignation letter written. I was history until you guys took me in the team room and promised to help."

"That was a wakeup call for all of us," Mickey said. "We met with the leadership team and told them we wanted to work out a plan to support Sandra and help the Hustlers get on track. They gave us two months but insisted on production improvement within two weeks. We put together a plan and all of us took responsibility for working with the team. It worked. Both the Hustlers and the team developers learned a lot about teamwork in that two months. We learned, you can't expect teamwork from the teams if the team developers don't know how to use it as well."

Summary

These teams illustrate many aspects of a developing Performance Culture. We can see that line teams:

- resolve conflicts within the team
- coordinate activities with other teams
- train and indoctrinate new team members
- set and measure goals
- ask for help from other teams or from the team developer
- give performance feedback to help team members improve
- plan much of their own schedules

Leadership teams:

- set and maintain boundaries
- reward and recognize teams without causing unhealthy competition
- maintain goal focus throughout the organization
- learn from their mistakes while helping the teams learn as well

In both companies the process took time and had to pass through a conflict stage. Once the teams learned how to deal with the conflict and use problem-solving skills, the benefits of the Performance Culture began to take hold.

In the coming chapters we will discuss the skills required on the part of team developers and leaders to achieve the results seen in these teams and the development of a Performance Culture.

CHAPTER 11

Navigating the Ups and Downs of Implementation

The task of the leadership is to manage the Performance Culture – to guide it through the stages of conflict, progress, regress and rejuvenation. Well-formed boundaries help eliminate many of the wide swings in organizational functioning by building organizational trust. Once trust is formed, game playing on both sides is reduced with a commensurate improvement in goal focus for the entire organization.

The problems the insurance and manufacturing teams in Chapter 10 faced had been present in the organizations for years, causing waste, bottlenecks and inefficiency. It was difficult, if not impossible, for management to see these inefficiencies because they were directly related to the manager's dependency relationships with the workers. In the supervisor's eyes, Sally and Jennifer were not hurting the company and the morale of the work group; they were good workers who simply liked going to lunch together. To the manufacturing manager, Juan was a good worker who took pride in his work. It was impossible to see how he could be hindering work or hurting the development of other employees until the team system was implemented.

Learning Point: The Performance Culture reveals weaknesses and problems in the old system that were never even suspected. Be careful not to blame the pain implementation causes on the new system.

The pain and discomfort that comes from dealing with these problems can easily be blamed on the team process, but that assumption is like "killing the messenger." The team process merely shows what was not clear before. It makes transparent work processes and interpersonal relationships that were invisible to the manager in a traditional system. It strikes at the very heart of dysfunctional status systems and the dependency relationships that support them.

As the team developers told us in Chapter 10, during the development of the teams a series of conflicts needed to be resolved. Almost all of the challenges dealt with issues related to the old system, not the personalities of the workers. This is an important lesson. At first, the people involved in the conflicts were simply living by the expectations and traditions of the old system. They were not bad employees trying to resist the team process. They were simply comfortable with the old way of doing things and did not want to change. Until a change has been in place for one to two years, it will not be completely believed and acted upon by the workers or culture carriers. Sally, Jennifer and Juan had been around the block long enough to know that what management says and what actually happens are usually two very different things. Juan was living proof that management would not stick to its boundaries when he appealed to the leadership team and received his transfer in spite of existing policy.

In the beginning of implementing a Performance Culture it is difficult to draw the boundaries and enforce them. People cannot see the necessity of upholding boundaries, especially when it affects them personally and management has defined boundaries poorly in the past.

As we saw in the case of Juan, poor boundary management not only hurt the Hustlers but many other teams as well, and eventually hurt Juan. In the growth of the organization there will inevitably be cycles of conflict over the first two to four years. These cycles are closely related to clarity of boundaries and expectations. If issues are clearly resolved in light of the new policy or expectations, the very act of resolution becomes an example and a precedent to the entire organization. For example: If the leadership team had encouraged Juan to go back to his team and complete the cross-training before he transferred, Juan might have seen the futility in maintaining his traditional approach. That action would also have sent the message to all other senior people that they have an obligation to fulfill to their team before they can transfer somewhere else.

Waves of Conflict

A great deal of conflict in the early stages of team development is related to the way the system is changing and the leadership's ability to maintain those changes. Every time leadership sends a contradictory message, it sends a wave of conflict through the organization.

We saw that happen across the entire organization when Juan transferred. In violating their own policy the leaders gave to the senior people hope that the new policy would not be enforced and they could go back to the traditional way of training people. At the time when the leadership group made the decision to let Juan transfer, it felt it had legitimate reasons for doing so but those reasons were based on outdated principles. They did not look at the issue as a present and future concern. The leaders were concerned that holding to the boundary would create conflict and hurt production. Their decision was to delay implementation of the policy for another month, so everyone could get used to it, even though the policy was widely known and had already been advertised for several months. In their efforts to be kind, they created problems in the whole system.

The wave of conflict picks up momentum and becomes a conflict cycle that feeds on itself. While it may seem insignificant at the leadership level, it is very disruptive to the culture. To management it is like looking at a large wave from an airplane whereas workers see it from a small boat. To managers it does not seem like much, but to the workers and the culture carriers it can threaten to swamp the boat.

Conflict resulting from poor boundary enforcement is expensive in terms of wasted resources and discouraged workers. When the waves of conflict come, employees spend a good deal of energy dealing with the emotional fallout and trying to figure out, "What does the leadership really want?" Like the person in the small boat who spends most of his energy trying to stay afloat, middle managers and line workers spend much of their discretionary effort dealing with the waves of conflict rather than achieving their full potential and reaching their organization's goals.

Every time leadership sends a contrary message it causes a wave of confusion that creates goal conflicts. These conflicts grow as they propagate from one department, team or level to another. They take on a life of their own and can cause massive upset in an organization.

Implementation Flow Chart

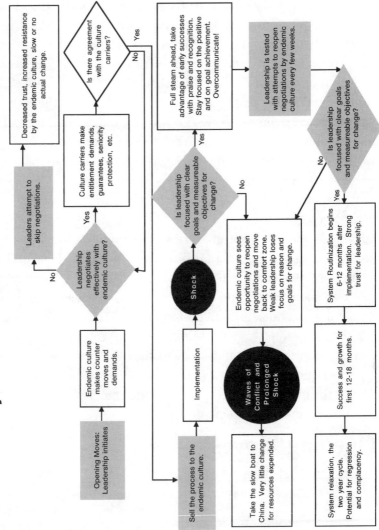

The Change Cycle:
How the Game Is Played

Regardless of the promised benefits of the Performance Culture, many cling to the old adage, better the pain you know than the one you don't. While most people readily understand the Performance Culture's benefits to themselves and the company, they have difficulty believing it will truly happen. In other words, the workers and culture carriers do not trust that the leaders will fulfill their promises. For this reason a game develops during the transition period between the company, the endemic culture and the individual, whereby each party takes a small, but risky step toward trusting the other. If there is any perceived betrayal, bets are off and the game starts over again.

It is somewhat like dating or the early stages of marriage when each party gives a little to see what happens. If one party takes advantage and does not give back something of equal or greater emotional value, the relationship may get stuck. It is useful to understand this emotional game and recognize how it is played. In this way management and the various constituencies (engineering, marketing, manufacturing, customer service, human resources, etc.) can focus on the goal – to develop trust toward higher performance – rather than getting sucked into the emotional morass of quid pro quo. In the following discussion we will look at one section of the chart at a time to better understand what is happening at each phase of implementation.

Opening Moves

The game begins as management makes the first move for self-concerned reasons – they want more efficiency or more profits. The countermove: Individuals and the culture carriers in marketing, engineering or the union counter with a step of their own–they, too, are self-concerned: "What are you going to give us in return for helping you with this change?"

Here are some of the typical moves:

- There will be many individual and small group countermoves that are very difficult to address with a single response.
- If there is a union, the individual issues may be communicated through this avenue. This allows management to respond to the union as a single entity, although it really consists of many subgroups with contradictory interests.
- The more dependent the work force, the more it will demand guarantees and entitlements from management. (Highly dependent employees are the result of a autocratic or nonparticipative approach to leading people.)

Many of these demands will be out of line with business needs such as insistence on maintaining old classification systems vs. developing a more cross-functional work force. But there is no reason to panic, these are just the "first offer," not the final bid.

Negotiations

The opening moves are followed by a period of negotiation between all concerned. This may be called a planning stage or a redesign – it is an opportunity for both sides to suspend the traditional rules and talk openly about what they want.

- This period is handled by volunteers or interested parties. They may work closely for several months to come up with a reasonable design, but in the end they have to go back and sell the design to the organization. It is not important or even possible to sell everyone on the new process, but for the plans to go anywhere, the key leaders, middle management and other culture carriers must "buy in" to a significant degree.
- In a union setting the bargaining unit is involved. Since they are the legally elected representatives of the work force, they can speak with some authority to make agreements, pending member approval or reelection. The process should never be adversarial but viewed as a win-win process. Development of trust is most important. Union officials are key culture carriers and must feel that the efforts they make to implement major change

will be worth the risk of cooperating with management. Their significant involvement from the beginning is essential.

Perils of skipping negotiations

If management skips the negotiation step by imposing its own design or team system, true change is unlikely to occur. Feeling railroaded, employees and middle management will dig in their heels and ensure that changes are effectively undermined. While some progress may be made, it will be slow and time-and energy-consuming.

Selling

A series of meetings are held with all concerned to explain the design and its purpose. It is best if the presenters are both management and nonmanagement. The idea is to begin developing trust and cooperation between representatives of all interested groups.

Implementation

The organization begins to systematically implement the changes necessary to bring about a Performance Culture. Initially many will be excited and a few will be resentful. The organization will have trouble staying focused on production or customer service as the teams are learning new skills and roles. Boundaries will be violated frequently by both the teams and management while they are learning how to use the new system. The more educated the work force, the easier the implementation. Professional organizations tend to make the transition fairly easily if the plan is sound and leadership is consistent.

Shock

The first real and effective change often sends the culture into shock. The culture carriers will attempt to slow down the process or reverse it altogether. Much like putting a foot into a cold swimming pool, the workers will want to withdraw and go back to the warmth and comfort of the old structure. The hallmark of this stage

No matter how fast or slow you put your foot into the water,
it is still cold and your strong inclination is not to jump in.

is the cry; "You are going too fast!" But, no matter how fast or slow
you put your foot into the pool, it is still cold and your strong inclination is to get out. While an organization can go too fast in making the transition, that is generally not the problem – going too
slow is usually the problem. The slower an organization imple-
ments the change process, the more likely the culture is to revert
back to its old warm and comfortable ways. The only sure way to
get over the shock is to get in the water and get used to it as
soon as possible. Prolonging the process only prolongs the
shock.

Think of cries like: "You are going too fast!" as similar to
the cries of Briar Rabbit, "Don't throw me in the briar patch,
anything but that!"

The endemic culture says, *"If you just slow down, we will be
able to make the changes much easier."*

What this really means is: *"If you slow down, it will give us
a chance to organize a proper defense against all these changes."*

practical tip

At this time the leadership must be clearly focused on the goal and the plan for implementation. In the process a wide range of people were involved, the transition was carefully planned and everyone was briefed and trained. Much of the emotional upset from this point on comes from fear people feel when they finally recognize that new skills and behaviors will be required. The level of discomfort goes up immeasurably when the process shifts from theory to practice. Stay focused on the goal and help people overcome their fears through constant coaching, praise and recognition for the desired behavior.

Taking the Slow Boat to China

If the organization chooses to take the slow route, the union or work force will see this as an opportunity to reopen negotiations. As a result, the game begins again more intensely with each side raising the stakes. Things that were once decided and agreed upon become open questions again. Moves and countermoves are made.

> *A new key idea based on contrasting experiences in changing an established plant versus starting up a new one emerges. Intensive change at the worker (micro) level cannot be brought about in a gradual manner; microlevel discontinuity is called for.*
> **Lyman D. Ketchum and Eric Trist, 1992, p. 86.**

- In non-union environments the process will get bogged down as each constituency fights to gain the upper hand. Engineers will make demands, marketing will refuse to participate, customer service will try to implement alone, while middle management will argue against certain changes that would reduce their authority, professionals will make dire predictions and **all** employees will feel fear due to loss of control.

- In a union environment there will be posturing on each side. Both sides will find themselves renegotiating and replanning everything. This is frustrating because boundaries become fuzzy, making it difficult to tell if you are going forward or losing ground. Commitment wavers and both sides try to back out or hedge their bets in the game.

Full Steam Ahead

If the organization stays the course and follows the plan (provided it is reasonable), the system will protest loudly, "This is too hard" or "This is not what we thought it would be." We saw this pattern in the story of Middle America Manufacturing and Juan. The whole system rebelled when the leadership waffled on the boundaries, seeing it as a chance to get out of the water. But as long as the organization stays in the water, the process will gradually move on and progress will be seen within 6-12 months.

In the meantime, leadership must focus on the many small successes in the organization, praising and recognizing all individuals and teams that are making progress.

Learning Point: The best way to tell the workers and culture carriers what you want is to recognize and praise those who are doing it.

This must be done consistently and with forethought. Know what you want to praise, then go out and find it. DO NOT wait for success to come to you. By the time you find out about it, it is too late.

The more leadership recognizes and praises the desired behavior, the less the workers and culture carriers will test and resist change. Leadership's task is to show the employees that there are more rewards and incentives by changing than by staying the same. To the degree that workers feel no reason to change, they will resist and attempt to test the new system. This stage will last several months as the organization gets used to the new "water temperature."

Prolonged Shock

If the organization makes several moves back and forth – in and out of the water – it will stay in shock, eventually moving entirely out or never getting more than their feet in the water. At this time new management is often brought in and the process starts all over again. The second time employees and middle management have less reason to cooperate. As a result, the negotiation stage will be much harder.

We have seen companies struggle with implementation for as long as five years, afraid to get in the water, but desperately needing to improve productivity, safety or customer satisfaction. This is frustrating to middle management and confusing to all employees. During such periods, any productivity improvements were marginal and mostly attributed to technology.

System Routinization

Once the system gets over the initial shock, new patterns of behavior begin to develop from the structure of the team design. If practiced diligently and modeled by management, these new behaviors can become the norms in 12-18 months. Employees will begin seeing benefits, but more importantly, the new structure will become as comfortable as the old. Improvements will be evident in productivity, customer service, safety and quality while conflicts and grievances will decrease. This stage will continue for about a year.

Trust Development

Organizational trust comes from: *a pattern of consistent and reliable management behaviors over time, within a set of well defined boundaries and clearly managed expectations.* The patterns begin to become believable to both sides, which allows for relaxation and less guardedness. Open discussion and problem solving become easier and conflict is greatly reduced. The game mentality is largely eliminated with much more focus on the mutual goals.

System Relaxation, the Two-Year Cycle

As we have discussed earlier, after the second year and into the third, leadership may begin to relax. They may reduce the amount of praise and recognition or get too distracted by business issues. But the system is still too new to be self-sustaining. It needs the praise and recognition of the intentional culture as a reassurance that it is going in the right direction.

With relaxation comes a reduction in system discipline. The habits, procedures and processes that were implemented with the new Performance Culture begin to get sloppy. If there is a leadership change at this time and the new leader is poorly trained or indoctrinated, the whole system can get sloppy.

At this time the system needs to take a hard look at itself. Because of the success of the leader who has brought the organization this far, he or she is often promoted or reassigned. The new leader may be unfamiliar with the process and does not have a high commitment to it, since he or she was not part of its design. As a result, the new leader may not provide the appropriate level of guidance and interaction with the culture.

Regression

The culture carriers rapidly slip back into old ways of leading. When crises hit, production falls, or market conditions change, the new tools for teamwork and problem solving are selectively forgotten. Some managers will use them, others will not. The disparity in the use of the new system opens the door to a rapid regression in favor of a crisis-management approach. Since the old system no longer exists and the new system is not being used, the only alternative is heavy management intervention.

If this continues, management will pay a severe price, since they are now carrying the entire system. Conflict and productivity problems will pop up. The more time and attention is paid to these issues, the less time is left for maintaining and coaching the teams. This becomes a vicious cycle. Regression becomes rampant and the system changes to a strongly management-driven system with employees behaving dependently once again.

We have seen systems in which the anger and bitterness resulting from the regression created an impossible labor situation where trust was no longer possible. People who jumped on the bandwagon, put their reputations on the line with their peers. When the process fails they must go back and face their peers and admit that they were "duped" by management into helping. These may be strong words but that is often how the early adopters feel. The longer an organization stays in the regression stage, the harder it is to move to consolidation and a Performance Culture. The "I told you so" crowd begins to take charge of the culture. It may be impossible to direct the culture back into a constructive and goal-focused mentality.

Consolidation

If the system recognizes when it has slipped into regression, it may regroup and move into consolidation. Consolidation begins with a thorough reassessment of the entire process by all the stakeholders and development of a plan to consolidate gains and move forward. Realignment or readjustment of the design is a likely outcome with stronger systems and more consensus on the boundaries and expectations of the system.

Energy and Development

As a result of consolidation, the system will reenergize and show strong gains for another two years. The steps taken at this stage will be solid and create real value for the company. The team discipline will become stable and people will gain confidence in its use. Elements of a Performance Culture will become institutionalized.

Complacency

Complacency can set in any time after a period of success and growth. The system relaxes, and although it may not regress totally, it will lose momentum and a competitive edge. Constant training and goal focus, regular movement of team developers among the teams, fun, energizing challenges to the organization, and so forth, will prevent or delay complacency.

Questions

1. Where have you seen cycles of conflict result from poor boundary management in your organization?
2. Have you found weaknesses in your system that only became clear when teams were implemented? How did management respond to these revelations? Was the team system blamed for the problem or did people recognize it as an old problem that needed to be addressed in the team process?
3. Where do you see the "implementation game" being played in your implementation efforts?
4. Has your organization maintained clear boundaries and a focus on the implementation goals?

12

Leadership Group:
Guiding the Process

A s we have mentioned throughout, the effectiveness of
organizational change depends upon the intentional culture's ability to involve the endemic culture and weave the
two together into a common cultural fabric. To move the organization steadily and rapidly toward a Performance Culture the leadership group must be structured in such a way that the two cultures
work together every day in the organization.

Leadership develops at every level in a Performance Culture
because many people are allowed and encouraged to use their
natural leadership abilities for the good of the organization.

Purpose of the Leadership Group

No matter how the leadership group is configured, it must be
structured to deal with two main issues:

1. To grow the business by focusing on organizational task goals:
   a. Quality
   b. Productivity
   c. Customer service
   d. Rapid turnaound, etc.

2. To grow the Performance Culture by focusing on the process goals:
   a. Process improvement
   b. Cross-training
   c. Interpersonal and cooperative skill development
   d. New technical skill development

With both task and process goals in place, the leadership can begin the development of the Performance Culture.

Four Duties of the Leadership Group

There are four things leadership must do to ensure goal accomplishment (for a full discussion of goals, refer to Chapter 9). These involve a cycle of goal setting through accountability for goals.

Setting Goals

To enable the teams to function, the leaders must set the broad goals for the organization including both task and process goals. Task goals include the direction of the business with respect to capital improvements, quality, turns on inventory, throughput, market share, and so on. It is important to make these as clear and measurable as possible, so the teams that actually do the work can plug their own goals into those of the organization.

Process goals must also be set. As we have mentioned, process goals look inside the organization to ensure that the skills and resources are developed to support the task goals. Process goals for the entire organization might relate to cross-training, technical skill development, conflict management, computer literacy, language proficiency, reduction in management overhead, dollar value of team improvements.

Discussing Goals

Once set, goals need to be discussed openly and directly with the entire work force. Simply posting goals on the bulletin board does not provide commitment and buy-in. Senior and middle management must systematically inform people of the goals and point out why they are important. As mentioned, personal communication is necessary to make the process effective.

Approving Team Goals

One of the key duties of the leadership team is to help hold teams accountable for their goals. Many organizations require teams to submit their annual goals for approval. A subcommittee of the leadership group might examine the goals to ensure that they are (a) measurable with supporting process as well as task goals and (b) congruent with those of the organization.

Accounting for Organizational and Team Goals

The last step in the goal process is reporting on goals. Throughout the year, teams are expected to report on goal progress at regular intervals, thus the leadership group has time to intervene if a team falls behind. At the end of the year each team is again required to report on its goal achievement to the leadership group. If this process is followed, there will be few surprises and the organization will have plenty of time to react to most problems before they become a crisis.

In Chapter 10, our visit with two teams, we saw the results when the leadership maintains the focus of the organization on both the process and task goals. The teams have a strong sense of direction and feel clear accountability to the organization for achieving them.

When process goals are not maintained, such as in the example of Juan, team development can suffer. When task goals are constantly evaluated as in the example of NE1 KAN's agent timeliness, teams can identify problems or weaknesses early and intervene effectively.

The purpose for reporting directly to the leadership team is to intentionally circumvent any hierarchical structure and to force direct vertical communication between the teams and the leadership of the organization.

A direct accounting procedure serves three purposes:

1. It makes it clear to managers and team developers that their function is to support the teams in achieving their goals.
2. It reduces territorial behavior on the part of managers and ensures that everyone recognizes that "we work for the company, not for any one manager." This is a powerful message both to the manager and the teams. It breaks the cycle of dependency between manager and team (or employee) and creates open accountability.
3. It spotlights the team as the unit of work, not the individual. Everyone needs to feel responsible for achieving goals, not just a few individuals or the leader.

As described earlier, when Dick Jarman was president of Butler Manufacturing Buildings Division, he instituted the practice of reviewing each engineering team's goals in a formal presentation. This was totally different from previous practices of having the local management account for the performance of the region. According to Dick, this approach allowed him to hear and see for himself the issues of concern to the teams. In addition, it gives the teams a sense of accountability to the corporation. That is, the local manager is not the only one taking the heat, the entire region is responsible for its performance, good or bad. If the teams do well, they deserve credit, and Dick is quick to give that recognition. If the region is doing poorly, the teams must feel the responsibility to some degree and make plans accordingly.

The Leadership Group

Since there is never a perfect overlap between the endemic and intentional cultures the leadership must find ways to weave the two cultures inextricably together. One way to do this is to bring the culture carriers into the decision-making process from the very beginning. These include key technical people, middle management, shop floor leaders and union leaders.

Management does not own the culture. It cannot be changed by fiat. It is a living thing that by its nature is constantly adapting to its environment. The environment contains traditions, taboos, relationships, seniority systems, peer pressure systems, customer and supplier relationships of which management has no direct experience. While these may seem irrelevant to the manager, they generally dictate the manner in which an organization responds to a challenge or crisis. As we discussed in the Middle America Manufacturing example, the endemic culture had its own system of training, quite different from that of the leadership group. The old system valued skill development in only a few people like Juan. Those people gained a strong sense of status from their position and guarded it closely.

In a Performance Culture the leadership group should consist of a combination of management, middle management and nonmanagement. Participants should be selected in a way that ensures the true leaders are involved, not just employees management likes. You cannot create a Performance Culture if the leadership of the endemic culture is left out of the process. In a union shop, this is fairly easy since the union representatives are clearly the leaders. In a nonunion company it is more difficult to select people for the leadership team. Some form of nomination system may be used, with management making the final selection. At this time in labor relations history, there is significant debate about how to make selections without violating U.S. National Labor Relations Board rulings on "company unions." Since the law is still evolving, you may wish to consult a legal advisor on the best way to select leaders.

The important principle is that the selection process be fair, yet have a high probability of selecting those people who are the most influential. Whether they are supportive of the process or not is irrelevant at this point. People know and understand the need for cooperation and maintenance of a strong competitive company. Their objections are generally based upon their experience with past management behavior and their traditional exclusion from the process. Some of the most negative and cynical endemic leaders become strong in their positive leadership qualities when given a chance to influence and work on designing and governing the team process.

Larry Schroyer at the Government Services Administration had this to say about leadership's role in creating a Performance Culture:

"Leaders should not be afraid to let employees see the personal side of them, to spend more time talking to people. Make it routine to have formal meetings. Stop and chat with people. Appreciate their diversity.

You can never stop talking about what the organization is doing. You must make them a part of the decision making in establishing goals and objectives. Communicating with employees is also essential.

I think one of the biggest challenges for leaders is not to get caught up in change for the sake of change. Change is vital, but it needs to be thought out and discussed at all levels of the organization.

Employees must be made part of the decision process. I have found that once employees get involved in what is going on, once management is honest about what is happening, they'll follow you through hot coals. But they have to understand! They can't just be told; they need to be a part of the change. Employees have to be part of the decision making and part of implementing change.

You can't just pay lip service. Leaders have to let go of some of the decision-making process. If you establish a team to make certain decisions, you have to give these employees the freedom to make decisions and to act on them. You have to be willing to accept their decision.

It is very demotivating if you just pay lip service and don't follow through. Employees will see right through it. They must be able to understand the process. Typically the employees can do it better because they are closer to the process of getting the work done.

Many managers underestimate employees. I see so many employees blossom now. They have demonstrated skills and abilities I would not have believed possible. It was a great experience. At the time it seemed tough to get through, but it did the organization good."

How Is the Leadership Group Configured?

The answer to this question depends on the type and size of the organization. Is it large or small? Is it in one physical location or geographically dispersed? Is it a technical high-skill or low-skill organization? Is it union or non-union? The following are general guidelines that need to be adapted to fit your organization.

First, the leadership group is often split into two, unless it is a very small organization. The first group we will call the leadership team, the second we will call the steering committee. Names for these groups may vary from company to company. It is their function, not the name, that is important.

- The leadership team (LT) is responsible for growing the business.

- The steering committee (SC) is responsible for growing the teams and the human infrastructure.

practical tip

Local Organizational Size

While there is no formula for the correct configuration, the larger the organization, the more effort must be placed on keeping people involved at all levels. Large organizations will need one LT and one SC to set policy and goals for the entire organization. It is very likely that such an organization would have a LT and SC for each business unit of 200 employees or less. These subgroups would be directly responsible to the organization-wide LT and SC. Other organizations combine the LT and SC into a single group for each business unit. This unified group still includes nonmanagers on a rotating basis and is charged with carrying out the policies and goals of the organization-wide LT and SC.

Leadership Team

The leadership team tends to focus on the task goals, whereas the steering committee focuses more on process goals. Together, the two comprise the leadership group, and as such they may meet as one group occasionally. The SC and LT processes are one way to weave the intentional and endemic cultures together to create a goal-focused Performance Culture. But this is only a small beginning. There are many ways to ensure that everyone is involved. We will discuss some of these here.

The leadership team is comprised of many of the top managers of the organization along with representation from the nonmanagement ranks. For example, the key manager is always a member of this group. At Standard Motor Products in New York City, the union president, Roberto Johnson, is a full member of the Polaris leadership team. The team also includes managers from marketing, finance, production, customer service, human resources and all other major departments – about 12 people in all. The team works directly with the vice president to run the business, set goals, and deal with budgets, market strategy, production, and so on. The group meets weekly to coordinate activities and set policy.

The Steering Committee

The steering committee is comprised of a wider selection of people with a heavier representation of nonmanagers, along with one or more senior managers, a middle manager and a team developer. Membership on this body should rotate at least every 18-24 months. Some companies rotate a few members off the steering committee every six months, while others rotate a large number once a year. The principle is to involve as many people from the endemic culture as possible in the decision-making process without getting it bogged down. The key manager is a member of this group as well. It is best to clearly limit membership to between 8 and 10.

Unlike the leadership team, this group is not a team; it is a committee. The distinction here is that members of the SC are not interdependent and do not work closely together every day. The SC is more a policy and guidance body that ensures the human infrastructure of the organization is developed and is able to support the goals of the company. These include policies on hiring, transfer between teams, cross-training requirements, performance feedback and coaching, auditing of team results and goals, and setting up the developmental levels of empowerment. The group in turn works to ensure that teams are conducting the prescribed cross-training, that teams are learning new leadership and problem-solving skills, that conflict management and resolution skills are taught and used and so forth. The SC also works with the team developers to help them understand their role in developing the teams.

The SC, or a subcommittee of the SC, is charged with ensuring that all teams have goals that are congruent with those of the organization. The SC may also hear regular presentations from teams on their progress towards self-development or their level of empowerment.

Relationship between the LT and the SC

While both of these groups have important work to do separately, there is sometimes overlap and even confusion about which group should do which tasks. Therefore, early in the process some agreed-upon guidelines should be developed to ensure that the groups do not duplicate work or undermine each other. The key manager and perhaps another person serve as members of both groups to help facilitate communication and coordinate efforts. The primary concern is to make sure the two groups function well in their own areas and coordinate well when there is overlap in duties.

Geographically Diverse Organizations

When a large organization is spread out over a wide area, it may be necessary to have a central coordinating group and local steering committees. This process has worked well at Butler Manufacturing's engineering group which has engineering offices in 13 regions. Each region has its own SC and sends a representative – either a manager or a nonmanager to the organization-wide SC for an 18-month period. When the term is up, the membership rotates. That is, a manager replaces a nonmanager or vice versa. In this way representation alternates.

This arrangement is complicated and probably not necessary unless the organization needs very tight coordination among its various regional groups. Butler wanted to ensure that all regions used the same team process so that the language and process developments would be similar. However, this has not hampered creativity. The regions still come up with creative ideas within their own offices that are then shared with the larger organization. The central region, for example, developed a strong technical skills training process, which many of the other divisions adapted or modified for their own use.

Creating Leadership at Every Level

practical tip In traditional organizations, the manager is the key person responsible for the business. In a Performance Culture the goal is get everyone to think, in part, like a manager. That is, everyone is responsible for how well the business runs, not just the manager. To this end it is important to structure the workplace in such a way that every team sees itself as a business responsible for running itself profitably, efficiently and within the structure and goals of the overall company. To do so, every person must have a task to perform, which heightens this sense of responsibility and teaches business skills.

As we have pointed out earlier, a Performance Culture cannot develop on a voluntary basis. The organization must set clear expectations about participation and performance. Once employees realize the expectations and get used to them, they will find them far more interesting and rewarding than the traditional role of the worker. However as we have mentioned, up to 10% of the work force cannot, or will not, choose to participate in the process. The coaching approach discussed earlier helps, many otherwise resistant employees become positive contributors once they realize the benefits to them and the organization. But a few will never respond and must not be allowed to hold back the process.

Other Leadership Opportunities

Since positive leadership can come from anywhere in the organization, it is important to make sure there are plenty of opportunities for people to participate.

Training

It is paramount to train line workers to carry the message of the organization very effectively. People listen to and respect their peers. To that end, routinely train teams of managers and nonmanagers to deliver much of the training. No one carries the message better than the culture carriers. Not only do these people make good trainers, they gain valuable skills that they take-back to the work place.

All kinds of training, including technical skills, problem-solving skills, interpersonal skills and conflict management skills can be learned and taught by nonmanagement trainers. It is gratifying to see someone who was once afraid to stand in front of a group learn to train groups of people in valuable skills. The confidence they gain and the skills they learn often lead them to contribute more value to the organization. They also become excellent models for others by displaying the values of the Performance Culture.

Problem solving and planning

Involve union or nonmanagers in key planning and change initiatives. In some cases they can even lead the charge. On two occasions Standard Motor Products in Kansas had to make major changes in product lines. In both cases management and union representatives came together and worked out the many details of the transition. The change included hiring temporary employees to build up inventory and temporary layoffs for others. Once management determined what needed to be done, Thom Norbury, the general manager, along with Ernest Lewis, the union chair, and the shop committee began working on the transition plan. In one case projections indicated that up to 45 people might be laid off. With a lead time of several months, a plan was put in place to retrain people who were interested, in new skill areas. The result of the plan was that only 15 people were laid off, and those who wanted to return to work were back in 60 days.

Both Thom and Ernest agree that this approach was only possible with the leaders of the culture being closely involved. Once management learns how to involve people in the process, many things become far easier to execute. With everyone involved in executing a plan that they support, there is less likelihood of unforeseen problems or sabotage.

Making Sure New People Support the Performance Culture

It is far easier to develop a Performance Culture in a new organization than in an established one because a new organization does not have an endemic culture but often has a fairly well-understood intentional culture. That means that new employees can be more carefully trained and developed in ways that are congruent with the goals of the organization.

A manager recently recounted to me his efforts to hire several new people into his team-based company. His interview teams asked every candidate if they had ever worked in a team-based system. Half of them said yes. But on further questioning, the interviewers found that everyone of these candidates described a single-leader work system that was simply called a team.

At the SMP plant in Wilson, North Carolina, general manager, Eric Sills, along with Tom Murray and others, took great pains to develop a culture of teamwork and empowerment when the new plant opened. Every employee was told that the organization was team-based. All team members and managers received training in the process and the leadership structure was implemented. The result was a relatively smooth implementation with teams getting a quick start and showing strong results after three years.

The most critical time for vigilance is when leadership changes. In a short time a new leader or owner, untrained and uninformed, can create chaos in a once well-functioning system. New leadership should be well trained and indoctrinated into the values of the culture and the appropriate behavior for managers and leaders. New managers are always tempted to put their mark on the organization soon after arriving without truly understanding the system they are working with. Moreover, most incoming managers have no idea of how a Performance Culture works. The company risks losing all the time, investment, good will and trust built up in the Performance Culture with one poor management move. Soon the endemic and intentional cultures split and the organization loses the competitive advantage of a highly cooperative culture.

Questions

1. Is your culture "business friendly" and goal-focused?
2. Does your leadership group involve people from different levels?
3. Is there strong emphasis on both task and process goals in the leadership group?
4. How have you involved the culture carriers in the process of change?
5. Does your leadership group adequately represent both parts of the organization's culture?

The Team Developer:
Facilitating Team Maturity

T he task of the team developer (TD) is quite different from that of the traditional supervisor or manager. In a Performance Culture the team is much less dependent upon the team developer than a traditional supervision. Many techniques and methods can be used to help a team develop, the most important include managing boundaries and following the team disciplines. Teamwork is a developmental process that people can only learn by practice.

Working with the Team

Due to the critical role of the team developer (TD) in a Performance Culture we are devoting a whole chapter to analyzing the main responsibilities. From the beginning it is important that the TD discusses expectations. Go over the charge or mission of the team and review the purpose of the team within the organization. The leadership team or steering committee probably has policies

> *The manager's function is not to make people work, but to make it possible for people to work.*
>
> **Tom DeMarco and Timothy Lister, 1999, p. 34.**

and procedures that govern the team structure itself. This should be a part of the early discussions with the team.

Next the TD must help the team organize itself. I recommend using the wheel concept[31] to ensure that the principle of shared leadership is practiced by all teams. No matter what structure is used, be aware that teams are very comfortable with the single-leader role and will do their best to place a permanent leader in charge of the team in some way. At the same time, there are frequently individuals who want to be leaders for life. Both of these tendencies must be avoided if the team is to become truly self-sufficient.

Levels of Empowerment

Teams, like families, grow and develop through stages. To guide this process we have found it helpful to develop a roadmap whereby teams can gauge their development and the steering committee can monitor progress.[32] Help the team understand and use this concept – not as a checklist to race through but as a ladder of opportunities, with each step taking the team to higher levels of functioning.

Setting Goals

Learning to set goals and achieve them is the most important lesson for the team. Much of the more difficult aspects of team development are made easier by a clear, focused goals. A team with a clear goal matures much faster. Early discussion of goals with milestones to mark progress helps the team understand the importance of working together (see Chapter 9).

Help the team set realistic goals; short-term at first. The idea is to get initial success by achieving some short-term goals and then moving on to higher goals. The first goals might be for a month or a quarter. Measure them rigorously, teach the team how to measure and coach them on reporting their results at each team business meeting.

Teaching the Team to Function as a Unit of Business

Since every team is a unit of business within a larger organization, the objective is to teach the team how to function like a business: how to plan, anticipate, produce, schedule, and cooperate with other units of the business. The more you teach teams and expect them to use the knowledge, the less dependent they will be on management. We encourage a mini-curriculum for skill development. The idea is not to make MBAs out of everyone but to give team members the skills they need to manage their part of the business.

The team developer is not expected to teach all of these skills, but is expected to find somebody who can. Within every organization there are experts or highly skilled people who can teach basic skills to the team. For example, someone from the accounting department may spend three half-hour sessions with your team teaching budget-related issues and how to calculate the cost of rework or waste. A maintenance or computer person might teach the team basic preventive maintenance for a machine or desktop computers. While these people are usually very busy, I have found that they are often quite willing to work with you and your team, especially if it makes their own work easier in the long run.

One payroll team took it upon itself to systematically teach all the other teams in the facility how to complete payroll forms as well as benefit applications, health care claims, and so on. The result was far fewer errors and mistakes on forms coming into the payroll office. In fact, the effort was so successful that the team began a regular rotation of update training for every team. Team members found that it was a lot easier to teach people how to do things right the first time than to complain about it and correct the problems later.

Teaching the Elements of Effective Team Business Meetings

Team business meetings are the heart and soul of effective team functioning. Meetings are to conduct the business of the team and should be well managed and focused. That is not to say they cannot be fun, but fun is not the focus, business is.

When team meetings begin to be ineffective, too many managers cancel them. In our view, when teams have trouble with meetings, it means the TD or manager has not taught the prerequisite skills and/or held the team accountable for using them. Canceling the meeting only ensures that the skills are not learned and keeps the team immature and dependent upon the manager.

We continue to be amazed at the number of organizations that try to implement teams without budgeting adequate time for meetings. Team business meetings are the way teams refuel and tune themselves up. But they must be clearly structured so that the teams learn the necessary discipline. Teach them how to structure the meetings and use time wisely. In our visit with two teams in Chapter 10 the NE1 KAN team conducted a very effective meeting that examined goals, problem solving, training and team development issues as well as an evaluation of the meeting, with no significant involvement from the team developer.

How often does the team meet? Usually teams meet at least once a week, but depending upon the type of team, they may meet less frequently. A rule of thumb is that the more interdependent a team is, the more often it should meet. Most teams with a reasonable level of interdependence need to meet weekly to ensure continuity of purpose and effective communication.

What should take place in the team business meeting? Each meeting should include a discussion of goals and coordination of tasks. The team needs to attend to both task and process goals. It is just as important to talk about performance goals as it is to talk about future skill development.

Sample Team
Business Meeting Agenda

The following is an example of the items that might appear on an agenda. Not all of these could or would be done in a single meeting.

Review & approve previous   5 minutes
meeting's minutes

Review agenda for current meeting   2 minutes

Review & update current action items   10 minutes

Review team performance indicators   10 minutes
    -recognize good performance
    -discuss improvement actions

Team recognition activities   8 minutes
    -achievements
    -personal milestones
    -awards

Team activities   10 minutes
    -training
    -training reinforcement
    -thought of the week
    -performance improvement tips
    -good news items
    -feedback
    -team building exercises

Review action items assigned   5 minutes
    -actions item
    -responsible individual
    -due date

Set agenda for next meeting   4 minutes

Meeting evaluation & suggestions   5 minutes
for improvement

Stressing the Importance of Performance Feedback

Teamwork relies on the ability to give one another feedback on performance in real time. Mature teams do this easily and non-judgmentally. The team should learn feedback skills as soon as possible. This takes regular practice with the whole group.

NEVER take a team's word that it already practices effective and timely feedback! Teams are extremely good at fooling themselves into thinking they are honest and open with one another, even as they are running a world class gossip column in the break room. Effective feedback skills are not taught in schools. Even most managers who have been trained in giving feedback have trouble doing it effectively. So it would be unrealistic to expect a team to demonstrate these skills without practice or training.

Until you see these skills clearly practiced on a daily basis, continue to expect the team to practice them in structured training and feedback meetings. It generally takes a team six months or more to get the basic skills and at least a year of diligent practice to master them. Hit-or-miss practice does not count. In fact it may do more damage than good. There is no substitute for using the skills weekly, if not daily. Remember we call this a "discipline," because it takes discipline for the team to learn and maintain the skills.

The use of regular verbal feedback and the coaching form (see Chapter 8) will help the team learn these skills. Your job is to ensure that they are used on a regular basis.

Designing and Offering Developmental Coaching

You will need to meet and coach the respective leaders on a weekly basis until they understand their duties and know how to perform them. If team members are well educated and experienced, they may take to the process easily, including running meetings and charting goals. Less-educated teams will need a good deal of training and coaching in the early stages. The more structured the procedures, the easier it will be for the teams to learn.

If you lay out a clear plan for skill development and follow it consistently every week, the teams will learn fast. On the other hand, when the process is disorganized, unplanned and poorly executed, there is often more confusion than learning. The better you plan and coordinate, the less time it will take for the team to learn the process and reduce its dependence on the team developer or manager.

To teach responsibility, give them responsibility that is commensurate with their level of maturity and competence. In a well-designed team-based system, everyone is responsible for a significant aspect of the team's business. No longer does management enable dependency behaviors by managing workers. Workers are expected to manage themselves and their part of the business.

Learning Point: "Having a job in our company means taking responsibility for yourself, your team and the goals of the team."

As you coach the various leaders, start where their skill level is – not where yours is. You have chaired many meetings, they don't even want to be in front of a group, let alone serve as the chairperson. Most people will learn very rapidly and take on more responsibility if coached in a nonthreatening, nonjudgmental way.

Setting up Healthy Competition

Be careful about how you structure competition within the team and between teams. Competition is worshiped in many organizations but it can be destructive. There are three types of competition. Two are positive – external and self-competition. One is destructive-internal competition. As a team leader make sure you emphasize the two positive types.

External Competition

The first kind of competition is *external competition*. This is competition between your company and other companies in your industry. Using this type of competition means you benchmark yourself against other companies or organizations to see where you stand. From the results of such a comparison, you can develop a plan for improvement and compete against the benchmark. The city of West Palm Beach successfully used this type of competition to develop its wastewater treatment plant teams. An independent consulting group assessed the performance of the private sector in wastewater treatment and the teams use this information to set their own goals. Gains over the goals is a major component of their process. This is healthy competition because it allows the teams to compete against an objective and an impersonal goal based on benchmarks from the private sector.

Self-Competition

The second positive type is *self-competition*. As the term implies, the team competes with itself. A Performance Culture avoids comparing people and teaches them how to compare themselves against a measurable standard or goal. Teams should strive to be the best they can be – not just better than some other team or company.

Teams carefully measure their performance in any given area and then set goals to improve that performance. This means that everyone is working to improve. A self-competition approach gives the steering committee and the team developer a wide variety of things to recognize and reward. Instead of having a single prize for "Best Team," there can be many prizes: most improved team in safety, most improved team in customer satisfaction for the third quarter, most cross-trained team in the department, and so on.

Recognition and rewards should be available to any team based upon its performance against an objective and measurable goal, not against another team. Dieting is a good analogy here. In losing weight the issue is not "Am I thinner than Joe or Sally?" but "What

Dieting is a good example of self-competition.
In losing weight the issue is not "Am I thinner than
Joe or Sally?" but "What is best for me and my body?"

is best for me and my body?" People who compare themselves to others generally feel guilty or angry at themselves or even at the person they are comparing themselves with, but they are not particularly motivated to lose the weight. While they may end up losing five more pounds than Joe or Sally, they may not be doing what is best for their body. Teams are exactly the same. They often spend great energy watching another team rather than doing the best they can. They end up winning the 8-minute race when they could have run 4:05.

It is important to emphasize that the whole company is the true team. One particular team is a subteam of the larger company team. American football has defensive, offensive and special teams – each contributing a unique set of skills to the overall effort. Teams need to keep in mind the greater goals of the organization, not just their own narrow world.

Internal Competition

The third type of competition is *internal competition* or competition between teams, shifts, departments or individuals. While there are rare times when this is appropriate, it is generally destructive and undermines cooperative team-based behavior. This type of competition is difficult to control and the measures are often easy to manipulate. It can too easily become personalized as well.

In our visit with the Middle America Manufacturing team, we noticed how the competition between shifts led to waste and conflict. This is not unusual. I have seen many examples of managers pitting one team or shift against another. The manager may never realize that the two groups undermine each another to win or that the bad blood created by the competition creates an internal focus so strong that people forget that the real competition is outside the organization.

Internal competition is appropriate when there is no major prize at stake. For example, many companies run successful United Way campaigns by allowing teams to compete. Other charitable drives and community service competitions may also be appropriate, but not within work related areas.

The team competition at the SMP plant in Wilson, North Carolina, is interesting. Each team has monthly and annual goals and receive points for meeting their respective goals. At the end of the year the number of points a team has accumulated determines the amount of money it can give to a designated charity. The company has a set budget for charity. If a team receives 25% of the points, it can donate 25% of the budgeted funds to the charity of its choice. No team benefits directly and the entire team must agree on the charity. This is a great way to encourage healthy competition. There is no incentive or reason to cheat or undermine other teams. Instead, the teams feel proud that they have been given control over the company's charitable giving.

Understanding the Dynamics of Teams

Within a new team there will be aggressive and passive individuals. Those with passive tendencies usually allow those who are more aggressive to set the agenda for the team. While this may be a natural way for a group to behave, it perpetuates dependency behavior and inhibits team development – dangerous to a Performance Culture. To avoid this all-too-familiar scenario, one of the boundaries you must set in the beginning is the principle of shared leadership.

Shared Leadership

practical tip Shared Leadership simply means that no individual is totally responsible for the leadership of the team. Leadership duties are shared on a rotating basis with each person taking a turn, for example, every three months to six months. Three to four months is generally optimal. This allows leaders to learn and settle into the role, while avoiding the temptation to feel they own it. In our visits to the two teams in Chapter 10, we met team leaders, quality leaders, safety leaders, huddle leaders, and so on. Each person has specific duties that support the team effort. Shared leadership is the only way to ensure that all carry their fair share in the support of the team.

Learning Point: The natural development of groups does not lead to teamwork; it frequently leads to dictatorships or abdication of responsibility by the entire group. Make sure you structure the process to encourage teamwork.

Shared leadership speaks to the issue of "Who owns the team?" Groups would like one person to take charge and "own the group." Such a model allows the group to simply follow rather than do the hard work of leading. Within such an environment, those who are not leaders are overly ready to complain or criticize the decisions of the leader. The abdication of leadership is the first step on the slippery slide down to single-leader groups. The only way for a team to mature is to function like a team, including sharing leadership and responsibility. Everyone has leadership potential. When leadership is expected of them, it is remarkable how often people respond favorably.

While many methods have been tried, the only fair way I have found to prevent dependency is to make sure that all leadership duties are shared and rotated often enough so that no one can escape leadership responsibility.

This system benefits everyone concerned. On a personal level, I have heard hundreds of people say that learning to take leadership responsibility on the team helped them take more responsibility for their own life. At the same time the organization benefits because people who take responsibility are far more productive and motivated than those who see themselves as dependent on a manager or supervisor. While workers generally do not like the idea of shared leadership at first setting the expectation, and following it as a boundary, creates important growth opportunities for everyone on the team.

This setup does not eliminate the natural leaders of the group, but it prevents them from becoming the dominant force. At the same time the natural leaders will learn a wider range of leadership skills. Often dominant people have a very narrow range of leadership skills that, if overused, can alienate and demotivate their teammates.

While shared leadership addresses many problems in team development, there are also psychological issues to consider such as how teams tend to avoid dealing with painful issues.

Fear of Change

New teams do not want to fail. This is reflected in two responses, abdication and defensiveness. Abdication means that team members would prefer that the TD take over as the leader. They do not want the responsibility because they are afraid of failure or conflict. With the TD as their authority figure they can remain dependent just as they were when they were working under a supervisor or manager. The desire for dependency is strong. The TD's task is to learn how to set proper boundaries and not overstep them, thereby leading the team or doing their emotional work for them.

Defensiveness comes in when the TD tries to set boundaries teams do not like. For example, when they are expected to use the principles of shared leadership, they may withdraw into a passive, defensive mode in which they may resist or refuse to carry out the duties initially or they may become aggressive and verbally attack the TD or manager. "If we are a team we should be able to decide how we organize ourselves." Both responses are present in some degree at the beginning.

Recognize that these responses come primarily from fear. Fear of failure, fear of conflict with others on the team, fear of the TD, fear that the team will have to do more work or that the new process will interfere with the current workload – fear of the unknown. Faced with fear many people become paralyzed and put a lot of energy into trying to keep things the same.

The task of the TD is to help the group develop its leadership skills across the entire team. Assume everyone can lead and proceed accordingly. Listen to their concerns, but remain gently and firmly insistent on following the principle of shared leadership.

Helping Teams Overcome Fear and Confusion

When we are in pain or fearful, we usually look around to find the cause in our environment. This is a form of external locus of control (discussed in Chapter 4). During the early stages of team development, individuals and teams will look desperately for the external cause of their conflict, anger or discomfort. In most cases they place the blame on the "teams." They will say things like:

- *"Until the team concept, Sara and Jane never had any problems with each other."*

  Looking at the process objectively, in the old system Sara and Jane did not have any problems, but that might have been because they had not spoken to one another for three years.

In the team process they are expected to work closely together and work out their differences.

- *"They made us go in teams and now we can't get any work done for all the confusion."*

  Objectively viewed, neither the work nor the policies and procedures have changed but there are no longer managers doing the scheduling and the team is uncomfortable with that role; therefore there is confusion.

- *"They make us do those useless team meetings and it puts us behind on our work."*

  If the team meetings are wasteful, it is because the team has not learned or is not using the discipline of meetings. The meetings are unproductive when the team fails to productively use the time for problem solving, training or conflict management.

- *"The managers put us in teams and when we have problems they won't help us."*

  The managers are willing to help the teams but the teams are uncomfortable with learning how to do things themselves; they would rather be dependent upon a manager. When managers do not buy into dependent behaviors on the part of teams, they are often blamed for the team's discomfort.

- *"The reason we are an hour behind in production is that we have to put all those numbers in the computer. That is the manager's job; we don't have time."*

  The team members don't want to learn computer skills; they just want to do their job the way they always have. Since the data input only takes 30 minutes of one person's time, it does not explain why the whole team is an hour behind on production.

In each of these cases the team has identified the source of pain, not just their own fear of failure or fear of conflict, but also fear as it relates to the team process or management. It is important to keep an eye on the goal and recognize that the team process is not the problem; it is an answer to many problems that were present in the old system. Because people are uncomfortable with their new roles, they will identify team-related issues as the problem in the hope of getting management to back off and allow them to return to their old, more comfortable way of doing things.

Taking Care of Yourself to Maximize Effectiveness

Traditional organizations tend to designate supervisors, give them a little training, and then let them sink or swim. In a Performance Culture this should never happen. Team developers are charged with developing teams and they need a lot of help and resources.

In order for a vital learning center to form, middle managers must communicate with each other and learn to work together in effective harmony. This is an extremely rare phenomenon.

Tom DeMarco and Timothy Lister, 1999, p. 212.

The most important resource is other team developers. No one has all the answers. Teams can get stuck and team developers can easily fall into dependency-creating behaviors.

practical tip

To function most effectively, we see team developers as a team themselves, charged with developing a whole range of teams. Avoid the use of phrases like "my team." The TD does not own the team. Teams own themselves. When team developers get locked into the idea of "my team," they tend to get too emotionally involved, taking on too much responsibility and failing to carry out proper development and coaching. Also, they are reluctant to call for help or get other team developer's advice. As a team themselves, TDs should meet at least once a month to discuss methods, techniques problems and solutions. No TD should be left alone to develop a team. Developing a team is a group effort. On one's own, it is far too easy to slip back into old supervisory habits while avoiding the hard work of coaching, teaching and developing others.

I recommend that an outside team developer attend team meetings at least once a month. This breaks the cycle of dependency between the TD and the team and gives some perspective on other teams. When the TD is on vacation or is gone for an extended period, use that as an opportunity to have other TDs work with the team. Their ideas and observations will refresh the team and give a more objective view of the its development.

Good development skills are important and difficult to learn. Any Performance Culture will place a high value on people who can take a group and make an effective team out of them.

practical tip

Look in the Mirror

When teams have trouble responding to the challenge, the first place to look is at yourself. Team developer behavior often enables dependency in the team just as managers did in the past. You can teach people to become dependent on you without even recognizing it. Coach and facilitate, but be aware of how much you do for the team. For example, if you wish to teach a team how to track its own budget, never do the task alone, always have a member of the team work with you on the budget. Make it mandatory that any task you do for the team requires the presence of a team member who is there to learn that skill. In this way you will not easily be seduced into doing the work and team members will find it hard to avoid learning the new skill.

Assessing Your Own Behavior

Defensive behavior in the TD creates problems for the team's development (you may wish to review internal and external locus of control in Chapter 4). Training in nondefensive communication can help team developers identify their defensive tendencies. It is not easy, but most team developers find that understanding their defensiveness helps them control their own inappropriate emotional responses to the team.

When things get hectic and conflict seems to overwhelm the team, or when the TD gets caught in a conflict with an individual or the team, the tendency is to get defensive.

Examples of team developer defensiveness include:

- Getting angry and criticizing a team member publicly
- Becoming frustrated and doing a task for the team that it should do itself
- Talking about a team member behind her back
- Withdrawing and avoiding the team or a certain member
- Rolling your eyes when someone says something you consider stupid
- Getting red in the face
- Pointing your finger at someone
- Shaking a leg or foot as you get upset

Any of these behaviors can be a dead giveaway to the team that the TD has lost control. The team can often see it even when the TD cannot. The opportunity to guide and coach is lost when the TD becomes defensive. The team loses respect for the TD and fails to respond. Because the TD does not recognize his own defensiveness, he cannot change the behavior. It becomes a vicious cycle where both lose. For these reasons, it is critical that TDs learn to asses their own behavior and the impact it has on others.

Many people have a strong need to be liked. Team developers are no different. In the effort to help the team, the TD often makes the mistake of over promising or over committing. Be careful. When the TD or manager promises something and then fails to deliver, trust is diminished. It is better to underpromise and overdeliver.

TDs can help management to define and set expectations as well. Managers are prone to make promises that they cannot deliver or do not follow up on. Over promising raises expectations and makes your job a lot more difficult when expectations are not met. Cynical team members will quickly say things like, "I told you management couldn't be trusted."

To help management, keep them informed of what teams really need and remind them when promises are due.

Note: Be sure to read the next chapter. Although it is directed at the key leader, the dynamics described for the leadership team can and will happen to teams as well.

Questions

1. Do you help the team focus on self-competition and avoid internal forms of competition?
2. Do you have a shared leadership system to help everyone take ownership for the team and its results?
3. Who is most likely to get the blame for the team's discomfort in learning new skills?
4. Where have you seen teams or individuals exhibiting an external locus of control? How would a team behave if it had a strong internal locus of control?
5. Do you have a performance feedback system that regularly involves the teams?

The Key Leader:
Sustaining the Process

The key leader in the Performance Culture leads the process by creating mutually trusting relationships with the culture carriers while also holding them accountable for high expectations. Leadership begins with modeling nondefensive ways of communicating and working together. The key leader and his or her team are the model that all other teams emulate. The transition between leaders must be carefully monitored to ensure that they are held accountable for the human as well as the material resources of the organization.

The Key Leader's Primary Task

Your primary task as key leader is to develop the goal focus of the organization, beginning with your leadership team. Tenacious goal focus is the most important function of your role. This begins with the development of clear, unambiguous goals for the organization. This is often a difficult step because many leadership teams are not accustomed to developing goals in such a way that every person in the organization can understand them and subsequently develop their own team's complementary goals.

practical tip

Three to five clearly written and measurable goals need to be set. Then, the leadership team needs to meet with the teams and thoroughly discuss the goals and what they mean to the organization. This information stage is followed by working closely with the teams to set their own goals, ensuring that the goals are both measurable and complementary to the organization.

The most effective Performance Culture leaders are those who place equal and consistent emphasis on task and process goals. These leaders teach and expect people to develop themselves and their teams, even as they are producing products or services for the company. The key leader must be involved in this process, meeting with teams, encouraging them and supporting the leadership team in getting everyone on board. In the course of the year, the key leader must keep the organization focused on the goals in many ways. These include:

- Prominently displayed charts with the organization's goals posted in every department, not just the front office
- Periodic public reviews of the organization's goals
- Periodic review of individual team's goals, on perhaps on a random basis
- Prominent recognition of teams who have achieved various goal-directed objectives

Meeting Expectations and Empowering Employees

In the course of leading an organization, leaders often lose focus, fail to follow up and forget commitments, without seeing this as having any serious consequences. People count on leaders to follow through on their initiatives, BUT there are consequences to those who took the risk to follow the leader and then found themselves hung out to dry. When the leader lets them down, they may not say anything but trust is hurt and future cooperation will be harder to get.

I worked with a plant manager once who was very exciting and motivational. During his talks he often made commitments like, "I will be visiting every shift once a month to talk with you and see what you are doing." Or, "I have committed to get the new press on line by October 1." Or, "I want you to feel free to talk to me about any concerns you have." While all the statements were reasonable, he had a bad habit of overcommitting himself. As a result, many things he "committed" himself to do never happened. Within a year after he took over, his credibility dropped so far that he was virtually unable to lead. People did not take him seriously and no one would risk following him.

One worker said, "I went out on a limb for him last year and worked a lot of extra time to get my group ready for the new equipment. When nothing happened, he told us it would be another month, then another month, then he told us it had been cut out of the budget. I was infuriated. I had my people all ready and excited, they went to a lot of trouble, then saw all their plans trashed. This has happened to me several times and to other managers as well. It has gotten so bad that I can't get excited about anything he says and I won't involve my people unless I have to."

The failure to keep intentions consistent with expectations caused such turmoil and ill will that this manager soon left the company. I believe he was very well intentioned, but not realistic in terms of what he could or would do. He had no clue about the risk others were taking for him and how they felt when he did not follow through with his part.

Learning Point: Congruence is the key to credibility in leadership. Whether you are an empowering manager or Attila the Hun, people want to be able to know that what you say is what you will do.

Almost as destructive is a commitment poorly executed. When the plant manager said, "I will be visiting every shift once a month to talk with you and see what you are doing," he did in fact visit the shift, but only spoke to a few supervisors and stayed for an hour or less. But based on his statement, people expected to see him on their shift and maybe even have a chance to speak with him occasionally. From their perspective, they never saw him or if they did it was only with a supervisor. Trying to explain this to him only got a very defensive response, "I do visit every shift each month just like I said." What he never understood was that his words had created an expectation that he would behave quite differently. His inability to understand the importance of congruence between words and deeds led, in part, to his downfall.

The need for approval or fear of conflict often leads leaders to say things or make commitments that they cannot or will not support later. The short-term consequence is to gain approval or avoid conflict but the long-term consequence is a slow but sure undermining of their credibility.

Overcommunicating

The most effective method of managing expectations is to overcommunicate. Sepa Lee, formerly human resources manager at Harmon, says, "If there is one thing I have learned in our implementation process it is that you cannot overcommunicate." Take the plant manager's case mentioned earlier. Since he did not want to disappoint people, he did not communicate the status of the new equipment except to say it was delayed. He did not keep managers updated or find out what plans they were making so he had no way of knowing that they were getting further and further out on the very limb he was sawing off!

Clear and well-developed communication structures ensure that such mistakes do not happen very often. They also maintain a two-way accountability, whereby the Performance Culture leader will get unambiguous feedback on how his or her statements or commitments are perceived by those who see and hear them. Use of the coaching form (see Appendix) or some kind of written feedback process every three to six months prevents this type of problem and helps the leader learn about the consequences of his behavior.

To ensure that leaders manage expectations effectively and proactively they can institute a number of communication structures that allow for rapid dissemination of information and two-way communication with the culture. These include monthly or quarterly information meetings, use of the open meetings technique, electronic broadcast of information, skip-level meetings.

Succession Planning

If the organization is serious about maintaining a strong Performance Culture, it must be very careful about who is put in charge. Although one division or manufacturing plant may be team-based, the rest of the corporation is probably not. In the organization's succession planning, the culture of the target organization often receives too little consideration. New fast-track managers may be given assignments for "developmental purposes" without considering the development of the organization. The hard work of the Performance Culture leader can be blown away by one uninformed, if even well-intentioned, new leader.

A new leader who is primarily interested in professional status in the company does things for short-term gain that get results, but at the cost of damaging a strong cooperative culture. Often the aftermath is realized only after the manager has moved on to her next assignment.

To avoid such setbacks, succession planning should consider the continued development of the culture at least as much as the development of a single leader. This requires that the incoming leader is well informed AND trained in how to work with the Performance Culture. Unfortunately, the culture he or she comes from is often very traditional and hierarchical with little understanding of what it means to develop a Performance Culture. You cannot expect such a person to have the skills or *even the interest* in developing Performance Cultures, especially if he knows his next career stop will be back in the hierarchical, non-team organization.

There is no easy solution to this problem. It is always difficult to mix the two types of cultures. Generally, the hierarchical system consumes the team system, not because of any superior processes but through shear force of tradition and political power.

One solution is to hire the leader from outside the organization and make the organization subject to special succession planning. This may solve part of the problem, but it may create many more. It is helpful for the new leader to know and understand the greater culture, so he can effectively move to protect the Performance Culture from the many vagaries of the larger traditional organization. Leaders who are unfamiliar with the larger organization's culture may not know how to do this and may not have sufficient political influence even if they do.

Additionally, hiring outsiders may incur the wrath of those who think the assignment should be theirs – even though their own leadership style is anything but team-based. This can lead to undermining and may limit the effectiveness of the new leader. With no built-in political base, he has a massive job to sell himself to the corporate management while effectively blending his leadership style with that of the team-based organization. This may be too much to ask of any human being.

Whatever is decided, recognize that the new leader needs to be accountable for maintaining the Performance Culture and developing it further. The leader is the steward of the human resources in her part of the organization. When she leaves, those resources should be better trained, more team-oriented and capable of responsibility than when she took over. Anything less is clearly a misappropriation of the company's assets, as much as if money were taken from the till.

Transition Planning

Far too little attention is given to transition planning in many organizations. When a leader is given a take-it or leave-it opportunity for advancement with a month's notice, he is effectively gone within a few days – mentally if not physically. Issues around transition and integrating the new leader into the system are glossed over. While this is not likely to change, there are certain steps the organization can take to ensure continuity between leaders.

1. *Make it clear that the new leader is responsible for the stewardship of the human as well as the material resources.* Emphasize that the corporate values have been incorporated into the culture and that the new leader's job is not to put her imprint on the organization, but to continue its growth and development. All too often new leaders arrive on the scene anxious to recreate the organization in their own image. This is often very ego-driven and based upon values that are quite different from those of a Performance Culture. There is nothing wrong with change, but in a Performance Culture all stakeholders have an important level of involvement in the planning and execution of that change.

2. *Make sure the new leader has learned the system before suggesting wholesale changes.* Teams can be as resistant to change as any other type of organization, especially if they do not respect or understand the leader.

3. *Plan an indoctrination period for the new leader.* This includes several meetings off site, not only with the leadership team, but with the steering committee and other nonmanagers. These meetings should focus on bringing the new leader up to speed on goals and goal development. They are also be aimed at developing the beginnings of trust among the various parts of the culture and setting the expectations of the new leader. *Any time there is a major change in leadership, there will be a need for systematic rebuilding of trust.* The system simply cannot perform efficiently if there is little trust in the new leader.

Learning Point: Any time there is a major change in the leadership, there will be a need for a systematic rebuilding of trust.

Trust from the previous leader is not easily transferred. It must be earned by the new leader with time and effort. Partial transference may be made by simply showing respect for the system the new leader inherited and for the people who helped create it. Beyond that, to create a responsive organization while continuing to steward the human resources, the leader must develop a great deal of social capital to draw from when deciding to make or stimulate change.

Leadership change brings up all the old fears that were seen when the teams first began:

- Will this new leader respect what we have accomplished?
- Will the new leader learn and listen before she starts making changes?
- Will the new leader involve us in decision making or simply retreat into decisions by management fiat?
- Will the new leader use a "problem frame" or a "blame frame" approach?
- Will this new leader display uncontrolled aggressive-defensive or passive-defensive behaviors?
- Does the new leader know how to function as a team member herself?

Until the culture carriers and workers can answer these questions positively, they will remain guarded and suspicious. The new leader must show herself openly and often to members of the endemic culture in her capacity as key leader. They must be able to see in meetings, in reviews, in skip-level meetings and on the floor that the new leader is concerned for their welfare and the continued development of the team process. They must feel confident that this new leader is not looking for another notch on her belt and is not already looking for her next assignment at their expense.

When the employees are reassured and feel confident about the new leader's positive intentions, the process of developing a Performance Culture can continue. Until that time, any major effort to improve the culture is likely to tear the newly formed fabric of trust between the leader and the endemic culture.

4. *Recognize that the people most critical to the success of leaders are the culture carriers.* These include middle management, union officials, team developers and other informal leaders in the organization. Key leaders must learn who the culture carriers are and bring them into meetings and the decision-making processes immediately. Help in this effort may come from the old key leader as well as the leadership team.

Questions

1. How well are your goals communicated to the line worker? How do you know?
2. Are new managers in your organization well coached in how to work in a Performance Culture?
3. Do you have communication structures that ensure two-way communication with every level of the culture?

CHAPTER 15

When the Two Cultures Merge

The focus of this book has been on helping organizations merge their endemic and intentional cultures to create a Performance Culture by capturing the power of teams. By eliminating the cultural friction found in most organizations the Performance Culture harnesses otherwise wasted energy to achieve higher sustained performance and, as a result, a true competitive edge.

In a Performance Culture everyone knows the goals and consistently values and achieves high performance.

Mark Payne, general manager of the SMP Wilson, plant says this about his efforts to create a Performance Culture, "Anything we do comes down to determining how to minimize resistance to change. Things can't be developed in a vacuum and then unleashed on folks. When plans are developed with employees, rather than imposed on them, you get fantastic results. That is the key to full commitment and use of everyone's energy. If you ask for input it unleashes an amount of work that far surpasses what you get if you just asked them to do something."

When employees use their skills and energy to the greatest extent possible, they learn the value and joy of achieving. As they learn the language of achievement and focus more on goals and less on obstacles, they find their work life more rewarding. At the same time, they learn how to self-reinforce they know what good performance looks like and the how to recognize and encourage it. As a result, in a Performance Culture, there is less need for management and more need for leaders.

Another characteristic of Performance Culture is that it is not dependent upon the good will of any one manager or leader because it is nurtured and developed by all the leadership – both formal and informal leaders participate in its creation and development. In addition, it cannot by copied or stolen because it is unique to each organization based on the trust that comes from an open and respectful relationship between the company and the work force.

Here is a short list of key characteristics.

A Performance Culture strives to:

- Ensure that every employee works toward specific weekly, monthly or yearly goals
- Ensure that every employee continuously learns new skills from formal training as well as from their team
- Provide every employee weekly or even daily recognition, feedback and support from their team mates or their team developer
- Develop care and concern among employees for one another and for performance
- Develop self-discipline at each level
- Develop leadership at every level
- Develop initiative in every team member
- Develop accountability at the organizational, team and individual levels
- Establish and manage ever-widening boundaries as teams develop

- Create high levels of involvement at and between all levels
- Develop a language of achievement that helps workers rise above entitlement and dependency towards responsibility, initiative and goal focus

Many of the organizations we have mentioned in this book have developed Performance

> *The institution provides guiding belief and creates a sense of excitement, a sense of being a part of the best, a sense of producing something of quality that is generally valued. And in this way it draws out the best ... The average worker in these companies is expected to contribute, to add ideas, to innovate in service to the customer and in producing quality products.*
>
> **Tom Peters, 1982, p. 323.**

Cultures with some or all of these characteristics. They are able to perform year after year and thrive through adversity while responding rapidly to markets and opportunities.

Everyone Leads

People who learn effective leadership skills generally learn effective "followership" skills as well, making teams work more effectively. Not everyone can lead all the time, but in a Performance Culture everyone leads some of the time. A culture that encourages and even expects leadership liberates a great deal of creative and motivational energy for the good of the company and the employees.

I have seen leadership come from the most unlikely people when the culture expected and supported it. I remember Mara at Harmon Industries, who left her team training session crying. She was scared to death that she would have to lead the team or stand in front of a group. She turned in her resignation that day but through the compassionate listening and support of Rick Garcia, her team developer, she agreed to stay and try. Four months later as I toured the facility, I looked in on Mara and her team. To my surprise she was the team leader, confidently leading a team meeting as if she were a vice president. She blossomed after that and made many valuable contributions to the team and the company. She later told me, "While I was very frightened, I felt enough support from my team and team developer to give it a try. Once I got over my fear, I found that I really liked it. I have greater confidence in myself and feel I can contribute much more."

Most people can learn to be effective leaders if they are supported by the right social structure. If people feel it is safe to take risks to learn and have new skills, leadership will evolve, sometimes quite rapidly. Leadership develops naturally within a Performance Culture.

The Competitive Advantage

Recall Chapter 10 when we looked at the Hustlers and NE1KAN teams. It took time and discipline for those organizations to achieve the high level of performance they now enjoy. Ask any manager, team member or team developer in those Performance Culture organizations how they feel about their culture. Virtually all will say, "I never want to work in a traditionally managed organization again. It is too much fun working in a friction free environment where goal achievement is the primary motivation."

Managers in those two organizations will tell you that they have far more time to lead and develop people and guide the company because people know how to take care of themselves. They don't need managers as much and when they do, they ask for help without the expectation that they will be rescued. As Mick Schneider of Butler Manufacturing is fond of saying, "My primary task as a manager is as a roadblock remover. Teams know what to do but sometimes they need help in removing the roadblocks."

Kenny Lynch, chairperson of the UAW at Standard Motor Products, says, "We have come a long way since we started team building 10 years ago. Teams are much more focused, people take a lot of pride in their work and we have an impact on the bottom line. We see our success every time we get a gain-sharing check each quarter."

Gary Henrie, of South Central Behavioral Services, Nebraska, talks about the consistent financial performance of his organization despite massive changes in the health care and mental health industries. Teams at South Central Behavioral know how their performance affects the bottom line and work hard to make South Central the most efficient and effective organization possible. Even as competitors are closing their doors, South Central has been able to thrive.

Robbie Robinson and rest of the teams at West Palm Beach Wastewater Treatment know that their high-performance teams beat the estimates of consultants who recommended privatization. Instead of privatizing, the city now enjoys a wastewater utility that consistently performs better than estimates for a private company. The teams know how to budget and control costs while improving service. Amazingly, they largely govern themselves with almost no management involvement.

As you begin or continue on the journey toward building your Performance Culture, consider the success Dick Jarman spoke of at the Butler Engineering Group. Remember the advantages Performance Culture has brought to Thom Norbury, Eric Sills, Mark Payne and others at Standard Motor Products, Lou Haddad and Robbie Robinson at the City of West Palm Beach, Celestia Ramm at Baptist Hospital, Jeff Utterback and Seepa Lee at Harmon, Larry Schroyer at the GSA, and many others as they told us of the benefits the new culture brought to their organizations and themselves.

Enjoy your journey and the prospect of bottom-line results only teams can achieve.

Endnotes

[1] See Karl Sabbagh, *Twenty-First Century Jet: The Making and Marketing of the Boeing 777.* (New York: Scribner, 1996) for a fascinating account of a massive dynamic team, Ben Rich and Leo Janos, *Skunkworks* (Boston: Little Brown and Co., 1994) for an interesting history of that famous institution and its research teams.

[2] For a full discussion on the structure of SDWTs, refer to D. Ray and H. Bronstein, *Teaming Up: Making the Transition to a Self-Directed Team-Based Organization* (New York: McGraw Hill, 1995).

[3] Taylorist refers to Fredrick Taylor (1856-1915), who could be called the father of modern industrial organizations along with Henry Ford. His concepts led to the time and motion studies of the 1920s and to the refinement of those techniques by the wife-and-husband team of Lillian Gilbreth, Ph.D., and Frank Gilbreth, on whose life the 1950 Clifton Webb and Myrna Loy movie "Cheaper by the Dozen" was based. Fredrick Taylor was a pioneer in the organization of machinery for greater efficiency. As an engineer manager and engineer at the Midvale Steel company in the 1880s, he developed and eventually perfected a system of organization. While it was more efficient, it had the effect of greatly diminishing the role of human judgment and dignity in the workplace. As a result, it caused much labor strife, among other things. The U.S. Congress in 1919 went so far as to ban Taylor's methods in any U.S. government facilities. Ironically, Taylor's methods were so much more efficient that they were soon adopted or adapted by many industries, including the U.S. government with or without the formal name of "Taylor." See Robert Kanigel, *The One Best Way: Frederick Winslow Taylor and the Enigma of Efficiency* (New York: Viking, 1997).

[4] J. Richard Hackman and Greg R. Oldham, *Work Redesign* (San Francisco: Addison-Wesley, 1980). Ricardo Semler, *Maverick: The Success Story Behind the World's Most Unusual Workplace* (New York: Warner Books, 1995).

[5] The more a team is organized along functions, the less it is able to load balance. People tend to stay in their functional areas, failing to see the big picture and how they could use their time to help others. At Butler Manufacturing, Kansas City, MO, the engineering teams in 13 regions across North America have learned how to load balance within and across teams. Both engineers and technicians work to load balance with major time and quality benefits. This is very different from their earlier functionalized design where the various specialties cared little for how their work affected others in the workflow. This has been made possible through high levels of training and cross-training throughout each regional office.

[6] Groucho Marx, *Grocho and Me* (New York: Random House. 1959), p. 26.

[7] See Hiring as a Statement of Cultural Norms in the Appendix.

[8] Kurt Vonnegut, *Cat's Cradle* (New York: Dell Publishing, 1963).

[9] 2000 International Conference on Work Teams, Dallas, Texas, sponsored by the University of North Texas.

[10] Refers to the seven rules for meetings used in the Teaming Up® system.

[11] See Aubrey Daniels, *Bringing out the Best in People* (New York: McGraw Hill, 2000) or Ferdinand Fournies, *Coaching for Improved Performance* (New York: Van Nostrand Reinhold, Co., 1978).

[12] John L. Ward, *Keeping the Family Business Healthy* (San Francisco: Jossey-Bass, 1987), p. 2. This classic work has only grown more relevant with time. If you are involved in a family or closely held business, it is a must read.

[13] See some of these authors for more in-depth discussion of performance evaluation: Aubrey Daniels, *Bringing Out the Best in People* (New York: McGraw-Hill, 2000); Tom Coens and Mary Jenkins, *Abolishing Performance Appraisals* (San Francisco: Barrett-Koehler Pub., 2000); Thomas Gilbert, *Human Competence* (New York: McGraw-Hill, 1978); Edward Lawler III, *High-Involvement Management* (San Francisco: Jossey-Bass Publishers, 1988).

[14] Peter Block, *Stewardship: Choosing Service Over Self-Interest* (San Francisco: Barrett-Koehler Publishers, 1993), p. 172.

[15] It is not my purpose to discuss compensation systems in detail here. Instead, I refer you to two good resources on the topic. See Jay Schuster, *The New Pay* (New York: Lexington Books, 1992) and Steven E. Gross, *Compensation for Teams* (New York: AMACOM, 1995).

[16] When first assessing a leadership team, I use the LSI from Human Synergistics, www.humansynergistics.com. This instrument, or one like it, is capable of giving the leader valuable standardized information about behavioral impacts and it can offer specific suggestions for behavioral change.

[17] For a discussion and guidelines on how to involve non-managers in management meetings, see Chapter 4 in D. Ray and H. Bronstein, *Teaming Up: Making the Transition to a Self-Directed Team-Based Organization* (New York: McGraw Hill, 1995). The principle of "open meetings" helps break down the barriers between the intentional and endemic culture.

[18] The complete "Brownie Point" program is explained in Chapter 8.

[19] Throughout this discussion we will compare the team development process to raising a child. I do this because child rearing is a developmental process familiar to most people.

[20] See D. Ray and H. Bronstein, *Teaming Up* (New York: McGraw Hill, 1995) p. 193.

[21] I use the *Team Based System Survey* to assess both individual teams and entire organizations. (Kansas City, KS: IPC Press, 2000).

[22] D. Ray and H. Bronstein, *Teaming Up* (New York: McGraw Hill, 1995), p. 143

[23] Steven R. Covey, *The 7 Habits of Highly Effective People: Powerful Lessons in Personal Change* (New York: Fireside Book, 1990).

[24] See the sample Coaching Form in the Appendix.

[25] Dick Grote, *Discipline Without Punishment* (New York: AMACOM, 1995).

[26] 1998 Teaming Up® Conference, Kansas City, Missouri 1998.

[27] Dan Dana, *Conflict Resolution: Mediation Tools for Everyday Worklife* (New York: McGraw-Hill, 2001). www.mediationworks.com.

[28] Teaming Up® is a proprietary implementation strategy designed to help organizations transition rapidly into a Performance Culture. The process is outlined in our book, *Teaming Up: Making the Transition to a Self-Directed Team-Based Organization* (New York: McGraw Hill, 1995).

[29] Peter Block, *Stewardship* (San Francisco: Barrett-Koehler Publishers, 1993).

[30] The FBI is a structured performance feedback system that all Teaming Up® organizations use. It teaches good listening skills and non-defensiveness in communication. Non-defensive, performance-based feedback is an essential ingredient for high-performance teamwork.

[31] D. Ray and H. Bronstein, *Teaming Up: Making the Transition to a Self Directed Team-Based Organization* (New York: McGraw Hill, 1995), p. 147.

[32] See discussion in Chapter 7. We also discussed this concept at length in D. Ray and H. Bronstein, *Teaming Up: Making the Transition to a Self-Directed Team-Based Organization* (New York: McGraw Hill, 1995), p. 64.

Bibliography

Adams, S. *Seven Years of Highly Defective People*. Kansas City, MO: Andrews McMeel Pub., 1997.

Adams, S. *Journey to Cubeville*. Kansas City, MO: Andrews McMeel Pub., 1998.

Adams, S. *Random Acts of Management*. Kansas City, MO: Andrews McMeel Pub., 2000.

Block, P. *Stewardship: Choosing Service Over Self-Interest*. San Francisco: Barrett-Koehler Pub., 1993.

Coens, T. and Jenkins, M. *Abolishing Performance Appraisals*. San Francisco: Barrett-Koehler Pub., 2000.

Covey, S. R. *The 7 Habits of Highly Effective People: Powerful Lessons in Personal Change*. New York: Fireside Book, 1990.

Dana, D. *Managing Differences*. Shawnee, KS: MTI Publications, 1993.

Dana, D. *Conflict Resolution: Mediation Tools for Everyday Worklife*. New York: McGraw-Hill, 2001.

Daniels, A. *Bringing out the Best in People*. New York: McGraw Hill, 2000.

DeMarco, T. and Lister, T. *Peopleware: Productive Projects and Teams*. New York: Dorset House Pub., 1999.

Fournies, F. *Coaching for Improved Performance*. New York: Van Nostrand Reinhold, Co., 1978.

Fukuyama, F. *Trust the Social Virtues and the Creation of Prosperity*. New York: Simon and Schuster, 1995.

Gilbert, T. *Human Competence*. New York: McGraw-Hill, 1978.

Gross, E. *Compensation for Teams*. New York: AMACOM, 1995.

Grote, D. *Discipline Without Punishment*. New York: AMACOM, 1995.

Hackman, J. and Oldham, G. R. *Work Redesign*. San Francisco: Addison-Wesley, 1980.

Hofstede, G. *Cultures and Organizations: Software of the Mind*. New York: McGraw Hill, 1997.

Kanigel, R. *One Best Way: Frederick Winslow Taylor and the Enigma of Efficiency*. New York: Viking, 1997.

Katzenbach, J. R. and Smith, D. K. *The Wisdom of Teams*. New York: HarperCollins Pub., 1993.

Ketchum, L. D. and Trist, E. *All Teams Are Not Created Equal*. Newbury Park, CA: Sage Pub., 1992.

Lawler, E., III. *High-Involvement Management*. San Francisco: Jossey-Bass, 1988.

Lawler, E., III. *The Ultimate Advantage*. San Francisco: Jossey-Bass, 1992.

Marx, G. *Groucho and Me*. New York: Random House, 1959.

Neave, R. *The Deming Dimension*. Knoxville, TN: SPC Press, 1990.

Oakley, E. and Krug, D. *Enlightened Leadership Getting to the Heart of Change*. New York: Simon and Schuster, 1994.

Peters, T. *In Search of Excellence*. New York: Harper and Row, 1982.

Postman, N. *Technopoly: The Surrender of Culture to Technology*. New York: Knoph, 1992.

Ray, D. and Bronstein, H. *Teaming Up: Making the Transition to a Self-Directed Team-Based Organization*. New York: McGraw Hill, 1995.

Ryan, K. and Oestreich, D. *Driving Fear Out of the Workplace*. San Francisco: Jossey-Bass, 1991.

Sabbagh, K. *Twenty-First Century Jet: The Making and Marketing of the Boeing 777*. New York: Scribner, 1996.

Schuster, J. *The New Pay*. New York: Lexington Books, 1992.

Semler, R. *Maverick: The Success Story Behind the World's Most Unusual Workplace*. New York: Warner Books, 1995.

Senge, P. *The Fifth Discipline: The Art and Practice of the Learning Organization*. New York: Doubleday, 1990.

Stack, J. *The Great Game of Business*. New York: Doubleday, 1992.

Ward, J. L. *Keeping the Family Business Healthy*. San Francisco: Jossey-Bass, 1987.

Appendix

Hiring as a Statement of Cultural Norms

When an employee first comes to pick up an employment application, the way he or she is treated tells a lot about your culture. If you only hire one in every 10 applicants, this means that there are other people in the world who have a positive or negative experience with your organization. Treating people with dignity and respect from the beginning, even if they are not hired, will gain positive word-of-mouth press in the community. Most organizations pay no attention to the early phases of hiring but this is exactly when strong messages can be sent about values and culture.

Do the questions on the application form emphasize your culture as well as the minimum qualifications? Is the first person an applicant meets trained in how to communicate the cultural expectations and norms to the applicant?

Questions might include:

We are a team-based organization that places great value on cooperative skills. If you had a good idea and implemented it with your team's help how would you feel if everyone on the team shared equally in any reward for the idea's implementation?

We are an organization that values diversity of all people and cultures. What experiences or training have you had in your work life that would help you work with and understand people who have very different backgrounds from your own?

We value self-development in our salaried employees. While the company is willing to help all employees improve their education, salaried employees are expected to attend specific professional certification courses and gain Level II Certification within one year after employment. Are you willing to meet this requirement by submitting a plan within three months and following that plan to completion before the end of your first anniversary date?

We are a company that values skill sharing and cross-training. Are you willing to cross-train with any employee on your team regardless of task or skill level, according to the team's training plan? This may mean that you would do lower-skilled tasks regularly if required by the team or company.

We value customer service and we want all employees to have as many skills as possible to serve our customers. Are you willing to learn whatever skills are required to serve the customer as efficiently as possible? For example, this might mean an engineer would be required to learn data entry skills to back up an absent team member. A maintenance person might be required to run a production machine when the team is short on production people. (Pay is always commensurate with the highest skill classification.)

We are a team-based company. Teams are responsible for determining vacations, overtime, some production scheduling, new employee interviewing and performance appraisal. Are you willing to perform these duties after proper training and coaching?

These statements and questions clearly show a company's values and expectations. Their presence on an application will discourage some applicants who are incompatible with the culture. For others it will provide an important taste of the expectations of the company and what role they may play.

Coaching Form for Team Members

Team Name _____ Date _____

Team Member's Name _____

   The purpose of this form is to provide a standard basis for coaching team members on the values and behaviors important for solid teamwork. This form is not intended to be all-encompassing but as a vehicle for solid communication and feedback to enable employee growth and development in a manner consistent with team goals. It is not a performance appraisal and does not go in any personnel file. Try to identify at least two specific areas of strength and two areas for development.

1.This team member shows respect and supports other team members. This member is a good team player and cares about the needs and wants of the overall group.

Strengths: Rating _____
Areas for improvement:

2.This team member focuses on our customers' satisfaction by meeting daily, weekly, and monthly goals.

Strengths: Rating _____
Areas for improvement:

3.This team member accepts responsibility and takes appropriate action to resolve issues.

Strengths: Rating _____
Areas for improvement:

4.This team member gives and receives constructive feedback.

Strengths: Rating _____
Areas for improvement:

5. This team member participates in the cross-training necessary to the team.

Strengths: Rating _____
Areas for improvement:

6. This team member performs his/her "Wheel" position responsibilities to the team's satisfaction.

Strengths: Rating _____
Areas for improvement:

7. This team member performs his/her "Task Assignments" to the team's satisfaction.

Strengths: Rating _____
Areas for improvement:

General comments regarding progress of team member from last quarter.

Documents reviewed by:
Team Members: _____, _____,

_____, _____, _____,

_____, _____
Team Developer: _____
Steering Committee _____, _____

Coaching Form for Team Developers

Team Name _____ Date _____

Team Member's Name _____

   The purpose of this form is to provide a standard basis for coaching team developers on the values and behaviors important for solid teamwork. This form is not intended to be all-encompassing but as a vehicle for solid communication and feedback to enable employee growth and development in a manner consistent with team goals. It is not a performance appraisal and does not go in any personnel file. Try to identify at least two specific areas of strength and two areas for development.

1. The team developer respects, cares for and supports team members.

Strengths: Rating _____
Areas for improvement:

2. The team developer effectively communicates and manages team boundaries.

Strengths: Rating _____
Areas for improvement:

3. The team developer effectively keeps team members focused on tasks.

Strengths: Rating _____
Areas for improvement:

4. The team developer clearly states management's objectives in terms that apply to the team and encourages the team to measure and chart its performance against these standards.

Strengths: Rating _____
Areas for improvement:

5. The team developer effectively mediates conflict within the team.

Strengths: Rating _____
Areas for improvement:

6. The team developer assists the team in managing cross-team conflict.

Strengths: Rating _____
Areas for improvement:

7. The team developer models effective feedback techniques.

Strengths: Rating _____
Areas for improvement:

8. The team developer approaches problems objectively and positively, modeling enthusiasm, integrity and honesty.

Strengths: Rating _____
Areas for improvement:

9. The team developer trains and coaches team members in meeting skills, goal setting, charting, and other team management skills.

Strengths: Rating _____
Areas for improvement:

10. The team developer is effective at keeping the team focused on activities associated with the team's current level of empowerment and the team is progressing through the levels as expected.

Strengths: Rating _____
Areas for improvement:

Team Members: _____, _____,

_____, _____, _____,

_____, _____

Team Developer: _____
Business Unit manager _____

Example Coaching form
from Human Dynamics, Inc.

Associate's Name: _____

Reviewed Date From: _____ To: _____

Place a check mark in the column that best describes the associate's typical behavior.

Add any specific comments in the space provided.

Item *Please cite specific examples*	1 Poor	2 Fair	3 Good	4 Excellent
1. **How does the associate relate with others? (Other associates, clients, etc.)** Does the associate communicate honestly and clearly, share ideas, build interpersonal skills, manage conflict (known and observed), use feedback appropriately, and solve problems effectively?	Comments: _____ _____ _____ _____ _____ _____ _____ _____ _____			
2. **How does the associate work within a team? (i.e., home team, or project team)** Does the associate cooperate, share ideas and skills, encourage team growth, accept responsibility, help reach team and company goals, act dependably in their role positions?	Comments: _____ _____ _____ _____ _____ _____ _____ _____			

Item *Please cite specific examples*	1 Poor	2 Fair	3 Good	4 Excellent
3. How does the associate apply the core values? Is the associate focused, fast, fair, friendly, flexible, and fun?	Comments: _____ _____ _____ _____ _____			
4. How is the associate growing within the company? Does the associate go across teams to get work done, recognize customers (internal and external), actively seek opportunities for self-improvement, contribute new ideas to make the company grow and become more profitable?	Comments: _____ _____ _____ _____ _____ _____ _____ _____ _____ _____			
5. Is the associate moving toward being self-directed, or dependent on others? Is the associate cooperative, punctual, trustworthy, enthusiastic, enterprising, diplomatic, organized, stable, etc.?	Comments: _____ _____ _____ _____ _____ _____ _____			

Index

About Darrel W. Ray, Ed.D.

D r. Darrel W. Ray, director of the Institute for Performance Culture, is a pioneer in the development of self-directed work teams in both union and non-union environments. He developed the Teaming Up® process that is now widely used across North America and the United Kingdom. Trained as a psychologist, Dr. Ray has studied groups and group dynamics since 1976 and specializes in organizational development, team building and self-directed work group implementation

A graduate of George Peabody College of Vanderbilt University, Dr. Ray holds a doctorate in counseling psychology and is a professional member of the American Psychological Association and American Society for Training and Development. He has taught at both the undergraduate and graduate level.

Dr. Ray's first book, *Teaming Up: Making the Transition to a Self-Directed Team-Based Organization* (McGraw-Hill 1995) continues to be the standard text for implementation of self-directed work teams. It is available at www.teaming-up.com or local bookstores.

Articles written about maximizing the power of teams can be read in: The Journal for Quality and Participation, Manage Magazine, Working Woman, Management World, Training and Development Journal, Human Resource Executive, NAPM Insights, and Supervisory Management.

To begin maximizing the power of teams in your company, contact:

The Institute of Performance Culture
913-724-3600
drdray@teaming-up.com
www.teaming-up.com

About Howard Bronstein

Howard Bronstein has been a teacher, newspaper correspondent, columnist, business instructor and consultant. Since 1988 he has been president of ODT, Inc., a human resource publishing and consulting company headquartered in Amherst, Massachusetts. When Dr. Ray was looking for a partner to help bring voice to his important work, he called ODT headquarters. As an associate and board member, Dr. Ray knew that Mr. Bronstein was familiar with his work and that they both share a vision of making organizations more efficient and effective by giving people control of their work.

About the Institute for Performance Culture

The institute is dedicated to helping leaders, managers, supervisors and team members learn and use team-based skills. Team skills are essential for today's precision performance workplace. The more individuals learn to use these skills, the more prosperous and satisfied everyone can be.

The People

Members of the institute are highly qualified and experienced professionals who believe team-based systems are generally a better more efficient way to organize a business than traditional systems. They also believe that team performance must be measured and proven to be effective.

Activities of the Institute

- Certification for team developers
- Implementation of self-directed work teams
- Training for executives and managers in team system development
- Training for mid-level managers in team leadership
- Training for teams and team leaders
- Coaching for team developers and leaders
- Publications: books, videos, CDs

See our web-site for current training sessions and schedules.

www.teaming-up.com

Useful products for Working with Teams and Leaders

Forte Interpersonal Communications Survey
©1996 The Forte Institute
3130 Wisconsin, Suite 5, P.O. Box 2543 Joplin, MO 64803-2543
For a free two page Forte Survey go to www.teaming-up.com

The Team Based System Survey
©2000 Institute for Performance Culture, www.teaming-up.com

The Team Development Series: 25 Case Studies for Self Directed Work Teams
©1999 Institute for Performance Culture, www.teaming-up.com
15699 Kansas Ave. Bonner Springs, KS, 66012 913-724-3600

The Life Styles Inventory, Self Description (LSI 1) ©1989

The Life Styles Inventory, Self Description (LSI 2) ©1990
Human Synergistics, Inc. 39819 Plymouth Rd. C8020, Plymouth, MI 48170-8020   www.humansynergistics.com

For a free two page report on your Communication Style go to:
http://www.teaming-up.com

THE FORTÉ INSTITUTE
•INTERPERSONAL COMMUNICATIONS•

Communication Style Survey

Survey 1

Date: _____

First Name: _____   Last Name: _____

E-Mail: _____   Gender: M F

Organization: _____   Position: _____

Address: _____   Phone: _____

Fax: _____

ZIP/Postal Code: _____

Circle the numbers below which best describe:

How You Feel You Really Are   (when not under outside pressure)

Mark your responses quickly, as your first response is usually best!
This is a survey. There are no right or wrong answers.

Guide: 1-Rarely   2-Seldom   3-Sometimes   4-Often   5-Usually

1. Individualistic	1 2 3 4 5	11. Daring	1 2 3 4 5	21. Aggressive	1 2 3 4 5
2. Spirited	1 2 3 4 5	12. Demanding	1 2 3 4 5	22. Industrious	1 2 3 4 5
3. Shy	1 2 3 4 5	13. Persuasive	1 2 3 4 5	23. Compassionate	1 2 3 4 5
4. Stick-to-it	1 2 3 4 5	14. Outgoing	1 2 3 4 5	24. Careful	1 2 3 4 5
5. Understanding	1 2 3 4 5	15. Earnest	1 2 3 4 5	25. Controlling	1 2 3 4 5
6. Precise	1 2 3 4 5	16. Pleasant	1 2 3 4 5	26. Thoughtful	1 2 3 4 5
7. Spontaneous	1 2 3 4 5	17. Stable	1 2 3 4 5	27. Charming	1 2 3 4 5
8. Logical	1 2 3 4 5	18. Kindhearted	1 2 3 4 5	28. Calm	1 2 3 4 5
9. Cautious	1 2 3 4 5	19. Enthusiastic	1 2 3 4 5	29. Fussy	1 2 3 4 5
10. Talkative	1 2 3 4 5	20. Impulsive	1 2 3 4 5	30. Agreeable	1 2 3 4 5

Be sure all 30 responses are circled. Then complete survey 2.

Survey 2

Complete after finishing survey 1 above.
Note: Instructions are different from survey 1.
Circle the numbers below which best describe:

How others expect you to act

Guide: 1-Rarely   2-Seldom   3-Sometimes   4-Often   5-Usually

1. Competitive	1 2 3 4 5		21. Forceful	1 2 3 4 5
2. Sophisticated	1 2 3 4 5		22. Confident	1 2 3 4 5
3. Tolerant	1 2 3 4 5		23. Sympathetic	1 2 3 4 5
4. Dynamic	1 2 3 4 5		24. Accurate	1 2 3 4 5
5. Serious	1 2 3 4 5		25. Conventional	1 2 3 4 5
6. Responsive	1 2 3 4 5		26. Charitable	1 2 3 4 5
7. Dominant	1 2 3 4 5		27. Appealing	1 2 3 4 5
8. Self-assured	1 2 3 4 5		28. Neighborly	1 2 3 4 5
9. Loyal	1 2 3 4 5		29. Assertive	1 2 3 4 5
10. Outstanding	1 2 3 4 5		30. Gentle	1 2 3 4 5
11. Persistent	1 2 3 4 5			
12. Bold	1 2 3 4 5			
13. Esteemed	1 2 3 4 5			
14. Eager	1 2 3 4 5			
15. Congenial	1 2 3 4 5			
16. Patient	1 2 3 4 5			
17. Steady	1 2 3 4 5			
18. Relaxed	1 2 3 4 5			
19. Convincing	1 2 3 4 5			
20. Popular	1 2 3 4 5			

For a free two page report on your
Communication Style go to:
http://www.teaming-up.com

THE FORTÉ® INSTITUTE

•INTERPERSONAL COMMUNICATIONS•

Order these books
and resources from
The Institute for Performance Culture

Call toll free: 1-866-847-8242 or Fax: 913-724-3463
Mail: 15699 Kansas Ave., Bonner Springs, KS 66012
www.teaming-up.com

The Performance Culture:
Maximizing the Power of Teams $29.95 X # _____ = _____

Teaming Up: Making the
Transition to a Self-Directed
Team-Based Organization $24.95 X # _____ = _____

Order both books and save! $44.95 X # _____ = _____

The Team Developer Series
(25 case studies) $24.95 X # _____ = _____

Shipping and handling $4.00 for each book
(Orders over $100.00 no S/H) $ 4.00 X # _____ = _____

KS residents add 7.5% sales tax   = _____
Overnight shipping extra – please call   **TOTAL** = _____

Volume discounts available

Name _____

Title _____

Organization _____

E-Mail _____

Phone (___) _____ Fax (___) _____

Address _____

City _____ State _____ Zip _____

AmEx. ❏   MC ❏   VISA ❏

Card No. _____

Exp. Date _____

Print name on card _____

Signature _____

Make checks payable to: *The Institute for Performance Culture*